NUCLEAR DESIRE

T0338064

Nuclear Desire

. . . .

Power and the
Postcolonial Nuclear Order

Shampa Biswas

University of Minnesota Press
Minneapolis
London

Published by the University of Minnesota Press
111 Third Avenue South, Suite 290
Minneapolis, MN 55401-2520
http://www.upress.umn.edu

Library of Congress Cataloging-in-Publication Data
Biswas, Shampa.
    Nuclear desire : power and the postcolonial nuclear order / Shampa Biswas.
    Includes bibliographical references and index.
    ISBN 978-0-8166-8097-9 (hc : alk. paper)
    ISBN 978-0-8166-8098-6 (pb : alk. paper)
    1. Nuclear nonproliferation—Political aspects—History. 2. Nuclear arms control—History. 3. Postcolonialism. I. Title.
JZ5675.B57 2014
327.1'747—dc23
                       2014005524

Printed in the United States of America on acid-free paper

The University of Minnesota is an equal-opportunity educator and employer.

20 19 18 17 16 15 14   10 9 8 7 6 5 4 3 2 1

To Sumita Biswas and Richard Ashford,
for keeping me intact

To build peace, now more than ever, it is necessary to build more than peace. To refuse nuclear weapons, we must refuse much more than nuclear weapons.

RAYMOND WILLIAMS
"THE POLITICS OF NUCLEAR DISARMAMENT"

Contents

Acknowledgments

I AM PLEASED TO HAVE THIS OPPORTUNITY to express my gratitude to some of the mentors, friends, and comrades who have shaped my intellectual formation and helped sustain my intellectual pursuits. Conditions of work are integral to all our labors. This is even more true for women and minority scholars in an increasingly neoliberal academy. In that context, the Department of Politics at Whitman College is a remarkable place to live and work. But one of the joys of working in this liberal arts college has been the vast network of colleagues from a variety of different disciplines who have enhanced my intellectual life in so many ways. I owe a special thanks to Tim Kaufman-Osborn for his generous mentorship over the years. Phil Brick, Paul Apostolidis, Susanne Beechey, Aaron Bobrow-Strain, Melisa Casumbal-Salazar, Kristy King, Leena Knight, Tom Knight, Gaurav Majumdar, Dalia Rokhsana, Nicole Simek, and Zahi Zalloua have enriched my professional and personal lives in so many ways. Elyse Semerdjian and Jon Walters have been wonderfully enlivening intellectual allies. Jeanne Morefield inspired and guided me in more ways than I can enumerate. Finally, the friendship, intellectual camaraderie, and support of Bruce Magnusson have been vital to my work. I have also had the good fortune of working with some of the brightest and edgiest students who sharpened my thinking and clarified my political commitments in ways that I could not have anticipated. There are too many of them to list here, but so many have gone on to make all manners of change in the world. Here I must thank Mitch Dunn, Marten King, and Sara Rasmussen for all their help with research and writing, and I must especially thank Thomas Friedenbach, without whose early help with research I could not have conceived or executed this project.

Outside Whitman, I have been sustained by a wide circle of friends and colleagues who have both carved out a space for the kind of work I am inspired to do and engaged with my work in many different ways. Bud Duvall and Naeem Inayatullah first taught me to trust my intellectual instincts and speak with honesty and clarity. Anna Agathangelou, Tarak Barkawi, Marshall Beier, David Blaney, Geeta Chowdhry, Carol Cohn, Lisa Disch, Siba Grovogui, Sankaran Krishna, Sheila Nair, Himadeep Muppidi, Eric Selbin, and Latha Varadarajan are all formidable scholars who have pushed, challenged, and helped form my thinking in ways that I can no longer even trace. I am deeply grateful to Marshall Beier for his sharp and attentive reading of the manuscript in its entirety.

My parents, Nirmal and Sumita Biswas, taught me all I know about love, integrity, and perseverance. Of the many gifts that she has given me, my mother was the first to give me my love of reading, writing, and politics. Amit, Swati, Nikhiel, and Neil have been among my fiercest and most generous cheerleaders. Elaine Ashford and Janet Axell have showed me great wisdom and given me much support.

I thank my editor, Pieter Martin, for his unflagging support and expert guidance.

I have learned so much about pacifism and justice from the intelligence, kindness, and many generosities of my sons, Ishan and Samir. I think they endured my many absences because they genuinely believed that my work may contribute in some measure to making a more peaceful and just world. Although my own ambitions are much more modest in this regard, for their sake I hope that they are right. Finally, there is nothing I can say that will adequately express the depth of my gratitude to my partner in all things, Richard Ashford. Without his constant encouragement, willingness to listen and engage with my work, and endless forms of daily nourishment, I could not have begun or finished this project. With him, so much more is possible.

Abbreviations

ABM	Anti-Ballistic Missile (Treaty)
ACDA	Arms Control and Disarmament Agency
ACDIS	Arms Control, Disarmament, and International Security
AEC	Atomic Energy Commission
ANA	Alliance for Nuclear Accountability
BAS	*Bulletin of the Atomic Scientists*
BESA	Begin–Sadat Center for Strategic Studies
CACNP	Center for Arms Control and Non-Proliferation
CDI	Center for Defense Information
CEA	Commissarait a L'Energie Atomique
CISAC	Center for International Security and Cooperation
CITS	Center for International Trade and Security
CNS	Center for Nonproliferation Studies
CRDF	(U.S.) Civilian and Research Development Foundation
CRS	Congressional Research Service
CSI	Container Security Initiative
CSIS	Center for Strategic and International Studies
CSP	Center for Security Policy
CTBT	Comprehensive (Nuclear) Test Ban Treaty
CTBTO	Comprehensive Test Ban Treaty Organization
CTR	(Nunn–Lugar) Cooperative Threat Reduction
DAE	Department of Atomic Energy
DPG	Delhi Policy Group
DTRA	Defense Threat Reduction Agency
ENDC	Eighteen Nation Committee on Disarmament
EURATOM	European Atomic Energy Community
FAS	Federation of American Scientists
FMCT	Fissile Material Cutoff Treaty
G8	Group of Eight
GDP	gross domestic product
GICNT	Global Initiative to Combat Nuclear Terrorism
GNEP	Global Nuclear Energy Partnership

HDI	Human Development Index
HEU	highly enriched uranium
IAEA	International Atomic Energy Association
ICBM	intercontinental ballistic missile
ICNND	International Commission on Nuclear Non-Proliferation and Disarmament
IGCC	Institute on Global Conflict and Cooperation
IISS	International Institute for Strategic Studies
INESAP	International Network of Engineers and Scientists Against Proliferation
INF	Intermediate-Range Nuclear Forces (Treaty)
INMM	Institute of Nuclear Materials Management
IPCS	Institute of Peace and Conflict Studies
IPPNW	International Physicians for the Prevention of Nuclear War
IR	international relations (the discipline)
IRBM	intermediate-range ballistic missile
ISIS	Institute for Science and International Security
ISTC	International Science and Technology Center
L&T	Larsen and Toubro
LAWS	Lawyers Alliance for World Security
LTBT	Limited Test Ban Treaty
MAD	mutually assured destruction
METI	Ministry of Economy, Trade, and Industry
MINATOM	(Russian) Ministry for Atomic Energy
MIRV	multiple independently targetable reentry vehicle
MPC&A	materials protection, control, and accounting
MPI	Middle Powers Initiative
MTCR	Missile Technology Control Regime
NACD	nonproliferation, arms control, and disarmament
NAM	Non-Aligned Movement
NCI	Nuclear Control Institute
NCPC	National Counterproliferation Center
NEI	Nuclear Energy Institute
NGO	nongovernmental organization
NIEO	new international economic order
NISA	Nuclear and Industrial Safety Administration
NMMSS	Nuclear Materials Management and Safeguard System

NNP	nuclear nonproliferation (regime)
NNSA	National Nuclear Security Administration
NNWS	non–nuclear weapons states (defined by NPT)
NPCIL	Nuclear Power Corporation of India, Ltd.
NPS Global	Nonproliferation for Global Security
NPT	Nuclear Non-Proliferation Treaty
NRC	Nuclear Regulatory Commission
NRDC	Natural Resources Defense Council
NSC	(Japanese) Nuclear Safety Commission
NSG	Nuclear Suppliers Group
NTI	Nuclear Threat Initiative
NWFZ	nuclear weapons free zones
NWS	nuclear weapons states (defined by NPT)
OECD	Organization for Economic Cooperation and Development
P5	Permanent Five (in the Security Council of the United Nations)
PGS	Partnership for Global Security
PIR	Center for Policy Studies in Russia
PNE	Peaceful Nuclear Explosions (Treaty)
PNND	Parliamentarians for Nuclear Non-Proliferation and Disarmament
PSI	Proliferation Security Initiative
PTBT	Partial Test Ban Treaty
RAND	Research and Development Corporation
ROSATOM	Russian State Atomic Energy Corporation
SALT	Strategic Arms Limitations Talks (I and II)
SASSI	South Asian Strategic Stability Institute
SCC WMD	Strategic Command Center for Combating Weapons of Mass Destruction
SGS	(Program on) Science and Global Security
SIPRI	Stockholm International Peace Research Institute
SLBM	submarine-launched ballistic missile
SORT	Strategic Offensive Reduction Treaty
START	Strategic Arms Reduction Treaty
STRATCOM	Strategic Command
TEPCO	Tokyo Electric Power Company
TTBT	Threshold Test Ban Treaty

UN	United Nations
UNDP	United Nations Development Program
UNSC	United Nations Security Council
WINEP	Washington Institute for Near East Policy
WMD	weapon of mass destruction

Use and Waste in the Global Nuclear Order

Three Nuclear Events: Tales of Order and Disorder

"Order" and "disorder" have shaped the nuclear world. Nuclear fission is the process of splitting the center of an atom to set in motion a process of radioactive decay. The remarkable scientific discovery of how to make and sustain such a chain reaction to generate incredible amounts of energy produced some of humankind's loftiest aspirations as well as its most apocalyptic nightmares. In its utopian incarnation of nuclear energy, nuclear fission can solve our most pressing energy needs—it can deliver us from the environmental limits of relentless capital accumulation and consumerism and, indeed, reign us back from the portending dystopia of global climate change. But in its dystopian incarnation, nuclear fission—now not so well contained within an exploding concrete structure (Fukushima Daiichi), now in the form of uncontrolled destruction inflicted on hapless innocents (Hiroshima and Nagasaki)—becomes a nuclear nightmare. An appreciation for this enormous potential of nuclear decentering and the desire to harness its possibilities and control its dangers generated a "global nuclear order," centered on a much-celebrated and extremely important treaty—the Nuclear Non-Proliferation Treaty (NPT). The NPT was one among many efforts to craft a global nuclear order to restrain the dangers of nuclear power, while liberating its "peaceful" possibilities for the larger collective good.

"Things fall apart; the centre cannot hold": the late Nigerian novelist Chinua Achebe picked from this fragment of Yeats's poem "The Second Coming" to title his best-known work on the unraveling of order that colonialism wrought. Implicit in the creation of any order are new centers and other peripheries. Where is the center of the global nuclear order? What happens when this center can no longer hold? Whose worlds fall apart? What kinds of new disorders, anxieties, and dystopias does that create? I would like to use this book to tell a larger story about this global nuclear order—its shape and form, its disruptions and frayings, its central players, its unexpected effects, and its marginal victims. Let me begin this story with three tales of "nuclear events" currently under way.

A Tale of Negotiation

International negotiations on Iran's nuclear program are currently in progress. There is euphoria in some quarters about the signing of a six-month "interim accord" that will temporarily pause Iran's nuclear program, as negotiations continue for a more "comprehensive solution" that might "fix the problem of Iranian nuclear weapons pursuit" in a more lasting fashion. Dignitaries from the United States, Russia, China, the United Kingdom, France, and Germany are in conversations with representatives from Iran over the nuts and bolts of Iran's nuclear program. The group negotiating with Iran is commonly referred to as the "P-5 plus 1"; the P-5 are the "permanent five" who hold veto power in the United Nations Security Council (UNSC) and are also the five states that the NPT recognizes as sole legitimate possessors of nuclear weapons. Iran has been a signatory of the treaty since its inception in 1968 and has always claimed that its interest is in nuclear energy (permitted by the NPT), not nuclear weapons. On the face of it, the negotiations have all the trappings of a dialogue among sovereign equals, with all the fanfare and high drama of international diplomacy at the highest levels of power on matters of life and death. Well-dressed, polished dignitaries meet in plush surroundings in the Palace of Nations in Geneva, Switzerland. They shake hands, they pose for cameras, and then they go behind closed doors and hammer out details of an agreement that will reign in Iran's nuclear ambitions. And the world appears to wait with bated breath.

This, after all, is a hopeful moment. The interim agreement is being called a "diplomatic breakthrough," portending a new global order in which Iran may be welcomed back as a member of the "family of nations." Iran commenced a civilian nuclear power program in the 1950s with considerable aid from the United States, at a time when Iran was a geopolitical ally of the West. The point of this deal and any future negotiations is to prevent this gesture of Western goodwill from being turned toward nuclear weapons building by this now unfriendly third world state. Since the 1979 Iranian revolution, the United States and Iran had been sworn enemies. In one of his more infamous State of the Union speeches, former U.S. president George W. Bush had referred to Iran as a member of the "Axis of Evil." Former Iranian president Mohammad Ahmedinejad routinely lambasted the United States (and its close ally, Israel) in his many colorful speeches. But the recent election of the "mild-mannered and soft-spoken" Hassan Rouhani, who has assembled a "Western-educated" foreign policy team, has inspired optimism in the "international community." Certainly there are detractors, as well, and anxieties about new disorders to follow this attempt to reorder Iran. For instance, this agreement is fraying U.S. relations with its allies. Israel has never publicly declared its possession of a very decent stockpile of nuclear weapons and has refused to sign the NPT. But the "well-mannered and Western-educated" Israeli prime minister Benjamin Netanyahu has mounted a public relations campaign to Western powers that Rouhani is a "wolf in sheep's clothing."[1] U.S. ally Saudi Arabia is miffed, too, and has hinted at starting a nuclear weapons program in retaliation.

How does this international community enforce its will? The military option—the willingness by the United States and Israel to preemptively strike Iran's nuclear facilities—has not been used but has remained on the table. But the United States and Israel have already successfully collaborated on more clandestine forms of intrusion—the smuggled computer virus Stuxnet brought Iran's centrifuges to a halt in 2010, and five nuclear scientists were assassinated in broad daylight on Tehran's streets between 2009 and 2011. Even more forcefully, sanctions imposed by the international community have been steadily expanded to virtually paralyze the Iranian economy, with devastating consequences for ordinary Iranian citizens. Iran, it is fair to say, is truly desperate. The P-5 plus 1 has offered to begin loosening the noose of these sanctions ever so slightly, if Iran is willing to halt its ambitions to acquire nuclear weapons. This is a minimal easing, President Obama has assured all, and easily reversible; the United States is willing to ratchet up the pressure in the future if need be.

We are reminded time and again by reasonable, thoughtful, concerned interlocuters that "we are all safer in a world with a denuclearized Iran." But who is this "we"—this mythical international community that speaks of peace and well-being for all made possible by reigning in this nuclear upstart? What kinds of questions about nuclear order and disorder are precluded when we invoke this "we"? Iran's current ability to produce even a single missile-deliverable nuclear weapon is fairly limited. Every single member of the P-5 (and Israel) has a sizeable nuclear weapons stockpile and considerable ability to deliver weapons. Each considers nuclear weapons as essential to its security, and none has ever engaged in any serious negotiations to eliminate its own nuclear ambitions. Nobody may be better off with Iranian nuclear weapons, but from what kinds of questions about the global nuclear order does this exaggerated attention to the disorderly conduct of Iran deflect attention?

But also, who is the "we" that talks in the form of the state at these international negotiations? For whom do the "well-mannered, Western-educated" representatives speak when they speak to each other? The current accord places certain limitations on Iran's ability to make and possess uranium enriched to a capacity more easily translated into weapons. But during the negotiations, Iran stood adamantly on demanding recognition from the international community of its "right to enrich uranium." This demand has been put on hold for now; at least on this question, the United States has been willing to agree to disagree. But what kind of right is the right to uranium enrichment, and who gains from that right—whether it be for the unremarkable case of the United States or for a so-called rogue state such as Iran? If sanctions are finally lifted, and Iran resumes its "peaceful" nuclear program *with* international approval, who will profit and who may be damaged from those pursuits?

A Tale of Conciliation

At one time, India, too, was considered a "problem" within the global nuclear order, albeit of a different kind than Iran. India has always refused to sign the NPT. For years, India had railed against the discriminatory aspects of an NPT that allowed members of the P-5 to retain custody of their nuclear weapons while barring everyone else from acquiring any. India had strenuously argued for the nuclear five to agree to a time-bound commitment to disarm. That is, publicly, India had waxed principled against the creation of an exclusive "nuclear club," while privately pursuing the path to joining that club. Embarking on a nuclear program to harness the liberatory powers of the atom to lift into modernity an economy ravaged by colonialism, India had called its first nuclear test in 1974 a "peaceful nuclear explosion." In 1998, however, it openly flexed its bellicose nationalist muscle to declare itself a nuclear weapons state.

Predictably, economic sanctions immediately followed India's nuclear brashness. States were forbidden to engage in any kind of trade with India that hinted at things nuclear, including for the peaceful purposes of nuclear energy. The integrity of the NPT—signed by practically the entire nonnuclear world—rested on branding India a "nuclear pariah," and so it was. Yet in less than a decade, India was no longer the nuclear problem it once was. In 2008, the United States and India successfully negotiated a nuclear fuel deal, followed by a more general exception made to nuclear trade rules that allowed worldwide nuclear trade with India. In effect, despite remaining a nonsignatory to the NPT, India's nuclear status had been normalized, rendered legitimate and unremarkable. This, for many, was considered to be major blow to the nuclear order fashioned out of the NPT.

Why and how was a disorderly India invited back into the orderly world of the international community? In the late 1980s, after four decades of following an economic model sympathetic to protectionist measures and socialist planning, the Indian state had opened its economy to global neoliberal forces, revealing the enormous market potential of a slumbering economic giant. India, after all, is second only to China in witnessing the most rapid expansion of nuclear energy demand. For a powerful global nuclear industry, the Indian nuclear tests of 1998 were a setback that the 2008 nuclear fuel deal duly rectified. A massive corporate lobby went to work in both the United States and India to secure a bilateral agreement to resume nuclear trade; shortly afterward, the United States went to work on the members of the Nuclear Suppliers Group to waive trade restrictions with this newfound nuclear ally. Israel and India, both nuclear weapons possessors who remain outside of the NPT but firmly within the embrace of the international community, are now participants in the making of the global nuclear order in which countries like Iran remain rogue. India, now, is on the side of the P-5 plus one, eager to ensure that Iran's nuclear program is entirely peaceful in nature, and looks forward to increasing oil imports from, and enhanced trade with, a de-rogued Iran.

Who profits from, and who disrupts, this reordering of the global nuclear order? The corporate interests that fought to legitimize India's nuclear standing now find themselves in a spot. The global nuclear industry sets up shop around the world in the name of a safe and reliable solution to energy needs and climate change yet everywhere compels local governments to indemnify them from any liability for nuclear accidents in the future, leaving those costs to be borne by victims and citizens of host countries. But disruptive activists in India demand democratic reckoning. As I write, the Indian prime minister wraps up a visit to the United States to negotiate the purchase of nuclear reactors from Westinghouse, even as groups within India refuse to yield the right to hold nuclear producers accountable to those affected by the pursuit of nuclear power. Powerful interests constitute the global nuclear order, but who are its victims?

A Tale of Horrors

In August 1945, two atomic bombs were dropped on Japanese cities by U.S. armed forces—"Little Boy" on Hiroshima on August 6, followed three days later by "Fat Man" on Nagasaki. More than one hundred thousand people were slaughtered on those two days, with many more deaths to follow. This brought an already exhausted Japanese imperial army finally to capitulate unconditionally, thus ending a major war that had consumed lives all over the world. In the triumphalist narrative that emerged from the conclusion of that war, the Allied forces, many of which had dragged their colonies into paying for the war effort in lives and resources, were the "good liberals" who had defeated the evil of fascism. The trauma of Hiroshima and Nagasaki has been a bare shadow in the narrative of Western historical progress that was written in the wake of that war.

In Japan, however, the immediately dead, forever maimed, and slowly dying of that moment have occupied an important commemorative place in the postwar national imagination. While the "greatest generation" in the United States helped start what would eventually become one of the two most lethal nuclear arsenals in the world, that same generation in Japan swore to honor the memory of this devastation by foreswearing nuclear weapons. Japan ratified the NPT in 1976 and has been a global proponent of universal nuclear disarmament. As may be expected, this nuclear-weary country needed to be convinced of the benefits of investing in any kind of nuclear power, even of the peaceful variety. So began an enormous project undertaken by closely aligned state and corporate interests, which together produced the "myth of absolute safety" to persuade Japanese citizens of the necessity, desirability, and complete reliability of nuclear power harnessed for such peaceful purposes. As a result of those enormous efforts, Japan came to be dependent on nuclear power to meet 30 percent of its energy needs. Also as a result of those efforts, Japan is now considered a "breakout" state, able to convert its peaceful nuclear program into a weapons program relatively easily and on quick notice.

The 2011 earthquake and tsunami that produced the reactor meltdowns at Fukushima also shook the confidence of the country. In their aftermath, a whole host of questions about the corruption of the nuclear industry, its collusions with the Japanese state, and its treatment of workers have led citizens to ask how a country that was the only victim of a wartime use of nuclear weapons let itself be victimized once again through its misplaced confidence in the magic of nuclear power. As nuclear energy is increasingly sold as the miracle cure for global climate change, how can we think about its future in ways that honor the effects of nuclear pursuits on all its victims, past, present, and future?

Nuclear weapons wreak immediate destruction, but one of the most vexing burdens that the pursuit of nuclear power poses is to a future world that must deal with its residues. Among the many problems that are currently plaguing the cleanup efforts at the Fukushima Daiichi nuclear plant is the matter of a large number of spent fuel rods—highly radioactive waste that emerges from the process of nuclear fission—that were being stored in the upper story of a now structurally compromised building. Using highly sophisticated robotic technology, the operator of the nuclear plant—Tokyo Electric Power Company (TEPCO)—has begun a major and delicate operation for the removal of these rods, some of which are now jammed together within the cooling pond. If successful, this will no doubt be hailed as a major success for TEPCO and likely help restore some of its lost credibility as a responsible manager of nuclear power. But the toxicity of this nuclear waste will still last thousands of years, and no adequate solutions on how to safely store and/or dispose of this waste have yet been devised. Who will be the future victims of the nuclear waste that comes from the process of creating nuclear energy for today's consumers of electricity? To bring it back full circle, how can we conceptualize the victims of nuclear proliferation and the global nuclear order in terms more expansive and inclusive than available to us when we look at the high-level diplomacy among "well-mannered and Western-educated" representatives of highly unequal states negotiating about weapons in the name of the "international community"?

Underlying all three tales is a larger story about the global nuclear order, inequality, and power that I would like to recount in this book, a story that begins with the dangers of nuclear weapons but continuously runs up against the larger effects of nuclear power more broadly. The story of nuclear weapons is almost always told through the medium of interstate relations. In the first tale, it is states that seek and possess nuclear weapons, and it is states that work together to prevent their spread. The field of international relations (IR) often refers to the metaphor of the billiard ball table to describe the relations between states, all of which are the sovereign equals of each other, even though so obviously unequal to each other. Some of these states speak in the name of the international community, others are rendered rogue or deemed acceptable in due course. But distinguishing rogues from allies requires, as other scholars of IR say, "opening the black box of the state," as in the second tale—this, of course, reveals a host of other powerful forces that work in, with, and through states but are barely contained by most of them. The game of IR—not unlike "the Great Game" of colonialism—is designed by these forces, its rules crafted by the most powerful among them. But I am most interested in drawing attention to those who are left out of this game altogether, even though profoundly affected by it. That is the lesson of the third tale. What kind of global order is crafted out of interstate relations on nuclear proliferation and who speaks in what ways in it? What are the different impacts of nuclear pursuits on different groups, interests, and bodies? Let me try, in the following section, to get at some of these questions about nuclear proliferation and its dangers by querying the "usefulness" of nuclear weapons and efforts to control their spread.

Rethinking Nuclear Use and Nuclear Waste

In his most recent book, titled *Atomic Obsession,* John Mueller (2010), in his characteristically witty, unsubtle, and provocative manner, offered a devastating account of the "usefulness" of nuclear weapons and nonproliferation efforts. In thrall to the alleged awesome powers of nuclear weapons, we live in such great fear of them and spend endless effort to prevent their proliferation. Yet nuclear weapons have been historically useless, Mueller suggested—unnecessary in bringing an end to World War II and irrelevant in keeping the peace during the Cold War. Hence spending massive resources on acquiring and keeping them has been wasteful. But also useless, he argues, have been the enormous and quite costly efforts expended on nonproliferation—useless, because most states don't want nukes, and the few who do won't be any the better for acquiring them. Nor are terrorists really able to buy or make or operate them, despite all the hyped-up drama around nuclear terrorism in policy and popular culture. Wasteful and costly expenditures pursuing useless nonproliferation initiatives trying to prevent the acquisition of useless weapons! Mueller's critique was brutal and controversial.

I don't find Mueller's arguments entirely persuasive, and there are parts of it that I find objectionable. I do, however, believe that thinking about our obsession with nuclear weapons through the lens of use and waste provides an instructive way into many current debates about nuclear proliferation and how to deal with it. Indeed, it is becoming much more common to question the military usefulness of nuclear weapons, including by some prominent military leaders such as Colin Powell. Ward Wilson's (2013) very recent book attempts to demolish what he calls the many myths about the historical and current usefulness of nuclear weapons. Many of these thinkers and leaders are trying to make a case for universal nuclear disarmament. Like them, I am interested in articulating a case for nuclear abolition *and* doing that via an analysis of the usefulness of nuclear weapons and nonproliferation efforts. However, as I hope to make clear in the rest of this chapter, my entry into the question of use and waste is from a quite different angle.

Mueller's (2010) book generated quite a bit of attention and a fair bit of criticism.[2] Some critics were naturally disappointed by Mueller's far too glib and even condescending dismissal of the dangers of nuclear weapons. One could suggest that some of this glibness is a product of the complacency born of a "long peace," in John Lewis Gaddis's terms, or, to put it differently, simply the fact that nuclear weapons have not been used since the bombing of Nagasaki in August 1945. Mueller did, after all, also suggest previously, in one of his other provocative and controversial books, *Retreat from Doomsday: The Obsolescence of Major War,* that most Western states had lost the appetite for major war and that we were headed to an even longer peace in a far more civilized world (Mueller 1989; Jervis 2009). Geoffrey Blainey (1973), speaking of the easy idealism generated in the calm of the interwar years in Europe, had once warned of the complacency born of living in a gentle time. Were Mueller's musings on the uselessness of nuclear weapons and the progress toward global peace, then, just the kind of careless utopian dreaming that comes from living in calm nuclear times?

Mueller's argument on nuclear dangers goes something like this. The fears of nuclear use mostly come from bombs possessed by small rogue-state or nonstate actors. But these are relatively simple devices, no more lethal than Fat Man and Little Boy—the atomic bombs dropped on Hiroshima and Nagasaki in 1945. They do not possess the explosive capacities of the far more lethal thermonuclear devices that established nuclear weapons states possess. The apocalyptic scripts of most nuclear armageddon scenarios are projections made from the power of these more deadly weapons. The detonation of a relatively simpler device by a rogue actor in downtown Manhattan will no doubt be devastating but not catastrophic. Such a detonation is unlikely to lead to the demise of an established, resilient state like the United States, let alone result in planetary annihilation. Framed in this manner, the dangers of nuclear weapons do, indeed, seem exaggerated. One could question Mueller's rendition of the extent of any such devastation caused by any such attack. What kind of political, social, and cultural formation might emerge from a nation-state that was able to withstand the *instantaneous* devastation of a nuclear attack? After all, time, in addition to scale, is as much a variable in the revolution that nuclear weapons are thought to have wrought. The United States might survive, and even return the favor in considerable kind, but in what form and with what long-term political and economic consequences?

But questioning the quality of survival of a relatively small-scale nuclear attack still leaves us with the issue of the massive overkill capacity that many states, such as the United States, continue to possess in the name of deterring just such an attack. Someone could reject Mueller's claim that nuclear weapons are simply not necessary for deterrence but still have no sound basis to argue for the massive stockpile of thermonuclear weapons that the United States and other nuclear weapons states have and continue to possess, during the Cold War and long after its supposed demise, far in excess of what may be necessary for deterrence. In that sense, I think Mueller pushes us to think about the usefulness of nuclear weapons in ensuring security, and I believe the case for the uselessness of nuclear weapons for poorer states, such as Iran and North Korea, with fewer resources to expend is stronger still. But I suggest that we think a little harder about *how* to think about this question of usefulness: if nuclear weapons are not just instruments of security, how else might they be useful for states that have a lot of them and want to keep many of them, and even for those who want to acquire them despite their massive expenses and the global opprobrium they now seem to invite?

Along with his dismissal of the usefulness of nuclear weapons, Mueller also, and in my mind more controversially, questions the usefulness of the countless efforts and initiatives undertaken on behalf of arms control and nuclear nonproliferation. On one hand, he suggests that many anti- and counterproliferation efforts aimed at particular rogue states have been enormously costly and essentially ineffective and, indeed, have only served to make nuclear weapons more attractive. In this respect, his attempts to document the costly *actual* toll in human life and suffering that the long and brutal sanctions imposed on Iraq and North Korea, to prevent a nuclearization that could have devastating *possible* effects in the future, are commendable. Sanctions against Iran to prevent its acquisition of nuclear weapons are taking a similar toll on ordinary citizens, while possibly only strengthening the resolve of sections of the regime. Any possible military action against Iran, as is suggested time and again by Israeli and sometimes U.S. leaders, will only make that worse. That preventing future nuclear weapons use is currently costly—in tragic human forms—is a singularly important point to make.

But Mueller is also skeptical of the outcomes of a massive undertaking of nuclear arms control and nonproliferation and disarmament efforts, efforts that he suggests have involved countless amounts of time, energy, and money yet have neither curtailed the ambitions of nuclear states nor made the world more or less safe. He takes a particularly hard swipe at various key treaties. The 1962 Partial Test Ban Treaty (PTBT) simply banned the kinds of tests that had already been discarded and drove more tests underground, where they are still conducted by the one state (North Korea) that continues to test explosively. The bilateral arms control treaties negotiated between the United States and the Soviet Union were quite ineffective—for instance, SALT I only offered a pretext to the two sides to innovate by adding more warheads to missiles when the former were limited, and SALT II capped the level of weapons, but at very high levels, and did not prohibit qualitative improvements. Most important, however, is the NPT—that linchpin of nuclear nonproliferation efforts—practically universal in scope, negotiated and extended indefinitely in 1995 with such great and heroic efforts, and yet, according to Mueller, so utterly useless in restraining the nuclear desires of those few hapless idiots who still want to pursue nuclear weapons. Most states refrain from acquiring nuclear weapons because they have smartly realized that they are a waste of time, money, and energy, not because of the force of the NPT. So can it be that such a well-regarded treaty such as the NPT and so many well-intentioned efforts to restrain the awesome destructive powers of nuclear weapons and create at least some semblance of nuclear peace are that useless?

At one level, much like his complacent disregard for the dangers of nuclear weapons and proliferation, Mueller's hasty dismissal of arms control and nonproliferation efforts appears flippant (Gusterson 2011). Surely one could not judge all efforts in a truly massive array of efforts to have been complete failures. There are some key treaties, such as the 1972 Anti-Ballistic Missile Treaty, that Mueller just fails to mention, and others, such as the Intermediate-Range Nuclear Forces (INF) Treaty, whose effects he underappreciates—these were quite important in ratcheting down the level and intensity of the arms race between the United States and the USSR. Other bilateral treaties have also played their part in significantly curtailing the number of nuclear weapons held by the United States and the USSR/Russia from the peak level of more than sixty-five thousand nuclear warheads held in 1986 closer to the more than seventeen thousand that still exist. There is now an enormous regulatory apparatus—centered on the International Atomic Energy Association (IAEA)—for tracking nuclear programs around the world. Even if states forsake nuclear weapons for smart budgetary and security reasons, the NPT provides an institutional and normative framework for mutual restraints among rivals and a mechanism for verification. These are no mean efforts, and Mueller is undoubtedly reckless in ignoring them. Yet I think that Mueller raises certain questions about use and waste that are enormously valuable, and well worth pursuing, if we think, not in terms of particular efforts and their outcomes, but in terms of a larger regime of institutions and practices that, despite internal contradictions and disagreements, works with a certain logic aimed toward solving the "nuclear weapons problem."

I am interested in interrogating this question of use from a very different angle than Mueller, by asking the question that I pose at the end of the first chapter of this book: what does the massive, sprawling, multi-billion-dollar nuclear nonproliferation (NNP) regime *do* that is more than the sum of all the good intentions of making nuclear peace as embodied in the many different parts and elements of it? My argument, in brief, is that the NNP regime helps produce and maintain a complex but hierarchical global nuclear order by effectively depoliticizing the problem of nuclear proliferation. Using an analysis heavily influenced by postcolonial IR theory, my attempt in this book is to reveal the (statist and capitalist) interests embedded within this order (driving the production of nuclear power) by politicizing the mechanisms that produce and sustain a desire for nuclear weapons. In other words, I suggest that examining the uses of the NNP regime in deflecting the inequalities that drive nuclear nonproliferation helps us grasp the ways that nuclear weapons and their pursuit are also quite useful, albeit by making only more insecure the already most vulnerable populations of the world. Thus, if we are genuinely interested in nuclear peace, we might be better served by pursuing a path that is attentive to the political economy of injustice rather than travel through the prism of "security."

A Postcolonial Approach to the Problem of Nuclear Weapons

I come at the study of nuclear nonproliferation as a postcolonial theorist rather than a security studies scholar. By way of explaining and as a gesture toward the kind of "critical inventory" that Edward Said (1979) suggests all intellectuals should undertake, let me describe my own trajectory into the "problem of nuclear weapons." I first became interested in nuclear nonproliferation for what may be considered largely parochial reasons. I was an Indian student in the United States in 1998 when India declared itself a nuclear weapons state by conducting a series of nuclear tests, to be followed immediately by Pakistan conducting its own series of tests. I knew that the ruling Hindu nationalist party at the time had promised just such a move in its election manifesto, but I was still surprised and dismayed. It seemed to me then, as it still does, to be such an utter and ultimately dangerous waste of resources for a country with such high levels of poverty and other socioeconomic problems, located in a politically charged region. I recalled that India had at one time taken a strong and proud international stand against nuclear weapons and had staked its own position as a nonsignatory of treaties like the NPT at least partially on that basis. But I was also unprepared, and this surprises me now, for the loud, vicious, sometimes racist, and very much hypocritical response that Indian and Pakistani nuclearization elicited in the United States. It was not uncommon to hear widespread condemnation of Indian and Pakistani actions without any accounting for the dangers that the U.S. possession of nuclear weapons pose. American political leaders and media commentators, striking an arrogant, paternalistic tone in many of their statements, seemed to be wagging their fingers at the actions of errant children. Refusing to defend what I have always thought is an indefensible decision, I nevertheless felt cornered and increasingly resentful as I searched for ways to express my frustrations. Watching the process through which the Indian nuclear program has now become legitimized, and through which India has positioned itself against other nuclear rogues while relinquishing the quest for universal disarmament, has not been reassuring in the least.

I also became increasingly aware, as I tried to make sense of this rampant hypocrisy, how little the trauma of the bombings of Hiroshima and Nagasaki was a part of the American historical psyche or, for that matter, the very American-centric discipline of IR in which I had been trained. For the last decade and a half, I have lived sixty miles downwind from Hanford, Washington, the most contaminated nuclear site in the United States, which produced the plutonium used for Fat Man. It has been disconcerting to see how severed the devastation inflicted on the seemingly far-away victims of Nagasaki appears from the lingering effects of the nuclear waste generated from the production of the commodity that wrought that devastation in my own backyard. These (dis)connections between aggressive nuclear pursuits and their diffuse and dispersed effects have made me think a lot harder about the obscured relationships between agents of power, structures of interests, and forms of victimization.

More recently, I have watched North Korean nuclear belligerence and Iranian nuclear recalcitrance with the same sense of despair and the continuing unreflective arrogance of U.S. (and other nuclear states') responses with the same sense of frustration. I vaguely remember the sense of excitement in some quarters when U.S. president Ronald Reagan and Soviet president Mikhail Gorbachev momentarily considered the question of nuclear abolition at the Reykjavik summit in 1986. Recently, there has been considerable excitement as U.S. president Obama and a few well-known cold warriors strongly attached to nuclear deterrence in the past have enunciated public positions advocating universal disarmament. It is not uncommon for many commentators in scholarly and media forums to urge the United States to lead the way to nuclear peace. I will confess to being somewhat puzzled by this. Continuing aggression by the most heavily armed state on the global stage—which includes claims to keep the military option on the table with respect to Iranian nuclearization—should offer little expectation of any significant change emanating from the U.S. foreign policy establishment. The even larger conventional weapons advantage that the United States would have in a nuclear-free world should also make one less sanguine about its motivations for peace. Why, then, petition the United States to assume leadership in carving out a path to nuclear zero? If nuclear weapons are worthwhile to abolish, where else could one look for change? It appears to me that answering these questions requires rethinking some of the questions that have previously been posed in the security studies literature: what drives nuclear proliferation and efforts to prevent it? Who benefits from those efforts? Who is harmed by nuclear pursuits?

I had an early inkling that nuclear proliferation and attempts at non-proliferation had something to do with economic power and interests, but within conventional IR, the former belonged to the subfield of security studies and the latter to the subfield of political economy, with little conversation between the two. The subfield of security studies is dominated by political realists, the subfield of international political economy by political liberals. In one sense, this book may be seen as an attempt to bridge those two subfields, but it does so via a critique of those dominant approaches within both subfields. There is now a growing body of post-colonial IR scholarship that has mounted a serious and thorough critique of the major institutions and practices of international relations as well as the discipline of IR, with a particular focus on systems of domination, structures of exploitation, and relations of alterity (Darby 1998; 2006; Krishna 2001; 2009a; Chowdhry and Nair 2002; Inayatullah and Blaney 2004; Grovogui 2006; Jones 2006b; Beier 2009; Agathangelou and Ling 2009; Muppidi 2012; Seth 2013a; Sajed 2013). Influenced to different degrees by different strains of Marxist, poststructural, anticolonial, and post-colonial thinkers, the focus of many of these scholars has been to theorize the (colonial) cultural encounters that have helped shape the structures and institutions of global modernity, and their continuing residues, albeit in new forms and with different expressions, in contemporary practices. Rather than provide an overarching alternative theory or replace a Eurocentric IR with a non-Western one, these scholars have offered a plurality of third world perspectives and voices that help us see both existing problems in new ways and new problems previously invisible to IR. My own intellectual formation within the discipline has been very much within this genre. Unfortunately, there is, as yet, too little engagement of these perspectives by those who study nuclear weapons policy and a generally dismissive attitude toward questions of inequality, powerlessness, and exploitation, seen as marginal to the more "serious" dangers of nuclear security. Even many critical security studies scholars who have problematized the concept, referents, and effectiveness of security, and have considered the intersections of security and political economy, have not, in my view, paid adequate attention to the insights of post-colonial theory (Campbell 1992; Dillon 1996; Krause and Williams 1997; Booth 2005).[3] I attempt, in this book, to make the case that the connections between global power, international hierarchies, and neocolonialism that postcolonial scholars raise are in fact quite central to thinking about the problems posed by nuclear weapons, and understanding them will be critical to solving those problems.

The broader field of postcolonial studies outside of the discipline of IR has occasionally witnessed some sharp debates on questions related to its intellectual foundations and ongoing political commitments. Critics have objected to the extent to which the excessive influence of the "linguistic turn" of postmodern and poststructural theory and overemphasis on the politics of representation and mimesis have led to inadequate attention to political economy and the contemporary forces of neoliberal capitalism. Although I am largely unsympathetic to the kinds of critique that disparage the metropolitan location of postcolonial critics (Ahmed 1992; Larsen 2000), or suggest that postcolonial theory serves as an apology for neoliberalism (Dirlik 1997), I find myself quite persuaded by the argument that accounting for the resilience and import of continuing relations of colonial power requires attention to exploitative global capitalism, in all its contemporary expressions (Dirlik 1997; Young 2001; Lazarus 2001; Parry 2004). As will be clear shortly, I am very much influenced by poststructural theory, especially the Foucault of *Discipline and Punish,* but the Marx (1977) of *Capital* remains quite central to my thinking. My readings of both poststructural theory and historical materialism, however, are strained through a reading of postcolonial history and politics, drawing intellectual inspiration from a whole series of postcolonial thinkers from a variety of disciplines, whose work I draw from heavily in this book. Thus my attempt to chart out the contours of the global nuclear order takes me to an examination of the politics of representation in the NNP regime, the operation of this regime through the mimetic medium of the modern nation-state, and the powerful transnational capitalist interests that underlie and belie the NNP regime in its exploitation of vulnerable and marginal communities and peoples.

Much of the literature in the area of nuclear proliferation is "empiricist," focused on assessing the causes and consequences of proliferation, much of it through quantitative analyses. By the standards of many of those studies, this book would be considered theoretical, even though I make ample use of empirical data. However, there is an important sense in which I consider myself very much to be an empiricist, engaged with the problems of the world as I see them and invested in contributing toward their alleviation. In a very influential piece that has inspired considerable work in the area of critical security studies, Robert Cox (1986) once distinguished between *problem-solving theory* and *critical theory* as they apply to the field of IR. Problem-solving theories largely take the world and its structures of power as given, he suggested, and, in providing conservative solutions that largely accept the existing frames, aid in the perpetuation of existing institutions and the interests underlying them. By contrast, critical theory stands apart from such structures, calling into question their constitution and ultimately contributing toward their dissolution. My own view is that much of the scholarship and thinking on nuclear proliferation within the security studies field—driven by a genuine concern about the dangers of nuclear weapons possession and proliferation—are mostly problem-solving exercises that ignore the larger structures of power that drive both proliferation and nonproliferation efforts and thus contribute to sustaining a global (nuclear) order that serves a very specific set of interests. Like Cox, I am interested in investigating and critiquing the ideology, institutions, and material bases of this order. But, and here troubling this divide between problem solving and critical theory, I consider the "problems" posed by nuclear weapons possession and proliferation to be pressing and urgent global problems, and the larger aim of the book is to provide readers with a way to think about them in a theoretically sophisticated, historically and contextually sensitive, and ultimately more productive way. In other words, I see the critical theory I undertake as a problem-solving exercise. I suggest that tackling urgent issues such as nuclear proliferation in an effective manner requires the kind of deeper and broader understanding that can conceptualize particular problems with an appreciation for history and complexity. In that sense, although the book is not conceived as a practical policy-making guide, as a good deal of the security studies literature tends to be, it hopes to help inspire a fuller and sounder understanding of what kinds of efforts will make nuclear disarmament ultimately possible and lasting.

Chapter Outline

The puzzle that begins chapter 1 is centered on security. Security is the primary problematic for realist IR theorists and states the primary agents for delivering it. In the self-help anarchy that describes international relations for realists, creating cooperative institutions that might restrain state action is generally challenging. In the area of security, where state interests are most effectively individuated, that challenge is considerably magnified. Yet there is in place a truly enormous regime of interstate treaties and organizations, international nongovernmental agencies, think tanks, watchdog groups, and transnational activists that have made it their business to track, monitor, regulate, and effectively constrain state actions with respect to the pursuit and possession of nuclear weapons. The NPT is one, albeit absolutely critical and perhaps even central, node of this massive regime. Chapter 1 describes this NNP regime in detail, showing the various linkages, cross-cutting ties, and quite different specific aims of different elements of this regime. What unifies these different aims—sometimes complementary, sometimes contradictory—is that they all recognize the "problem" that nuclear weapons pose and attempt to solve it. They do so largely by focusing on the state—urging it, placing demands on it, cracking its secrecy, tracking it, monitoring it, and regulating it—and they all are engaged in the very well-intentioned task of constraining state actions toward the end of nuclear peace. Good intentions are fragile in the Hobbesian anarchy of realists, and so it is liberal IR theorists to whom I turn to see how well they explain the evolution of these mutually enabling identities and interests working toward a common end. The debate between realists and liberals over the emergence of cooperation under anarchy is interesting to an extent, I suggest, but doesn't really get us too far in understanding how *effective* this kind of cooperation is, when it does actually emerge, as it has with the problem of nuclear weapons. It is this question of effectiveness that is the actual puzzle of chapter 1 and one that I suggest neither realists nor liberals are particularly good at theorizing.

I suggest that there is a very important sense in which gauging the effectiveness of the vast, sprawling, complex, multi-billion-dollar regime in terms of the overall goal of creating nuclear peace reveals failure. I am compelled by the arguments made by Mueller, Ward, and others on the military uselessness of nuclear weapons. But the case for nuclear abolition has been well made, many times over, long before Mueller's book. That case is now also being made by highly placed conservative policy leaders in heavily armed nuclear states that were previously committed adherents of deterrence. Numerous proposals and blueprints outline the steps to a nuclear-free world. But nuclear abolition has always been a receding goal, relegated to the future when all the other problems of nuclear weapons—especially proliferation—have been solved. The number of nuclear warheads that exist in the world, and the power to deliver them across great distances in relatively short time, remains unacceptably high, even in the eyes of many experts who find nuclear weapons useful for security. It is not the well-meaning intentions driving the regime that I question, nor even the specific successes in restraining the superpower arms race or preventing the spread of weapons material or technology, but the "liberal progress" this massive constellation of efforts should portend. Whatever progress we make via this or that treaty or organization, we are not, in my view, progressing toward a nuclear-free world; if anything, anxieties about nuclear attacks have only increased recently. Here I am on ground similar to Mueller's in questioning the usefulness of this multi-billion-dollar enterprise in ensuring nuclear peace. But my interest is in querying this so-called failure further, asking if this failure itself can teach us something about the way the world works.

It is with this in mind that I turn to a Foucauldian analysis of the NNP regime, using James Ferguson's (1994) brilliant analysis of the development regime in *The Anti-Politics Machine* as a guide which, in turn, borrows Foucault's (1995) brilliant analysis of the prison regime in *Discipline and Punish*. Foucault suggests that "failures" (in prisoner rehabilitation, in poverty alleviation, in creating nuclear peace) are *productive*, that is, they have effects that exceed the particular aims of the regime and specific policies within it. This is what explains the perpetuation of the regime, despite persistent failures, through a plethora of redundant efforts that tackle the same problem in seemingly new ways. So the question I ask in chapter 1, and in the book more generally, is, what does the NNP regime *do* that is not just about the creation of nuclear peace? Answering this question, I believe, helps us understand the ways that the NNP regime continues to be useful, whether or not the various efforts contained within it actually make the world safer from the dangers of nuclear weapons. I suggest, with Ferguson, that one effect of the expertise-guided ways that the NNP articulates the problem of nuclear weapons is to depoliticize nuclearization, which in turn occludes a deeply hierarchical global nuclear order that helps produce nuclear desire as well as deflecting from the interests that benefit from the pursuit of those desires.

William Walker also articulates an account of the order-producing effects of the NNP regime, but from a liberal perspective. It is this account and the debate surrounding it that is the subject of chapter 2. Walker's lucidly argued, well-circulated account is largely centered on the NPT, which, he suggests, helps instantiate a global, progressive "Enlightenment Order" that evidences the triumph of reason over dogma, cooperation over mistrust, morality over evil. Certainly Walker is well aware of the hypocrisy of the nuclear five—recognized by the treaty as having a monopoly over the forces of nuclear destruction—and berates them for not doing their part to honor the (nonbinding) commitment they made to undertake "in good faith" the steps toward nuclear disarmament. But this does not impair in any serious fashion his championing and celebration of this most successful international venture of peace and goodwill. Walker's is a bold and generous narrative, and it is hard not to be uplifted by it, especially if you are persuaded of the dangers of nuclear weapons and interested in eliminating them. But his realist critics will have none of this utopianism. The world is already dangerous, full of suspicion and distrust; the point, then, is to keep dangerous weapons from those who are the most untrustworthy. The NPT, they suggest, was not some gesture of benign goodwill but a cynical attempt to freeze the nuclear status quo. Rather than disarm, nuclear weapons must and will be retained by those who can wield them responsibly, only more so as more rogue nonstate actors proliferate. Power is a central fact for realists, and Walker's critics underscore the centrality of power in maintaining the order of international relations. The NPT, in their view, very much reflects this power, and this is as it should be.

In this debate between Walker and his critics, I find myself quite buoyed by Walker but more swayed by his critics. I do not subscribe to the prejudices of Walker's critics; indeed, I find the distribution of irrationality quite evenly distributed across the world, the appetite to use preponderant violence and force against "foreign others" when deemed necessary much larger among the currently recognized nuclear states than the wannabes, and I am not persuaded that all the institutional restraints on nuclear use currently in place can, in fact, restrain aggressive, megalomaniacal foreign policy aggressors like the United States from redefining "responsible nuclear use" as they please. Indeed, I worry about the possession of nuclear weapons by the United States, Russia, the United Kingdom, France, China, Israel, and India[4] as much as I worry about their possession by Pakistan, North Korea, or Iran. Yet I find the prejudices that Walker's critics wear on their sleeves almost more refreshing than the vaunted liberal benevolence and goodwill of Walker's account. Liberal accounts such as Walker's will occasionally acknowledge inequality but brush it aside too quickly; power, here, appears incidental and extraneous. As E. H. Carr (1940) pointed out so long ago in *The Twenty Year Crisis,* one must always scrutinize the interested character of liberal morality in a world in which even the most belligerent actors act in the name of peace. The NPT, like the rest of the NNP regime, acts in the name of peace, but what kind of peaceful order does it really instantiate?

Instead of quarreling with Walker's account of the NPT as a liberal Enlightenment Order, I suggest, drawing from a series of postcolonial theorists (Timothy Mitchell, Edward Said, Uday Mehta and Dipesh Chakraborty, and Tzvetan Todorov, among others), that the order of the Enlightenment was itself constituted out of various exclusions—of those irrational others who could be neither assimilated nor contained. Nuclear disarmament by the powerful states of the world will always remain a receding goal in the face of this radical diversity. The global order instantiated by the NPT and the larger regime surrounding it is framed through this logic of alterity, and whatever good it might have done to contain the spread of nuclear weapons, materials, and technology (as I believe it has), it also plays a central part in keeping alive this hierarchical order premised on a whole series of prejudices about the geography and limits of Enlightenment rationality. Occasionally, the institutionalization of this hierarchy becomes symbolic material, cynically wielded by third world leaders in the form of the "nuclear apartheid" argument to justify expensive and unsafe nuclear weapons programs that only bolster their own authorities and serve transnational capitalist interests. But nevertheless, whether or not particular states choose to pursue a nuclear weapons program, this hierarchy also helps keep alive the desire for nuclear weapons.

It is to this question of nuclear desire that chapter 3 turns, in an attempt to *politicize* the process through which nuclear weapons acquire social value. Generally cast as a nonproliferation treaty, the NPT prohibits nuclear weapons proliferation but actually encourages nuclear energy proliferation. Marking an ontological break that is, in reality, difficult to identify and sustain, this distinction has been criticized, especially for its proliferation-inducing effects. Iran claims to pursue its NPT-protected legitimate rights to nuclear energy; the members of the P-5 plus one and Israel insist that Iran intends to weaponize. But implicit in this ontological distinction is the premise that the power of the atom, when intended for the expansion of goods and markets, is liberatory and "peaceful," but when wielded for violence and war, it is utterly and devastatingly damaging. For postcolonial states, the Green promise for easy deliverance from poverty and weakness that nuclear power provides and the massive global opprobrium that the pursuit of nuclear weapons invite only makes that

line dividing the two sides more bright with significance. Many nonproliferation efforts are aimed at preventing the slide from the utopian side of
that line to the dystopian side. But also implicit in these efforts is the premise that nuclear weapons are deeply desirable, and sinful well-meaning
states with access to some of the infrastructure for their production may
always be tempted to slide from one side to the other. States pursue nuclear weapons or must *resist* pursuing them—as the widespread use of
the terms *nuclear restraint* and *nuclear abstinence* would seem to indicate.
Some states have the requisite maturity for selective ownership, but for
others, the temptation must be eradicated. It is this underlying desire that
I am most interested in theorizing, not the long list of demand-side reasons offered by security studies scholars for why states decide to pursue
or refrain from pursuing nuclear weapons. I theorize this desire through
an analysis of *commodity fetishism*, analyzing two interrelated logics that
make nuclear weapons valuable—first, the logic of deterrence as a semiotic economy of meanings through which nuclear weapons become "useful in their uselessness," and second, the logic of regulation through which
nuclear weapons emerge as a particular class of luxury goods.

First I turn to Marx to understand how nuclear weapons emerge as a
very particular sort of fetishized commodity. The question I ask, following Marx's analysis of commodities in volume 1 of *Capital*, is how nuclear
weapons accrue value. Marx analyzes how the operations of capital dis-
articulate *use value* from *exchange value* so that the market value of a commodity is increasingly removed from the real value of the labor that produces a commodity. The market in which nuclear weapons circulate is an
odd one, in which states are the sole customers. But so are the ways that
states think of the use value of nuclear weapons. The use of nuclear weapons, as states claim, is for deterrence—that is, the threat to visit the kind of
unacceptable damage that nuclear weapons promise to deter aggression.
In other words, the way that states manage the enormously destructive
uses of nuclear weapons is by arguing for their *nonuse*. Here I am back to
discussing the alleged uselessness of nuclear weapons, as Mueller does,
but in a way quite different from him. I don't question the dangers that
nuclear weapons pose, but I am interested in the ways that those dangers
have been strategically mobilized by states to make a case for their usefulness *as useless*. Deterrence, in other words, along with the technostrategic
language that forms its frame, both helps evacuate the enormous potential
for harms that nuclear weapons possess and helps make nuclear weapons

that absolute weapon that can guarantee absolute security without being *used*. In the final chapter, I turn to the implications of this sort of domestication of the nuclear threat for the state's ability to monopolize violence in the nuclear age, but here I am most interested in what deterrence, as a mechanism of fetishization, obscures, which is the larger political economy of nuclear production that the following chapter surveys.

Nuclear value has another dimension. In *The Social Life of Things*, Arjun Appadurai (1986) suggests that Marx's focus on labor and production makes him insufficiently attentive to the generation of value from the process of exchange itself. To fully understand the ways that nuclear weapons have emerged as fetishized objects of state desire, one needs also to attend to the highly regulated market of nuclear weapons knowledge, materials, and technology. Here the role of the NPT as a technology of regulation, which works in association with many other parts of the larger nonproliferation regime that tracks, monitors, and controls the spread of nuclear weapons, becomes important. The hierarchical global nuclear order that the NNP constitutes also helps produce and sustain nuclear weapons as objects available only to those who have the requisite credentials (the institutional apparatus, adequate maturity) and legitimate access (to fissile materials, technological know-how) to possess—making them luxury goods that confer status and ranking. Nuclear weapons may never be used, but they are useful for signifying who belongs where in the global nuclear order.

What does this usefulness of nuclear weapons in the name of their nonuse conceal? What could we learn if we saw nuclear weapons—shorn of their glamour as those most desirable instruments of security and ranking—as commodities that emerge from a process of production? It is to this question that I turn in chapter 4, where I try to assess the costs of unused nuclear weapons. There is simply no easy way to calculate these costs. My attempt is not to provide any comprehensive accounting of these costs but instead to show the many different dimensions of it and, more important, the ways that those dimensions point us toward the *already occurring harms of these allegedly unused weapons*. Any assessment of these costs, yet again, destabilizes the neat break between nuclear energy and weapons on which the NPT relies. Although my reach is global, I try to make the task a bit more manageable by focusing on three case studies, each exemplifying a different stage of nuclear weapons development. The United States is the longest established nuclear weapons states, one of the two largest producers of them, and a founding member of the NPT; India is a relatively newer nuclear weapons state with also a quite active and expanding nuclear energy market and one of four nuclear weapons states that are not party to the NPT; and Japan, the only victim of a wartime nuclear use, that had until the nuclear reactor meltdowns at Fukushima Daiichi in 2011 a fairly massive nuclear energy program, is a state that has decided not to pursue a nuclear weapons program but is fully capable of breaking out, if it so chooses, at relatively quick notice. I move back and forth between the global level and these three cases to show how we may think of the larger effects of investments in nuclear weapons that may never be used.

Starting from the most general level and moving closer to the production process, chapter 4 examines three kinds of costs. At the *first*, most obvious level, I provide existing estimates for the amount spent on nuclear weapons, which, when available, includes not just defense expenditures on the procurement of weapons but also their maintenance, enhancements, deployments, storage, waste disposal, environmental cleanup, and so on. These are massive costs, but more important are the *opportunity costs* these entail, the consequences of which are only more severe for poorer countries, such as India, with high levels of poverty. At the *second* level, I examine the collusion of state and corporate interests invested in the pursuit of nuclear power, and the effects of that on safety and security. The "regulatory capture" of the state by corporate interests in nuclear power is evident in all three cases. In the Indian case, it is also clear how much the enormous potential of India's energy markets mattered in normalizing the Indian nuclear weapons program, corporate interests helping to neutralize India's rogueness as a recalcitrant nuclear power unwilling to submit to the nuclear order of the NPT. The Japanese case shows how much the state colluded with corporate interests in making nuclear power palatable to an understandably nuclear-weary nation after World War II, interests that are regrouping in the wake of the resistance to nuclear power that has emerged after the Fukushima Daiichi disaster. In this second kind of measure, my attempt is to get at the costs of nuclear pursuits in the production of a consolidated neoliberal security state compromised in its ability to guarantee nuclear security. At the *third* and final level, I turn to an assessment of nuclear costs in terms of labor and bodily exploitation by turning to what may be considered to be the origins and end points of nuclear production—in uranium mining most specifically, but also in nuclear testing, waste storage, and nuclear cleanup efforts. Here I examine the effects of the collusions of statist and global corporate interests on those vulnerable bodies and indigenous communities around the world that have been rendered the most insecure by nuclear proliferation and are the least visible in most accountings of nuclear costs. Although it is far from comprehensive, my overall attempt in chapter 4 is to tackle the question of nuclear costs to demystify and politicize the very real effects of fetishized, unused nuclear weapons. However little wartime use of nuclear weapons there might have been since the end of the Second World War, the damages they have wrought are considerable and, more significantly, borne by the most marginal, vulnerable populations of the world—the "subaltern," as conceptualized by Gayatri Spivak (2010) in her well-known essay "Can the Subaltern Speak?"

In the concluding chapter of the book, I return to the question of nuclear order and its political effects, but from this problematic of the subaltern. The first part of the chapter is essentially a summary of the arguments of the book via the concept of the subaltern, but the second part scrutinizes the logic of state centricity in a nuclear world and the extent to which the state can speak for the subaltern in such a world. In the IR literature, Mohammed Ayoob has offered the framework of subaltern realism to discuss the fraught place of what he calls the subaltern state—the third world state attempting to consolidate its internal authority against numerous challenges in a state-centric world. Ayoob is quite adamant about the need for a state—as a vehicle of security—to speak for the concerns and aspirations of third world peoples within a hierarchical global order whose rules have been crafted by richer, more powerful states, as we already saw with the NNP regime. However, as some of the classical realists understood better than their neorealist inheritors, the qualitative change in the potential for destruction that thermonuclear weapons wrought raises serious questions about the ability of the state to secure its citizens. Some of these thinkers and others argued that the advent of nuclear weapons intimated a possibly different organization of world politics that was not centered on states as the agents of security. But deterrence, as we already saw, provides the state a mechanism to contain the threat that nuclear weapons pose to its own existence as a state. In that sense, deterrence may well have helped evacuate this possible radical restructuring of world politics toward which some of these early realists and others began to gesture. But what results from this statist resolution of the excessive dangers of nuclear weapons is an authoritarian national-security state, whose "nuclear guardians," in Robert Dahl's (1985) words, frequently remain publicly unaccountable.

The compromised neoliberal nuclear state that chapter 4 examines is also an authoritarian state, only further removed from the subaltern peoples and communities most impacted by nuclear pursuits.

Embedded within the hierarchies of the global order, the subaltern (nuclear) state, as Ayoob suggests, may find a voice as a state, but it is seldom the voice of the subaltern. How may the subaltern, then, speak? I ask at the very end of the concluding chapter. With Spivak, I suggest that the subaltern are already speaking, in all sorts of forms and expressions, all around the world—in the first, what remains of the second, the third, and, most important, the fourth worlds—but the vehicle of the state does not let us hear them, and the frame of security does not let us attend to them. From the perspective of the subaltern, nuclear weapons are, indeed, useless in providing security, and so the massive amounts of resources invested into nuclear projects may be considered a colossal waste, resources that could well have been used for life-preserving and life-enhancing goals. Looked at from another angle, this waste of resources has left the planet littered with radioactive waste, much of which, too, will be left to rot on some of the world's most vulnerable territories and peoples. Nuclear weapons are dangerous, in the present and the future, and nuclear abolition is a worthwhile goal. Offering his book as a "remedy for insomnia," John Mueller (2010) ends his criticisms of the unnecessary obsession with nuclear weapons and fears of their proliferation with the call to "sleep well." But perhaps, if we really want to reach that goal of nuclear abolition that is Mueller's interest, too, instead of sleeping well, it may serve us better to wake up to the plight of the subaltern.

CHAPTER 1

Intentions and Effects

The Proliferation of the Nuclear Nonproliferation Regime

The Case for Nuclear Arms Control and Disarmament

An odd constellation of forces arguing for nuclear disarmament suddenly appears to have emerged on the global scene. Even though the lively antinuclear movement of the Cold War era dissipated in anticipation of the "peace dividend" that was to follow the end of U.S.–Soviet nuclear antagonism, many cautious voices on the left continued to urge restraint and advocate disarmament by the infamous club of the "nuclear five."[1] What is interesting, however, is to see this chorus expand to include voices that, though always nervous about the perils of proliferation outside the club, were at one time fierce defenders of nuclear weapons for the club, many of them architects of nuclear deterrence doctrines that justified the possession of those weapons. So, for instance, two former secretaries of state (George Shultz and Henry Kissinger), one former secretary of defense (William J. Perry), and one former chairman of the Senate Foreign Relations Committee (Sam Nunn)—all well-known cold warriors in the United States—have together mounted a fairly visible public relations campaign to persuade current leaders and policy makers of the wisdom of moving to global nuclear zero.[2] Many strategic thinkers and scholars continue to argue that nuclear deterrence—long heralded for its contributions to keeping the peace between two hostile armed-to-the-teeth superpowers—still works quite effectively in relations between states, including the new nuclear states outside of the original club.[3] But the fears that drive the current calls for disarmament are not just from the slow horizontal spread of nuclear weapons to states outside the nuclear club but also from its diagonal spread to actors who can no longer be counted on to behave with the requisite rationality necessary for deterrence to function.[4] Although some of this concern is directed toward "rogue states,"[5] the rise of transnational terrorist groups, such as al-Qaeda, and their stated or presumed desire and ability to acquire nuclear weapons (perhaps from rogue states), is the primary source of anxiety here.[6] It is interesting, then, that the rise of global terrorism that has, on one hand, activated a whole new set of practices of violence has, on the other hand, arguably made peaceniks out of former nuclear hawks.

Efforts to abolish nuclear weapons have long existed alongside efforts to prevent their spread. Almost immediately after the first and only wartime use of nuclear weapons in Hiroshima and Nagasaki, proposals were under way to delegitimize the possession of nuclear weapons by any state.[7] However, as the Soviet nuclear weapons program gathered steam, efforts to halt the further spread of these weapons began taking precedence over desires for abolition. In the enormous nuclear arms control regime that emerged from these efforts, the Nuclear Non-Proliferation Treaty (NPT) has long been considered the shining star and foundational anchor for the entire regime. However, the NPT exists in close association with a number of other treaties, organizations, and agencies, working, if not always in perfect symmetry, in what may be considered an alignment of similar interests. In other words, the NPT may be considered one, albeit very prominent, node of what is a vast regime of agreements, associations, and interests that see their collective task as making the world safe from the horrific possible use of nuclear weapons. How can we understand the mechanisms that sustain this enormous regime, and how do we gauge its effectiveness?

The field of international relations (IR) has always had some difficulty in conceptualizing the emergence of cooperative regimes, especially in the area of security. This is largely because of the predominance of political realism, which is premised on an ontology of individuated, autonomous states in pursuit of power and security in an anarchic world riddled with potential threats, and hence prone to suspicion and mistrust. But with the emergence of political liberalism within IR, the possibilities of state cooperation came to be recognized in areas where sheer survival is not at stake, or areas which, in the commonly deployed game-theoretic language of that genre, are characterized by possible win-win or positive-sum combinations emergent from absolute gains. But why, how, and when states might collaborate where security is concerned—an area where relative gains in a zero-sum game are most at play—continued to remain somewhat of a puzzle. Thus it is that the academic division of labor within IR split the subfield of international security, in which political realism dominated, from the subfield of international political economy, to which political liberalism was generally seen to apply. Most efforts at explaining cooperation focused on forms of economic cooperation, while states were considered largely mistrusting and uncooperative in the realm of security. So it might be considered quite remarkable that an enormous and sprawling global architecture with respect to preventing the spread and use of nuclear weapons has now established itself so firmly within international politics, especially as the pursuit of nuclear security might well be considered "high politics" of the highest order.[8] Owing to the centrality of the NPT within it, I am referring to this regime as the Nuclear Non-Proliferation (NNP) regime, but its shape and scope are considerably larger, more complex, and multilayered, and the regime involves a variety of different kinds of actors, institutions, and organizations, all of which are invested quite simply in preventing the use of the massive (and spreading) stockpiles of nuclear weapons around the world.[9]

This chapter is an attempt to chart out the contours of this NNP regime and understand its existence and the functions it serves in global politics. The chapter begins by discussing how the field of IR conceptualizes and understands the existence of international regimes, before turning to an elaboration of this complex regime. Suggesting that liberal IR understandings of the NNP regime fall short of adequately grasping the complexity and functions of this regime, the chapter then discusses a Foucauldian-inspired understanding of this regime as a set of discursive practices whose effects exceed the purported aims of nonproliferation and violence prevention. In other words, the chapter asks what this massive constellation of actors, institutions, and interests involved in the NNP *does* that is more than the sum of the various liberal interests in simply ensuring the existence of a peaceful world.

Regimes in International Relations

The concept of a regime is now well established in the IR literature. Emerging from the genre of liberal IR, Stephen Krasner's definition of a regime as "principles, norms, rules, and decision-making procedures around which actor expectations converge in a given issue-area" has become the starting point for many scholarly analyses that attempt to account for the ways that cooperative relations among egoistic states motivated by self-preservation can be facilitated by the emergence of institutions and norms that guide and regulate state behavior (Krasner 1982b, 185). Regimes, in other words, are cooperative arrangements created by states to manage and contain the potential for conflict in an anarchic world. The special issue of the IR journal *International Organization* in which Krasner elaborated this definition takes as its task examining the importance of international regimes in a world of sovereign nation-states.[10] The purpose of the volume is to quite decidedly make the case that "regimes matter," although there is some disagreement among the contributors as to how much their presence mitigates the effects of a realist world in which brute power predominates. The bulk of the essays in the volume—categorized as "modified structural"— see regimes as emergent under fairly restrictive conditions from the coordinated actions of power-maximizing, sovereign states who find it in their rational self-interest to tame some of the excesses of international anarchy.[11] There are a few others—categorized as "Groatian" in inspiration— that see regimes as more pervasive and durable features of the fabric of international relations.[12] But the general theoretical framework of the volume understands regimes as "intervening variables" that help trace how the causal variables of power and interest affect outcomes and behavior so that the underlying realist structure of an anarchic world composed of security-motivated, power-seeking, self-interested states remains more or less the backdrop from which regimes emerge and in which they function.

It should come as no surprise, then, that of all the regimes conceptualized as possible in this volume, a security regime appears the most challenging.[13] In an anarchic world run by self-interested states whose prime motivation is their own survival in the face of an abundance of potential threats, cooperative security regimes appear notoriously difficult to fashion. Robert Jervis's (1982) article in the volume is a study in the trying conditions in the security arena that make a cooperative regime exceedingly difficult to design. The primacy of national security, the competitiveness among states in the pursuit of security, the high stakes of misplaced trust and mistakes, and the general secrecy and uncertainty related to state security all make the prisoner's dilemma more acutely operational in the arena of security. Jervis outlines a series of conditions that must be present to help overcome the "security dilemma" of anarchy, followed by an empirical analysis of the Concert of Europe that demonstrates how fragile, ultimately, any successful attempt to institutionalize security cooperation can be. Thus it is not particularly surprising that in the enormous industry of empirical studies generated by the regimes literature in IR, very little attention has been devoted to the study of security regimes, especially at the global level.[14] After expressing some pessimism about the ability of the two Cold War superpowers to create a viable regime that would regulate their behavior, Jervis ends his piece with a rather dramatic note from Herman Kahn's imaginings of the kind of nuclear crisis that might well lead the two superpowers, albeit unhappily, toward a world government. Yet he fails to reflect at all on the NNP regime, already well under way in its establishment by 1982, when the article was published, the attempt of which is precisely to prevent such a nuclear crisis from developing.[15] Some years later, Joseph Nye (1987) expressed a little more optimism than Jervis in the existence of a mosaic of partial security regimes that had emerged from a history of U.S.–Soviet "nuclear learning,"[16] and here he identified the NNP regime as one of these "partial regimes" that include the NPT, the International Atomic Energy Agency (IAEA), and the Nuclear Suppliers Group (NSG), supplemented by U.S.–Soviet bilateral talks. But there is, generally, very minimal scholarship that explores the NNP regime in any systematic fashion as a global security regime.

The fact that self-interested states so thoroughly invested in their own survival and security have actually cooperated in a variety of ways to prevent conflict, especially in a nuclear world, thus remained a puzzle not just for realists but also for the previously mentioned neoliberal institutionalists generally more sanguine about state collaboration. However, two lines of scholarly inquiry that emerged from the regimes literature tried somewhat harder to explain state cooperation by targeting particular causal variables that pushed states toward a reconfiguration of their own interests and showed more promise for understanding security regimes. First was the literature spawned by work on knowledge networks that came to be known as the epistemic communities literature. The importance of knowledge and expertise in the creation of regimes was hinted at in Ernst Haas's contribution to the 1982 special issue on international regimes cited earlier, but the concept of epistemic communities—networks of empowered experts, both domestic and transnational, who can bring their shared consensual knowledge to help transform the narrow self-interests of states away from conflict and toward collaboration and coordination—was developed systematically in subsequent work by Peter Haas, Emanuel Adler, and others (see Haas 1989). Thus, another special issue of the journal *International Organization* came to be devoted to the influence of epistemic communities in the production and sustenance of international regimes.[17]

In the introduction to that volume, Peter Haas (1992, 3) defines an epistemic community as "a network of professionals with recognized expertise and competence in a particular domain and an authoritative claim to policy-relevant knowledge within that domain or issue-area" who also share, in addition to certain causal beliefs and criteria of validity, a "set of normative and principled beliefs." It is this normative orientation that becomes the focus of the soon-to-follow norms-based accounts of international relations that proliferated in the 1990s (discussed later), but the focus of the epistemic communities literature was to show how expertise is wielded by cross-nationally connected elite professionals in ways that not only shape the identification and delineation of various "global problems" but also help reformulate state understandings and interests toward the goals of collective solutions and collaboration in a wide range of "issue areas" that include trade in services, nuclear arms control, management of whaling and other forms of environmental protections, food aid, and monetary policy. In the concluding essay of the volume, authored by Emanuel Adler and Peter Haas (1992), whose purpose is to elaborate a future research agenda, the authors point to the "nuclear nonproliferation field" as a particularly promising area in which to examine the influence of epistemic communities, yet with the exception of the piece by Emanuel Adler (1992) that studies the influence of the U.S. arms control epistemic community on the creation of an antiballistic missile arms control regime in the same volume, there has been little work to document the extensive contours of a global NNP regime in which technical and policy expertise plays a crucial authoritative role.[18] Although studies of epistemic communities in other international areas have abounded, particularly with respect to environmental policy making, there has been relatively scant attention paid to security in general and nuclear security in particular. Here one sees, once again, the further entrenchment of the academic division of IR labor between political realism–dominated security studies and political liberalism–dominated international political economy.

The emergence in the 1990s of an entire corpus of norms-based accounts of various international phenomena can be partially traced to these earlier discussions of cooperation and regimes and might be seen as one somewhat successful attempt to breach the previously mentioned academic labor divide. Most of the scholars who came to define this area claimed to situate themselves at some distance from the realist–rationalist accounts that drove the study of international regimes and institutions.

Expressing their dissatisfaction with the shared presuppositions of both realist and neoliberal institutionalist scholars in a rather thin conceptualization of individuated, autonomous, and fully bounded actors, this group of IR theorists was motivated to take seriously the *relational* end of international relations. In doing so, they helped steer what came to be called the "constructivist" turn in IR, attentive to the social construction of state identities and interests. A volume edited by Peter Katzenstein in 1996 was an explicit attempt to understand the realm of international security through the constitutive and regulative effects of ideas and norms. Despite the positivist traces in its claim to exceed the materialist ontology of realist IR by inserting "culture" as a "causal explanatory variable," there was here a conscious effort to take account of the ways that norms shape identities and practices. The volume identifies three layers of "the international cultural environment in which national security policies are made"—a first layer of "formal institutions or security regimes," of which the NPT is identified as one example of an arms control regime, a second layer of a "world political culture," which includes rules and norms of sovereignty as well as various standardized social and political technologies carried by epistemic communities, and a third layer of "patterns of amity and enmity," which have important cultural dimensions (Jepperson, Wendt, and Katzenstein 1996, 34).[19] However, despite the framing of a research agenda with the promise of a serious analysis of institutions, rules, and culture, the empirical studies in the area of security that emerged from this school focused much more narrowly on "ideas."

This is the case, for instance, with the most substantive work on nuclear security produced from this norms-based scholarly tradition—Nina Tannenwald's (2007) fairly influential study of the "nuclear taboo."[20] Though she goes to some length to distinguish between norms and the much stronger prohibitive notion of a taboo, Tannenwald makes a very strong case for how certain ideas and values about weapons use take hold and constrain state actions. Arguing against the realist understanding of deterrence and nuclear restraint, Tannenwald argues that rather than being motivated by a prudential fear of nuclear retaliation, U.S. policy makers obeyed a nuclear taboo that stemmed as much from moral revulsion as it did from "political" concerns like retaliation. To make this argument, she traces U.S. military thinking on nuclear use from the Korean War to the Gulf War with extensive primary research. She concludes that, because of a combination of factors, ranging from political concerns about

escalation and proliferation to moral concerns based in the memory of
Hiroshima and Nagasaki and antinuclear activism, U.S. decision makers
have consistently seen nuclear weapons as less useable than conventional
weapons, particularly after the second term of the Eisenhower administration. Although she hesitates to conclude that the taboo can indefinitely
prevent nuclear use, citing genuine temptation during the Korean War and
thinly veiled threats made during the first Bush administration, she sees
it as holding substantial explanatory weight in the long nonuse of nuclear
weapons.

To find the "objective" existence of this taboo, Tannenwald (2007, 13)
looks for evidence in "discourse," which she defines as "the way people
talk and think about nuclear weapons," which includes "public opinion,
the diplomatic statements of states and leaders, the resolutions of international organizations, and the private moral concerns of individual de-
cisionmakers." International laws, arms control agreements, state policies
on nuclear weapons, all "supplement" this discourse, and in her chrono-
logical narrative, the taboo emerges "bottom-up" as a result of "societal
pressure" and is *subsequently* "institutionalized in bilateral (U.S.–Soviet)
and multilayered arms control agreements and regimes" (56). Indeed, it is
only in chapter 7 of a very long book that Tannenwald takes up the question of institutionalization and discusses the different arms of the NNP
regime that helped delegitimize the use of nuclear weapons. Even though
different in emphasis and more attuned to societal processes of norms
diffusion, Tannenwald's characterization of institutions and regimes, and
that of the norms-based accounts of IR more generally, is ultimately fairly
consistent with the neoliberal institutionalist understanding of regimes as
mechanisms to instantiate the good intentions of policy makers in collaborative state actions toward the ends of global peace. Thus both Adler's
account of the ways that the work and strategic assumptions of the arms
control epistemic community helped draw the United States and the Soviet
Union toward negotiations on the Anti-Ballistic Missile (ABM) Treaty and
Tannenwald's account of the many bilateral and multilateral arms control
treaties as emergent from the efforts of policy makers to stabilize deterrence and circumscribe the use of nuclear weapons see the institutions and
agreements of the NNP as well-intentioned steps toward a more peaceful
nuclear world.

Indeed, very much in the vein of liberal IR more generally, all these accounts are also, ultimately, narratives of progress. Although Tannenwald

argues that her story is not one of moral progress, and points out that the "dark side" of the nuclear taboo is its indirect "permissive" effect of legitimizing more conventional forms of violence (25), the very structure of her account portends to the historical process through which a lethal and abominable weapons system gradually becomes abhorrent and illegitimate for use, with some occasional setbacks, but in a decidedly progressive, even if not entirely predetermined, direction. While Haas's introduction to the 1992 special issue of *International Organization* on epistemic communities alluded to earlier reminds us to be mindful of the realist context of material and structural power that shapes the influence of epistemic communities, the volume ends by reiterating the faith that liberal IR places in the possibility of "progressive change" that occurs through a "redefinition of values" and "the reconciliation of national interests with human interests in general, such as security, welfare, and human rights" (Adler and Haas 1992, 389–90). Adler and Haas's concluding essay thus ends by suggesting that the use of "reason" by epistemic communities in the solving of global problems paves the path to a possibly "better international order" (390). Adler and Barnett (1998), rejecting the general pessimism of realist IR regarding the immutability of a conflict-ridden world, similarly echo the hope that states dwelling within a "security community" may develop a pacific disposition. Thus it appears that even though liberal IR theorists have not attended to the NNP regime in any serious empirical fashion, the most likely way to conceptualize it in that literature is as a security regime that, in mitigating the most violent possibilities of international anarchy, establishes a well-intentioned, progressive order in the service of global peace.[21] But how does one measure progress in this regime?

Before we get to that question, it may be useful to document the truly staggering scale, scope, and reach of the NNP regime, a point that gets short shrift in most of the regimes literature, which focuses on how and why particular agreements get negotiated. To get a full sense of the enormity and complexity of the efforts involved in preventing the proliferation and use of nuclear weapons requires mapping out the infrastructural contours of this massive enterprise, which, although polyvalent in emphases and commitments, are all engaged in the task of making peace in a nuclear world. Those interested in focusing on the analysis can either skim through this next section, which largely describes the different elements of this regime and some of the connections and disconnections among them, or look at the list of these different elements in the appendix. This regime includes a series of multilateral and bilateral treaties; organizations and agencies tasked with implementing those treaties; government-affiliated, university-generated, and independent civil society–based think tanks and nongovernmental organizations (NGOs) engaged in a variety of tracking, monitoring, advocacy, and public service efforts; and reams and reams of publications of various kinds. The NPT is one, albeit crucial, node of this enormous regime but intersects with and is connected to many of the other nodes, all of which together form a complex network of scientific and public policy expertise, weighty political interests, huge economic stakes, and massive investment of financial, bureaucratic, and voluntary resources.

The Nuclear Nonproliferation Regime

The enormous fecundity of the NNP regime is evident in the sheer numbers of institutions, treaties, policies, organizations, think tanks, agencies, journals, and newsletters whose task, quite simply, is to halt or prevent nuclear weapons proliferation and/or reduce or eliminate the number of nuclear weapons that exist in the world, and all in the name of making our collective lives more secure. Needless to say, these tasks are conducted in multiple ways, from controlling and managing possible proliferation through officially sanctioned processes to advocacy efforts that document or suggest the harmful effects of nuclear weapons and nuclear weapons programs. What follows is a survey of this massive regime, showing the various points of connection between its different nodes and demonstrating its vast and deep reach. Though it is far from exhaustive, this survey should communicate how large and complex this security architecture is.[22] The section is divided into three central parts: the first discusses various international treaties and agreements; the second surveys different international organizations, agencies, and initiatives; and the third provides an overview of think tanks and NGOs. Please see the appendix for the Web addresses of each of the different treaties, organizations, and groups discussed in this section. Figure 1 provides a very partial sketch of the regime.

Treaties and Agreements

The most visible aspect of cooperative regimes are international treaties. Negotiated and ratified by sovereign nation-states, these are, at least on the

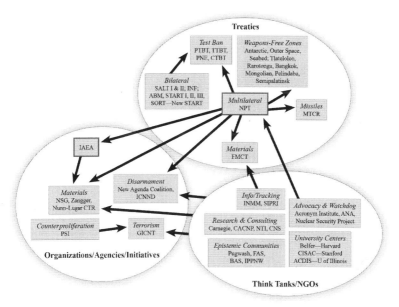

Figure 1. The nuclear nonproliferation regime.

surface, voluntary agreements to regulate and constrain particular kinds of state action. Although the NPT is the obvious backbone of the global nonproliferation regime, and the international treaty widely celebrated as having the widest possible reach, there are various other multilateral and bilateral treaties whose overall purpose is also to ensure the global reduction or elimination of nuclear weapons.

The NPT was first signed in 1968, came into force in 1970, and was indefinitely and unconditionally extended when it came up for review in 1995. The explicit purpose of the NPT is quite simple—to prevent the horizontal proliferation of nuclear weapons. Recognizing the peaceful uses of nuclear energy, the treaty enables nonnuclear weapons signatories to partake in such benefits by requiring nuclear weapons states (NWS) to share technology and materials that could be put to such use (Articles IV and V). In return, non–nuclear weapons states (NNWS) bind themselves to the agreement to not obtain or build a nuclear weapons capability (Article II) as well as accept IAEA jurisdiction to inspect its peaceful nuclear facilities (Article III), and NWS are prohibited from transferring any nuclear weapons technology or any fissionable, weapons-grade material to

NNWS (Article I). The NPT is often described as truly international in its scope, with every country in the world, except India, Israel, North Korea, and Pakistan, being party to it. The IAEA (to be discussed later) is the main verification agency associated with the NPT as well as with many of its associated treaties. The NPT has never stood in isolation as an arms control treaty and is always seen to work in conjunction with a variety of other kinds of supporting treaties:

- a series of bilateral treaties, particularly between the United States and Soviet Union/Russia, to reduce their mutual levels of nuclear arsenals, whether those be delivery vehicles (the Strategic Arms Limitations Talks [SALT] agreements) or warheads (the Strategic Arms Reduction Treaty [START] agreements), and which are the most significant efforts to reduce the sheer number of nuclear weapons in the world and may be considered the only evidence that the two largest NWS are serious not just about horizontal proliferation but about vertical proliferation as well
- a set of multilateral treaties that aim to create nuclear weapons free zones (NWFZs) among existing NNWS and show a real commitment exceeding the already accepted limitations of the NPT not to allow any kind of nuclear weapons activity in particular territories
- another set of supplemental multilateral treaties that attempt to prohibit nuclear testing and control the spread of fissionable materials, missile technology, and missiles, all working toward the general goal of preventing the proliferation of nuclear weapons

Bilateral Arms Reductions Treaties and Talks

SALT I (November 1969–May 1972) represented the first major negotiation between the United States and the Soviet Union to limit and restrain specific types of nuclear arms. SALT I addressed three specific nuclear issues: intercontinental ballistic missiles (ICBMs), submarine-launched ballistic missiles (SLBMs), and anti–ballistic missile defense systems. After a number of failed negotiations, especially over the definition of *strategic,* the talks finally yielded the ABM Treaty. Based on the logic of mutual assured destruction, which recognized the second strike capability of both superpowers, the ABM Treaty (entry into force on October 3, 1972) was an attempt to prevent the first use of nuclear weapons through the prohibition of the development of a nationwide defense. On December 13, 2001, the Bush administration gave formal notice of the United States' withdrawal from the ABM Treaty for the creation of the Missile Defense Agency. The ABM Treaty resurfaced in popular debate in 2008 and 2009 as the United States sought to construct missile defense shields in Poland and the Czech Republic. Current plans are to take a "phased adaptive" approach, with construction on a U.S. base at a Romanian site starting in October 2013. The SALT II (November 1972–June 1979) negotiations began as an attempt to equalize the number of strategic nuclear delivery vehicles, but after early discussions that largely stalled until November 1974, President Ford and General Secretary Brezhnev agreed to a basic framework that included an aggregate limit of twenty-four hundred delivery vehicles, with specific guidelines for which delivery systems were permitted (ICBMs, SLBMs, heavy bombers, and air-to-surface missiles would be allowed on both sides) and certain specific limits (such as on multiple independently targetable reentry vehicled [MIRVed] systems) and prohibitions. President Carter signed the SALT II treaty on June 18, 1979, but requested the Senate delay ratification in light of the Soviet invasion of Afghanistan. Although the treaty never entered into force, both sides agreed to follow its limits, pending reciprocation from the other side.

The Intermediate-Range Nuclear Forces (INF) Treaty (entry into force on June 1, 1988) called for the destruction of all ground-launched ballistic and cruise missiles with ranges between five hundred and fifty-five hundred kilometers. Motivated by the technological increases in the accuracy of Russian medium-ranged MIRVed missiles, the United States therefore agreed to eliminate its Pershing II missiles in exchange for the elimination of all Russian SS-20s, SS-4s, and SS-5s. Far and away the most important aspect of the treaty was its on-site inspection regime, which allowed for on-site inspection of intermediate-range missile operating bases (listed in the Memorandum on Data) by treaty parties thirty days after entry into force. Likewise, each party had the right to inspect facilities for thirteen years after entry into force (three during the elimination period and ten subsequent years for verification). In 2000, the last inspection rights were terminated, and INF missile systems have been successfully eliminated. In contrast to many earlier treaties, START I (entry into force on December 5, 1994) featured tremendously dense technical language and called for each element of the agreement to have the same status as the treaty text (rather than subordinate implementing agreements). Nonetheless, it set down several important limitations on delivery vehicles and warheads and the delineation of specific rules for counting nuclear weapons (based on warheads), which had previously been subject to significant disputes (Article III). In the aftermath of the Soviet Union's collapse in 1991, the ongoing START negotiations also stipulated that all nuclear weapons scattered throughout the former Soviet Union be returned to the Russian Federation. The resultant Lisbon Protocol provided that Russia, Kazakhstan, Ukraine, and Belarus all be party to the final treaty and that Belarus, Ukraine, and Kazakhstan all adhere to the NPT as NNWS as soon as possible. START I expired on December 5, 2009. On April 2, 2010, the United States and Russia signed a new START treaty, intended to provide a short addendum to the comprehensive START I agreement and, most significantly, aimed at utilizing "downloading" (reducing the number of warheads attached to existing MIRVed missiles) methods to achieve necessary reductions and eventually eliminate all MIRVed ICBMs. However, START II did not enter into force. Although the treaty was ratified by the U.S. Senate, the Russian Duma did not approve it until 2000, and notwithstanding several amendments. The Bush administration opted not to pursue the START II negotiations further, opting instead to sign a simple agreement limiting the deployed arsenals of each side to between seventeen hundred and twenty-two hundred (Strategic Offensive Reductions Treaty [SORT]). When the United States announced its withdrawal from the ABM Treaty, Russia likewise withdrew its ratification of START II. START III was never signed. In addition to significant cutbacks in the number of strategic nuclear warheads, START III also intended to negotiate new deals relating to the transparency of nuclear warhead inventories and destruction thereof in an effort to make reductions irreversible. The U.S. withdrawal from the ABM Treaty all but killed the START III negotiations.

SORT (entry into force on June 1, 2003) was a short treaty in which both nations agreed to reduce the number of operationally deployed nuclear warheads to between seventeen hundred and twenty-two hundred. The treaty allowed either party to leave the treaty following a three-month-period withdrawal notice. Significantly, the treaty contained no procedures for verification, but it did establish a Consultative Group for Strategic Security, intended to build confidence and transparency between the United States and Russia. SORT was replaced by the recently signed and ratified New Strategic Arms Reduction Treaty (New START) (entry into force on February 5, 2011), which limits the number of deployed nuclear warheads to 1,550 and the number of ICBMs, SLBMs, and heavy bombers to 800. All New START obligations must be met within seven years after entry into force. Like previous START agreements, the New START does not regulate inactive nuclear stockpiles, meaning they will likely remain in the high thousands in both countries.

Nuclear Weapons Free Zones and Related Treaties

NWFZs are attempts to mark off areas and territories that may not house, develop, and/or test nuclear weapons. As protected "zones of nuclear exception," these treaties may be seen as supplementary efforts to bolster the nonproliferation aims of the NPT. Forty-six states are party to the Antarctic Treaty (entry into force on June 23, 1961), the first post–World War II arms limitation agreement and one that internationalized and demilitarized the Antarctic continent. Although the specifics of the treaty itself hold little bearing on the current global nonproliferation regime, its logic served as a model for "nonarmament" treaties, such as those excluding nuclear weapons from outer space and the seabed as well as those that established regional NWFZs. Most states are party to the Outer Space Treaty (entry into force on October 10, 1967), which limits certain types of space exploration and forbids the use of nuclear weapons in outer space. The significant article, Article IV, prohibits placing any weapon of mass destruction (WMD) in orbit around earth or any other celestial body and limits the use of the moon and other celestial bodies to peaceful purposes (including prohibiting weapons testing). Most states are party to the Seabed Arms Control Treaty (entry into force on May 18, 1972), which prohibits parties from placing nuclear weapons or other WMDs on the seabed or ocean floor outside of a twelve-mile coastal zone. The treaty also called on parties to take future actions limiting the possibility of a seabed arms race; consequently, subsequent developments in SALT and START extended prohibition to the beds of internal waters.

The NWFZs prohibit testing, possession, and stationing of nuclear weapons in large geographic areas in an attempt to reduce regional security motivations for proliferation. The Treaty of Tlatelolco/Latin American and Caribbean NWFZ (entry into force on April 22, 1968) was the first

NWFZ treaty to be negotiated and implemented. Beyond the standard provisions, the treaty also demands that territories belonging to nations outside the NWFZ abide by the NWFZ regime. The treaty distinguishes between peaceful and nonpeaceful nuclear technology, although it strictly regulates the transfer of peaceful nuclear technology. The treaty undertakes enforcement through individual negotiations with the IAEA and an internal verification organization—the Agency for the Prohibition of Nuclear Weapons in Latin America. In addition to the standard provisions, and unlike the Treaty of Tlatelolco, the Treaty of Rarotonga/South Pacific Nuclear Weapons Free Zone (entry into force on December 11, 1986) prohibits all nuclear explosive devices, regardless of purpose. Likewise, the treaty prohibits dumping of radioactive materials. Verification takes place under the IAEA. Additional protocols call on territories owned by nations not under the treaty (the United States, the United Kingdom, and France) to abide by its terms, to not threaten treaty parties, and to discontinue nuclear testing in the region. Excluding the United States, all extraregional parties (including Russia and China) have signed and ratified the treaty. The Treaty of Bangkok/Southeast Asia Nuclear Weapons Free Zone (entry into force on March 27, 1997) prohibits testing, development, possession, and stationing of nuclear weapons as well as dumping of radioactive material anywhere in the zone's territory unless disposal follows IAEA guidelines. Verification is undertaken through the IAEA and an independent commission—the Commission for the Southeast Asia Nuclear Weapon Free Zone. All five extraterritorial members have refused to sign (the United States, Russia, China, the United Kingdom, and France). The Mongolian Nuclear Weapons Free Zone (entry into force on February 3, 2000; declared in September 1992) was created after the collapse of the Soviet Union and is unique as the only NWFZ comprising only one nation. The Mongolian NWFZ prohibits developing, possessing, stationing, and transporting nuclear weapons in addition to banning dumping of weapons-grade nuclear material. The Treaty of Pelindaba/African Nuclear Weapons Free Zone (entry into force on July 15, 2009) goes beyond other NWFZ treaties by forbidding signatories from conducting research or seeking assistance for research on nuclear explosives. Nonetheless, in an exception to standard provisions, signatories are permitted to decide whether to allow transit of nuclear material through airspace, airfields, and territorial waters. Verification takes place through the IAEA. Extrazonal protocols forbid nuclear threats on treaty signatories (Protocol I), testing anywhere in the African NWFZ (protocol II), and compliance by all territories held by nations outside the NWFZ (protocol III). U.S. ratifications of Protocols I and II are still pending; France has signed and ratified Protocol III. The Treaty of Semipalatinsk/Central Asian Nuclear Weapons Free Zone (entry into force on March 21, 2009) prohibits producing, purchasing, and deploying nuclear weapons and is the first to mandate adherence to enhanced IAEA protocols. NWFZs have also been proposed in Northeast Asia, Central and Eastern Europe, and the Middle East.

Test Ban Treaties and Other Efforts to Control the Spread of Nuclear Materials and Technology

Recognizing the harmful environmental effects of nuclear testing, and in an attempt to curtail the further development of nuclear weapons, the test ban treaties have involved a set of progressive attempts to limit the testing of nuclear weapons. These efforts both precede and follow the NPT and are generally seen to work in conjunction with the NPT. The efforts began with the Limited Test Ban Treaty (LTBT) or Partial Test Ban Treaty (PTBT) (entry into force on October 10, 1963), which prohibited any nuclear tests or other explosions in the atmosphere, outer space, and underwater. Initiated by the Soviet Union after a few radioactive accidents in both the United States and the USSR, negotiations took place over eight years, with careful attention to technical concerns regarding verification. Negotiations stalled until, in 1958, President Eisenhower declared a moratorium on U.S. nuclear testing. China, France, and North Korea were notably absent signatories. With the United States, Soviet Union, and United Kingdom as parties to the treaty, the Threshold Test Ban Treaty (TTBT) (entry into force on October 10, 1963) prohibited nuclear tests with a yield exceeding 150 kilotons. At slightly more than ten times the yield of the atomic explosion at Hiroshima, the 150 kiloton limit did little to prevent future states from producing small-yield bombs but did remove the possibility of testing new or existing high-yield weapons. Verification involved an exchange of technical data related to designated test sites (including detailed geological data) and data pertaining to a limited number of tests for calibration purposes. Negotiated between the United States and the Soviet Union, the Peaceful Nuclear Explosions Treaty (PNE) (entry into force on December 11, 1990) governed all nuclear explosions carried out at locations outside of the weapons sites specified by the TTBT in an effort to allow for "peaceful" underground nuclear explosions.[23] The treaty specified that individual explosions must not exceed 150 kilotons and that group explosions must not have an aggregate yield higher than 1,500 kilotons (likewise, group explosions were required to be coordinated so that each individual explosion could be identified and measured). The treaty also created the Joint Consultative Commission to address compliance with PNE and TTBT.

Finally, and most significantly, the Comprehensive Nuclear Test Ban Treaty (CTBT) was adopted by the United Nations (UN) on September 10, 1996, but is still pending ratification by China, Egypt, India, Indonesia, Iran, Israel, North Korea, Pakistan, and the United States. A logical extension of the LTBT and the TTBT, the CTBT would prohibit any nuclear weapons testing by treaty parties. Nonetheless, the treaty does not prohibit all activities relating to nuclear activities (including subcritical experiments). Verification of the CTBT would take place under the Comprehensive Test Ban Treaty Organization (CTBTO) and would involve extensive use of geophysical models. The treaty likewise contains provisions for on-site verification pending an affirmative vote from thirty of the fifty-one executive members (a clause added to assuage Chinese concerns); most scholars, however, suggest that few circumstances would come to so close a vote as seismological data would conclusively determine the need for on-site inspection. Many expressed hope for ratification by the United States under the Obama administration, but such ratification depends on several conditions, all of which have to do with ensuring U.S. capacity to maintain and upgrade its nuclear weapons readiness.[24]

Not yet negotiated, the Fissile Material Cutoff Treaty (FMCT) is a U.S.-proposed agreement that would prohibit the production of fissile materials for nuclear explosives and weapons. Parties at the 2000 NPT review agreed to negotiate an FMCT treaty within five years. Although no such treaty was concluded by 2005, renewed efforts resulted in the 2006 founding of the International Panel on Fissile Materials. Later in the year, President Bush submitted a draft FMCT at the Conference on Disarmament in Geneva that lacked verification provisions but banned new production of plutonium and highly enriched uranium (HEU) for nuclear weapons for fifteen years. The Obama administration continued to endorse the FMCT but called for the addition of verification measures (presumably through the IAEA). The Conference on Disarmament unanimously agreed in 2009 to set up a working group on the FMCT. Nonetheless, many countries, such as Israel, China, Pakistan, and North Korea, continue to hold reservations, which may prevent its passage. Also not yet negotiated, the Hiroshima–Nagasaki Protocol is a proposed initiative to complement the 2020 campaign for a nuclear-free world.[25] The protocol aims to reduce nuclear stockpiles in existing nuclear powers in accordance with Article VI of the NPT. As of yet, the protocol has three articles: Article I calls for the complete cessation of "all activities related to the acquisition of nuclear weapons which non-nuclear-weapon States Parties are prohibited from pursuing" and the prohibition of all military doctrines and practices that incorporate nuclear weapons; Article II calls for an international negotiating forum open to all states relating to complete nuclear disarmament by 2020; and Article III calls for renewed commitment to the NPT and all of its obligations.[26]

An agreement to which most states are party, the Convention on the Physical Protection of Nuclear Material (entry into force on February 8, 1987) provides for physical protection during international transport of nuclear material and establishes a framework for international cooperation on recovery of stolen nuclear material. The treaty was amended at a diplomatic conference in July 2005 to make it legally binding for treaty parties to protect nuclear facilities and material in peaceful domestic use. It also provided for expanded cooperation between states on rapid measures to locate stolen material. The International Convention for the Suppression of Acts of Nuclear Terrorism (entry into force on July 6, 2007) obligates parties to establish a number of offenses related to nuclear terrorism within their national legal systems and to make those offenses punishable. The treaty offers a definition of *terrorist* as any person who possesses radioactive material with the intent to cause death or to damage property or the environment but makes an exception for nuclear weapons possession and use during armed conflict. The treaty also encourages international cooperation on nuclear terror issues such as data and intelligence sharing. Established in 1987, the Missile Technology Control Regime is an informal, voluntary partnership between thirty-four countries to prevent and slow missile proliferation. The treaty bans neither missile technology nor their sale but does place voluntary restraints on the transfer of missile technology, particularly those missiles capable of carrying WMDs. Claimed successes include the cessation of the Condor II ballistic missile program in Argentina, Egypt, and Iraq and abandoned missile programs in Brazil, South Africa, Taiwan, Poland, and the Czech Republic. Independent of the Missile Technology Control Regime, the

Hague Code of Conduct Against Ballistic Missile Proliferation (brought into effect on November 25, 2002) intends to curb the spread of ballistic missiles and to delegitimize their proliferation. The treaty does not ban ballistic missiles or their production but does call for some degree of restraint in their production, testing, and export. Finally, the Wassenaar Arrangement on Export Controls for Conventional Arms and Dual-Use Goods and Technologies (established on July 12, 1996) is a multilateral export control regime with forty participating states designed to replace the now-defunct Coordinating Committee for Multilateral Export Controls. The agreement is far less strict than its predecessor and focuses largely on transparency of national export controls. Of course, in addition to all these international treaties, different states have their domestic statutes, laws, and funds that pertain to the regulation of nuclear weapons and related matters and that are too numerous to mention here.

Organizations, Agencies, and Initiatives

As is clear from the preceding discussion, one result of the number of treaties and agreements regulating nuclear weapons production, use, and transfer is the creation of an extensive bureaucratic apparatus with wide reach across and within states. Both the NPT and the CTBT, the two nuclear treaties with the greatest global scope, have associated bodies whose intrusive reach is quite deep. Of these, the IAEA is perhaps the best known. An international organization established in 1957 through the UN, the IAEA is the fundamental verification agency for the NPT and a forum for scientific and technical cooperation on peaceful nuclear technology. The IAEA has 151 member states and negotiates individual safeguard agreements with each NPT state as a condition for ascendance into the treaty. Guidelines and individual negotiations range in specifics, but all allow the use of nuclear reactors and materials for energy purposes. The IAEA can conduct four types of inspections: ad hoc (verifying a state's initial nuclear report), routine, special (supplementary inspections in unusual circumstances), and safeguard visits (inspections to declared facilities to confirm safeguards). The voluntary IAEA Additional Protocol involves more intensive safeguarding and inspections. The CTBTO is the international organization that will officially be established on full entry into force of the CTBT and that will be responsible for creating and overseeing the International Monitoring System and other related CTBT programs. However, the CTBTO Preparatory Commission has been in operation since 1997. Several of the treaties mentioned earlier have their own associated bodies, and many also work closely through the IAEA.

A series of organizations have also arisen in conjunction with attempts to control the spread of nuclear materials and technology. The NSG is a multinational body concerned with reducing nuclear proliferation by controlling the export and transfer of possible nuclear weapons materials. The NSG was founded in 1974 in response to the first Indian nuclear test and currently hosts forty-six nuclear supplier states. Potential recipients of nuclear materials from NSG states must not contribute to nuclear weapons production, must have in place physical security measures to prevent theft, and must have negotiated and comply with an IAEA safeguards agreement. The Zangger Committee is a relatively informal committee established as a response to Article III of the NPT on nuclear transfer. The Zangger Committee oversees some aspects of nuclear materials transfers in combination with the NSG and makes decisions that would often be too difficult to make within the stricter framework of the more formal NSG. The list of items controlled by the Zangger Committee is known as the trigger list because export of such items triggers IAEA safeguards.[27] The Global Partnership Against the Spread of Weapons and Materials of Mass Destruction is a G8 partnership arranged at a Canadian summit in June 2002 as a response to the September 11, 2001, terrorist attack on the United States. The initiative encouraged cooperation on WMD nonproliferation issues, particularly with Russia, and committed the nations to raise twenty billion dollars over the next ten years for its purposes. The arrangement also had eight guidelines for cooperation emphasizing standard concerns on export controls and information sharing.[28]

Fears of proliferating nuclear materials have triggered a number of other, more focused and often interlinked approaches, many emerging from the United States. The quite well known Nunn–Lugar Cooperative Threat Reduction (CTR) is a U.S. program within the Defense Threat Reduction Agency (see later) that aims to secure and dismantle WMDs in former Soviet Union states. The CTR program provides funding and expertise in the former USSR to decommission nuclear, biological, and chemical weapons stockpiles within the limits of agreed treaties (such as START). Despite some concerns over cost, the CTR program is considered quite successful, having deactivated and destroyed more than six thousand nuclear warheads and five hundred ICBMs. Consequently, the

CTR program has been a model for other cooperative programs such as the Global Threat Reduction Initiative. The Global Threat Reduction Initiative is a U.S. initiative with the IAEA launched in 2004, based on and as an expansion of the CTR program. Under the initiative, the United States, with other IAEA partners, will accelerate efforts to repatriate all Russian-origin HEU by 2010, accelerate and complete the repatriation of all U.S.-origin research reactor spent fuel, convert the cores of civilian research reactors that use HEU to allow them to use low-enriched uranium, and identify and manage nuclear and radiological materials not covered by existing threat reduction programs. Progress has been moderate, owing in part, many claim, to a lack of funding. Within the United States, the Defense Threat Reduction Agency (DTRA) is a Department of Defense agency created in 1998 to safeguard the United States from WMD attacks and is responsible for overseeing programs such as the CTR program and for participating in various arms control treaties such as the Conventional Forces in Europe treaty. DTRA also heads the United States Strategic Command (STRATCOM) Center for Combating Weapons of Mass Destruction and oversees the journal *WMD Insights.* The STRATCOM Center for Combating Weapons of Mass Destruction was built to cooperate with the DTRA. It exists largely to coordinate programs headed by the DTRA.

Concerns about the security of nuclear weapons, materials, and know-how in Russia and the former Soviet republics ran quite deep and led to the creation of a whole host of other less well-known initiatives. The Nuclear Cities Initiative was a short-lived program between the United States and Russia centered on helping scientists and nuclear experts in closed Russian nuclear cities find employment and work after the fall of the Soviet Union. The program began in 1998 and ended in 2003, when its five-year term expired and the United States refused to renew it. Despite its brief run, the program is often seen as a model for evaluating U.S.–Russian cooperation on brain drain and related proliferation concerns. On a similar note, the International Science and Technology Center (ISTC) is an international organization established in 1992 to prevent WMD and nuclear weapons proliferation by giving Russian scientists and engineers opportunities in international research. Indeed, the state corporation in Russia that regulates the Russian nuclear complex—Minatom/Rosatom—in addition to the usual duties of a nuclear regulatory body, works with international initiatives such as the ISTC to employ and maintain security in Russian nuclear programs. Outside of the Russian context, the Brazilian–Argentine Agency for Accounting and Control of Nuclear Materials is a bi-national safeguards agency formed in 1991 that shapes verification procedures on nuclear programs in Argentina and Brazil to prevent arms races after the end of each nation's nuclear program in the 1980s. It is the only bi-national safeguards organization in the world.

The Proliferation Security Initiative (PSI) is a controversial U.S.-led initiative to prevent the spread of nuclear materials that involves the interdiction of third-party ships suspected of carrying nuclear materials. The initiative has more than ninety member states, though a number of states, notably China, have refused to join and question its legality. The organization was founded in specific response to North Korean transfers of SCUD missiles that were not preventable under international law. PSI has successfully apprehended a number of proliferation materials in the past, though it is often criticized as exceptionalist and illegal. Both the Container Security Initiative (CSI) and the Megaports Initiative are U.S. government programs established to bolster the security of container cargo shipped to U.S. ports through the use of intelligence and sophisticated radiation detection technology. The former was established in 2002 by the Department of Homeland Security, and the latter, established in 2003, is overseen by the Nuclear National Security Administration with assistance and cooperation from the Department of Homeland Security. CSI is also set to be expanded throughout the European Community. In addition, the Secure Freights Initiative is another initiative launched by the Department of Homeland Security in 2006–7 that uses nonintrusive inspection for radiation detection. All of these efforts partially depend on the Nuclear Materials Management and Safeguard System, which is a centralized U.S. government database used to track and account for nuclear material. The system contains historic data on possession, use, and transfer of such material and is operated by the Department of Energy, despite some funding from the Nuclear Regulatory Commission (NRC).

Many of the preceding initiatives, organizations, and agencies arose in response to the September 11, 2001, terrorist attacks against the United States, and needless to say, the U.S. nuclear bureaucracy has become significantly bloated in attempts to prevent nuclear terrorism. The NRC is a U.S. government agency that has existed since 1974 to oversee nuclear reactor safety, radioactive material safety, and fuel management. But despite issuing licenses for nuclear and radioactive material, most of the government's nonproliferation and counterterrorism initiatives are handled by other agencies, such as the Department of Energy or the Department of Homeland Security. In addition to the agencies already referenced, the National Counterproliferation Center (NCPC) is an organization within the U.S. intelligence community that was formed in 2005 to combat the spread of WMD. The NCPC works with the intelligence community to identify intelligence gaps and to find and fund new technologies to combat proliferation. In a somewhat different vein, the Global Initiative to Combat Nuclear Terrorism (GICNT) is an international program launched in 2006 by President Bush and President Putin that hosts workshops, conferences, and exercises to combat global terrorism. GICNT is currently host to eighty-one states and four official observers. Although its activities have thus far been relatively minimal, a number of officials and scholars, notably President Obama, have called for expansion and improvement in the future.

There is, however, clearly a concern that the prohibitions on nuclear weapons spread should not adversely impact the transfers of nuclear energy (the peaceful uses of which are permitted by the NPT). The Global Nuclear Energy Partnership (GNEP) was a U.S.-proposed agreement to promote nuclear fuel and energy use without proliferation risks. The agreement divides members into suppliers and users, with the understanding that by separating nuclear supplies from nuclear power plants, no state could acquire all of the necessary components for indigenous weapons capability. The agreement had twenty-five partner countries and twenty-eight observer countries but faced significant opposition from political organizations and arms control groups. It had been criticized for encouraging new nuclear materials reprocessing, thereby undermining nonproliferation commitments, and for failing to resolve nuclear waste problems. Others have criticized its hierarchical structure and likened the agreement to the problematic and controversial divisions within the NPT.[29] In 2009, the U.S. Department of Energy cancelled the U.S. domestic component of GNEP, striking a major blow to the arrangement, and it has now been reconstituted as the International Framework for Nuclear Energy Commission. The European Atomic Energy Community (EURATOM) is an international organization established in 1957 by the Treaty of Rome that oversees and facilitates nuclear energy programs on a European rather than national scale. EURATOM safeguards predated and shaped the safeguard system of the IAEA, and the EURATOM structure has been proposed as a treaty model for other regions such as Asia and the Middle East. The Next Steps in Strategic Partnership is a working partnership between the United States and India designed to expand cooperation into three areas: civilian nuclear activities, civilian space programs, and high-technology trade. To ensure nonproliferation, the agreement applies a "presumption of approval" policy for all dual-use items not controlled by the NSG, assuming they are for Indian nuclear energy facilities under IAEA safeguards.

Finally, there are the occasional official attempts to advance the agenda of disarmament. The New Agenda Coalition is a collection of middle-power countries (Brazil, Egypt, Ireland, Mexico, New Zealand, South Africa, and Sweden) working to build international consensus on progress toward nuclear disarmament. The group was founded after the perceived failure of the 1995 NPT review conference, which indefinitely extended the NPT without making any new or firm commitments on disarmament by the existing NWS. The coalition published an eighteen-point declaration in 1998 calling for a new agenda on nuclear disarmament. The coalition also played a key role in crafting the thirteen steps that emerged from the 2000 NPT review conference. The International Commission on Nuclear Non-Proliferation and Disarmament (ICNND) is a joint initiative of the Australian and Japanese governments aimed at "reinvigorating international efforts on nuclear non-proliferation and disarmament." The ICNND hosts conferences, works with other research centers, and commissions research papers. These research papers differ in perspective and conclusions, but common themes include non–first use policy and the negotiation and creation of new international treaties.[30] And of course, there is the Arms Control and Disarmament Agency (ACDA), which was an independent agency of the U.S. federal government established by the Arms Control and Disarmament Act but merged in 1999 with the State Department and became headed by the under secretary of state for arms control and international security affairs; it seeks to fully integrate arms control into U.S. conduct and security policy. Interestingly, despite gesturing toward "disarmament" in the title of the organization, none of the bureaus into which it is currently divided—the Bureau of Political-Military Affairs, the Bureau of International Security and Nonproliferation, and the Bureau of Arms Control, Verification, and Compliance—refer to that goal.

Think Tanks and Nongovernmental Organizations

Grasping the full scope of the efforts involved in preventing the proliferation and possession of nuclear weapons requires attention to the enormous number of NGOs and think tanks that deal with nuclear weapons nonproliferation. Indeed, the extent of civil society efforts that support, complement, and critique state and interstate efforts in this area is truly huge. Although many of these groups claim to be nonpartisan, their policy positions span the political spectrum, and many are involved in research, analysis, and advocacy work that attempts to influence policy makers as well as create public awareness. Whereas some of these groups attempt to prevent and control proliferation, others support and push for nuclear disarmament. Some of the most useful work done by many of these groups is to track movements of materials, technology, and weapons, and many are drawn on by or connected to the official organizations and agencies discussed in the previous section. Formed by scientists, lawyers, environmentalists, and many former policy makers, among others, and although with a particularly heavy concentration within the United States, these groups span the globe, with some focused on particular "problem countries," such as Iran and North Korea; others on particular contentious relations, such as between the United States and Russia or between India and Pakistan; and others on regions, such as the Middle East.

Research and Consulting

There are certain major think tanks whose research and analysis on nuclear security have become significant for academics, advocates, and activists as well as policy makers. Though the Carnegie Endowment for International Peace is a nonprofit, Washington, D.C.–based think tank focused on international engagement and U.S. foreign policy more generally, its Nuclear Policy Program releases frequent publications and policy pieces from the Carnegie Endowment's board of experts. Often deriding U.S. policy for ill-advised unilateralism, it was named by the *National Journal* as one of three organizations most likely to impact the Obama administration's nuclear policies. The other organization to be so named was the Center for Arms Control and Non-Proliferation, which is a nonprofit, Washington, D.C.–based research organization focused on security issues, with nuclear weapons and nonproliferation being two of its four focuses. Its publications most frequently focus on factual assessments of budgets, policies, and technological capacities. The final organization to be named most likely to influence the Obama administration's nuclear policies was the Nuclear Threat Initiative (NTI). The NTI is a Washington, D.C.–based public charity founded by Ted Turner and Sam Nunn and dedicated to countering the proliferation of nuclear, biological, and chemical weapons. Large publications are occasional, with most being coordinated with the James Martin Center for Nonproliferation Studies (CNS). Most publications are smaller press releases and brief assessments of situations and issues.[31]

Another influential think tank is the CNS, which is an NGO subsidiary program of the Monterey Institute for International Studies. The CNS works to train nonproliferation specialists and publish information and analysis. Three times a year, it publishes the peer-reviewed journal *The Nonproliferation Review*. Sister organization to the CNS is the Council for a Livable World, which is a Washington, D.C.–based nonprofit advocacy group dedicated to reducing the dangers of nuclear weapons and increasing national security. Publications are usually short policy assessments and news articles as most of its major publishing takes place through the CNS. The majority of the council's activities focus on the election of supported candidates, almost all of whom are democrats. Nonproliferation for Global Security is a private, nonprofit institution dedicated to reducing risks of proliferation and use of arms, with particular emphasis on WMDs, and engages in both public information and awareness campaigns as well as public policy research support. Publications are usually short policy assessments and proposals.

Most NGOs that deal with arms control and security have fairly dedicated sections devoted to nuclear nonproliferation. For instance, the Henry L. Stimson Center is a Washington, D.C.–based, nonprofit, global security think tank that maintains a large program dedicated to nuclear issues. Publications are frequent and focus on issues from multiple perspectives and are not (usually) directed toward U.S. policy makers. In addition to in-depth analyses, Stimson also produces reports, issue briefs, and background papers. Similarly, the World Security Institute is a Washington, D.C.–based think tank that emerged from the Center for Defense Information and is headed by nuclear weapons specialist Bruce Blair. The World Security Institute runs two divisions related to nuclear nonproliferation: the Center for Defense Information and Global Zero, a movement launched in 2008 and dedicated to reaching a world without nuclear weapons and strengthening U.S. and Russian commitments under START. The World Security Institute publishes monographs, newsletters, and documentaries related to global security and nuclear proliferation. The Center for Defense Information (CDI) was a nongovernment research organization founded in 1972 by retired U.S. naval officer Gene La Rocque and then worked under the World Security Institute. The CDI was composed of academics and high-ranking retired U.S. military officers who conduct critical analyses of U.S. defense and security policy. Publications were diverse but focused largely on U.S. policy options regarding nuclear issues and nuclear diplomacy. The CDI also published *The Defense Monitor* on U.S. defense policy. Recently, it joined the Project on Government Oversight. The Arms Control Association is another Washington, D.C.–based national organization dedicated to achieving effective arms control policies. Publications are diverse and cover news, articles, fact sheets, reports, treaties, and forums. The Arms Control Association publishes a monthly non-peer-reviewed magazine *Arms Control Today.* The International Institute for Strategic Studies (IISS) is a British-based think tank dedicated to political–military conflict. The IISS does not focus exclusively on nonproliferation or nuclear issues but does release frequent in-depth assessments of nuclear security situations regarding Iran, North Korea, and other nation-states. The IISS also runs a monograph series, the *Adelphi Papers,* which has published some very influential pieces on nuclear nonproliferation.

Not all groups are nonprofit organizations. Policy Architects International is a private, Washington, D.C.–based research and consulting organization that concentrates on services in international policy areas, with a number of publications in nuclear proliferation and strategic arms negotiations. Publications are in depth, usually fairly long, and often released through other organizations. Smaller but focused groups often emerge even outside the policy-connected East Coast cities of the United States. The Stanley Foundation is a nonprofit policy institute focused on international relations and based in Muscatine, Iowa. The Stanley Foundation runs a nuclear security program that aims to analyze and bolster international nonproliferation goals. Publications are usually short policy analyses. The Wisconsin Project on Nuclear Arms Control is a nonprofit, Washington, D.C.–based organization established to curb the proliferation of nuclear weapons through research and advocacy. The Wisconsin Project has provided assistance directly to U.S. and foreign governments to help improve export controls and has trained nearly eight hundred export control officials around the globe. The Wisconsin Project has also released three significant publications: its risk report, which claims to be "the leading source of unclassified information on companies around the world suspected of building WMDs"; *Iran Watch,* which publishes documents and private analyses on Iranian nuclear developments; and the now-defunct *Iraq Watch,* which tracked WMD programs in Iraq.

Many large research universities have their own institutes that produce expertise on nuclear security. The Belfer Center for Science and International Affairs is a research center located within Harvard University's Kennedy School of Government that publishes on a host of international issues. It has a dedicated section on nuclear issues and runs an affiliate program, Managing the Atom, which brings together an international group of scholars and officials to conduct research on nuclear technology. Publications are expansive and cover a wide variety of nuclear issues. The Center for International Security and Cooperation is a research center at Stanford University that studies and publishes on a range of issues, but with a particularly strong program on nuclear issues and arms control. The Center for International Trade and Security (CITS) is a University of Georgia School of Public and International Affairs affiliate. CITS focuses on trade in, and theft of, weapons and weapons components, with a particular emphasis on WMD materials. CITS releases publications routinely through a number of channels, including its own quarterly report, *The Monitor.* The Institute on Global Conflict and Cooperation (IGCC) is a research unit based in the University of California system that covers a range of topics in international policy. Although not explicitly focused on nonproliferation, the IGCC occasionally publishes materials and studies on nuclear and nonproliferation issues. These publications vary in length from short policy briefs and news coverage to large research papers and books. The Program in Arms Control, Disarmament, and International Security (ACDIS) is a University of Illinois at Urbana-Champaign program aimed at informing international security policy decision making. Publications range from short policy briefs to journal articles, books, and major research papers. ACDIS also runs a periodic journal, *Swords and Ploughshares.* The Program on Science and Global Security (SGS) is an affiliate of Princeton University's Woodrow Wilson School of Public and

International Affairs. SGS carries out research and policy analysis in nuclear arms control and nonproliferation and runs several publications: the
International Panel on Fissile Material; an independent group of nuclear
experts that releases reports; *Science and Global Security,* a peer-reviewed
journal on arms control and nonproliferation policy; and a number of independent publications.

Advocacy and Watchdog Groups

Although many of the preceding organizations claim to be nonpartisan,
they are clearly involved in advocacy work with particular political agendas. However, some groups' political and/or policy positions are much
more explicit. For instance, and not surprisingly, some of the strongest disarmament efforts come from civil society groups. Some organizations take
a stronger position than others with respect to disarmament. The Acronym
Institute for Disarmament Diplomacy is a U.K.-based NGO dedicated
to arms control and disarmament. The Acronym Institute publishes the
bimonthly journal *Disarmament Diplomacy,* which does not claim to be
peer reviewed, although many of its articles appear in other peer-reviewed
journals. Publications are left-moderate but call for larger changes to the
nonproliferation regime than publications by Carnegie or other more
moderate organizations. The Acronym Institute also runs the *Acronym
Institute Blog,* which offers brief analysis and coverage on disarmament
developments. In addition to its own analysis, the Acronym Institute also
maintains an expansive online catalog of government speeches and documents. The Middle Powers Initiative (MPI) is a program of the Global
Security Institute dedicated to the elimination of nuclear weapons. MPI
committed eight NGOs to work with middle-power governments to encourage NWS to engage in disarmament policies. In the wake of the breakdown at the 2005 NPT review conference, the Middle Powers Initiative
has organized and overseen an Article VI Forum calling on NWS to re-
commit to Article VI of the NPT. The more renowned Nuclear Security
Project is a project of George Shultz, William Perry, Henry Kissinger, and
Sam Nunn aimed at reducing nuclear dangers through analysis and activism. The project has conducted three major analytic studies on verification, fuel cycles, and "base camps" in achieving a nuclear-free world. Most
publications, however, are short news articles and op-ed pieces that have
received a fair bit of public attention. The Nuclear Age Peace Foundation

is a nonprofit international organization focused on nuclear weapons issues and a consultant to the UN Economic and Social Council. The foundation works toward the elimination of nuclear weapons through sponsoring of international efforts and organizations and through the publication of policy analyses. Publications are usually short, aimed at the general public, and focused on nuclear activism.

On the other end of the spectrum are think tanks that take a much more conservative position on disarmament. The well-known Research and Development Corporation (RAND) is a nonprofit global policy think tank that offers research and analysis to the U.S. armed forces. RAND is currently financed by a combination of private contributions and the U.S. government. Although RAND does not run a program dedicated explicitly to nonproliferation, it routinely publishes reports and assessments on nuclear issues and on U.S. nonproliferation policy. The Center for Security Policy (CSP) is a neoconservative, Washington, D.C.–based think tank focused on national security issues that claims to advocate "peace through strength." Although CSP is not focused explicitly on nuclear nonproliferation issues, it publishes occasionally on nuclear issues, particularly U.S. deterrence policies. The National Institute for Public Policy is a Washington, D.C.–based think tank dedicated to assessing U.S. foreign and defense policies in the aftermath of the Cold War. Publications frequently focus on nuclear issues, with particular attention to the role of nuclear weapons in U.S. military policy and the viability of certain deterrence practices; it is quite clear about not advocating for total nuclear disarmament. The Jamestown Foundation is a Washington, D.C.–based think tank dedicated to informing policy makers on events and trends of strategic importance to the United States. Although Jamestown does not feature a dedicated program on nuclear issues, it routinely publishes policy analyses (usually short) on nonproliferation and nuclear issues. Jamestown has received criticism for maintaining a neoconservative agenda with unannounced ties to the Central Intelligence Agency. It has also been criticized for a bitterly anti-Russian policy stance.

In addition, watchdog groups attempt to keep state efforts in check. The Alliance for Nuclear Accountability is a network of thirty-five local, regional, and national organizations "representing the concerns of communities in the shadows of the U.S. nuclear weapons sites and radioactive waste dumps." The organization primarily serves as a watchdog group for the Department of Energy and a policy advocate pushing to ban testing and construction of nuclear weapons in the United States. The group periodically issues press releases consisting of short analyses of events regarding nuclear weapons and maintains a library of local publications from its affiliate members. The Partnership for Global Security (PGS), formerly the Russian American Nuclear Security Advisory Council, is a nonpartisan organization dedicated to WMD security and elimination efforts. PGS runs a nonproliferation tracker that tracks the Obama administration's policies on nonproliferation in various categories; it also runs a Nuclear Threat Reduction Project that releases policy briefs. Most publications are short and published through news agencies or the *Bulletin of the Atomic Scientists*.

Information and Tracking

Several organizations have taken on somewhat specialized roles in the generation of important information and databases related to nuclear materials and weapons. Complementing the many state-led efforts in this area, some organizations focus on tracking the proliferation of nuclear materials. The Institute of Nuclear Materials Management (INMM) is an international technical and professional organization dedicated to the safe handling of nuclear material and safe nuclear management and maintains six technical divisions pertaining to safeguards, materials control, packaging and transportation, physical controls, and waste management. INMM frequently hosts events internationally dedicated to international cooperation on nuclear materials management. Publications are frequent, technical in nature, and usually occur through the institute's quarterly peer-reviewed journal, the *Journal of Nuclear Materials Management*, but smaller publications are released through the website. The George Soros Foundations are a network of foundations mostly in Central and Eastern Europe created by international financier and philanthropist George Soros. Although the foundations differ in activities, they largely aim to support the "open society" functions in countries behind "the iron curtain." With regard to nonproliferation, a number of George Soros Foundations aid and donate money to programs aimed at securing fissile material and nuclear knowledge from the former Soviet Union. The Nuclear Control Institute (NCI) is a nonprofit Washington, D.C., and Web-based research and advocacy center for preventing nuclear proliferation and nuclear terrorism. NCI is primarily focused on the elimination of plutonium and

HEU and the means of using peaceful nuclear technology for weapons technology. NCI publishes fairly detailed reports on international nuclear issues and brief policy analyses and news pieces, but publications have been relatively few in recent years.

Other organizations specialize in the more general compilation of information. Whereas some of these organizations are affiliated with governments, others are NGOs serving wider publics. For example, the Congressional Research Service (CRS) is an arm of the Library of Congress that conducts research on legislative issues for members of congress. Though CRS does not maintain an exclusive focus on nuclear issues or nuclear nonproliferation, it frequently publishes on those topics, producing well-researched, thoroughly documented publications that are around thirty pages in length. The Alsos Digital Library for Nuclear Issues is a searchable collection of more than twenty-seven hundred annotations and bibliographic information related to nuclear topics that is part of the U.S. National Science Digital Library. The quite large Stockholm International Peace Research Institute (SIPRI) is an organization that conducts scientific research on conflict and international security funded in large part by the Swedish government. The project conducts research on nuclear proliferation that tracks developments related to nuclear weapons policy and arms control, with a focus on the technical dimensions of arms control. SIPRI publishes through a number of sources: an annual yearbook that covers developments in arms control and security; a SIPRI series of monographs; a series of research reports; in-depth policy reports with topical policy recommendations; and *SIPRI Insights,* which provides brief overviews and research findings.

Epistemic Communities

In line with the epistemic communities literature, the number of researchers and experts involved in the nuclear nonproliferation field has given rise to several epistemic organizations composed of specialists in particular areas. On the question of nuclear nonproliferation, the influence of scientists in particular is noteworthy. The Pugwash Conferences on Science and World Affairs is an international organization that brings together scholars and public figures to reduce the danger of armed conflict and solve global security threats. Pugwash has played an important historical role during crises or at times of otherwise strained relations. Though its influence before and during the negotiation for the ABM Treaty has been noted in the epistemic communities literature, it has also provided important background work for the PTBT, the NPT, and other treaties. Pugwash releases publications ranging from briefing books to workshop reports that feature in-depth analyses of policy events and issues. The Federation of American Scientists (FAS) may now be the best known and most influential of an epistemic organization in the area of nuclear nonproliferation. A nonprofit organization focused primarily on global security issues, FAS publications for the most part focus on factual assessments of the existing security situation. FAS is closely affiliated with the *Bulletin of the Atomic Scientists* and the CRS. Publications from its current Nuclear Information Project, a subset of its Strategic Security Program, are mostly authored by Hans M. Kristensen, who also runs a major portion of the *FAS Security Blog,* which routinely publishes brief assessments of major issues. The Union of Concerned Scientists is another nonprofit science advocacy and watchdog group based in Cambridge that runs dedicated programs on nuclear weapons and nuclear energy. Generally considered liberal, publications are usually short and frequently focused on technical aspects of nonproliferation. The International Physicians for the Prevention of Nuclear War is a group of doctors, medical students, and other health workers established in 1980, spanning sixty-three countries but based in Somerville, Massachusetts. The group was awarded the 1985 Nobel Peace Prize for its work in raising public awareness of the health impacts of atomic weapons. The International Network of Engineers and Scientists Against Proliferation (INESAP) is a network of scientists who work toward nonproliferation and global disarmament through critical analyses of (primarily) technical and scientific issues associated with WMDs. Although most reports are technical, INESAP also releases books that conduct political analyses. The U.S. Civilian and Research Development Foundation (CRDF) is a nonprofit organization authorized by the U.S. Congress and established by the National Science Foundation and is dedicated to international scientific collaboration. Among its focuses, CRDF maintains a dedicated nonproliferation program that engages scientists from the former Soviet Union on nonproliferation issues, usually focused on technical aspects of nonproliferation or the medical ramifications of nuclear weapons programs.

Among other specialized groups, the Natural Resources Defense Council (NRDC) is a New York City–based, nonprofit, international environmental advocacy group. NRDC runs a nuclear program that has published a number of articles and monographs on nuclear stockpiles and nonproliferation. Publications frequently focus on the environmental effects of nuclear waste, the proliferation risks of the nuclear energy renaissance, or the economics of nuclear power and weapons. The Lawyers Alliance for World Security was a nongovernmental, Washington, D.C.–based organization concerned with nuclear and WMD proliferation. Publications usually took a legal perspective on proliferation issues ranging from START negotiations to North Korea and Iran. In a somewhat different vein, Parliamentarians for Nuclear Non-Proliferation and Disarmament is a global network of more than seven hundred parliamentarians aimed at achieving nuclear disarmament organized through the Global Security Institute. The organization disseminates information on nuclear disarmament through international events, forums, and UN meetings and encourages parliamentary action toward disarmament.

Regionally Focused

There are also organizations whose main focus with respect to nuclear proliferation is in a particular region of the world. The Begin–Sadat Center for Strategic Studies (BESA) is an independent academic body directed at achieving peace and security in the Middle East through policy-oriented research. BESA publications are on diverse topics and only occasionally related to nuclear proliferation issues but are almost always peer reviewed and generally respected in scholarly circles (see especially the *BESA Perspectives*). The Washington Institute for Near East Policy (WINEP) is a Washington, D.C.–based think tank focused on U.S. foreign policy in the Middle East established by the American Israel Public Affairs Committee and hence carries a fairly clear pro-Israel bias. WINEP maintains a program on Middle East proliferation that releases short policy analyses and monographs on U.S. policy in the region. The Center for Policy Studies in Russia (PIR) is an independent nongovernmental organization focused on international security and nonproliferation. Publication takes place through the center's quarterly peer-reviewed journal *Security Index* or through the PIR monograph series. Publications cover a number of issues but have a general focus on Russia and U.S.–Russian relations. The Eisenhower Institute is a Washington, D.C.–based nonpartisan, nonprofit presidential legacy organization affiliated with Gettysburg College that runs a program dedicated to nonproliferation called Safeguarding the Atom, funded by the NTI. Safeguarding the Atom aims at building an informal bilateral process focused on U.S.–Russian nonproliferation efforts. Publications are occasional. The Institute for Science and International Security (ISIS) is a nonprofit, Washington, D.C.–based institution geared toward international security founded by former IAEA inspector David Albright. ISIS provides reports and publications about existing and emerging nuclear weapons programs, with a particularly extensive focus on Iran. ISIS also releases and analyzes satellite data on said nuclear programs. Publications are in depth and detailed. The Woodrow Wilson International Center for Scholars is a Washington, D.C.–based institution founded as part of the Smithsonian Institution, with a sweeping focus on world issues. The Woodrow Wilson International Center runs a number of programs related to nuclear and nonproliferation issues, particularly their International Security Studies and North Korea International Documentation Project. Publications range in length and depth from brief policy summaries to full-length books and can frequently be accessed on their website. The Lowy Institute for International Policy is an independent Sydney-based think tank dedicated to international, strategy, and economic issues from an Australian perspective. The Lowy Institute maintains a dedicated nuclear policy center that focuses largely on nuclear security in Asia but also on Australia's nuclear policy. Publications range in length and political orientation.

South Asian nuclear security has spawned several organizations. The Delhi Policy Group (DPG) is a NGO focused on India and Asia. DPG's interests are diverse; its Nuclear Policy Stewardship Project works with the NTI to analyze and understand India's nuclear policy and its role in regional security. Publications, particularly on nuclear issues, are relatively infrequent, but DPG does host seminars, roundtables, and other events with some frequency. The South Asia Analysis Group is a nonprofit, India-based think tank composed of Indian academics and former government officials that seeks to advance strategic analysis and promote public understanding. South Asia Analysis Group runs a dedicated nonproliferation center that publishes brief policy analyses on global proliferation issues with some regularity, although publications in this area have slowed recently. The group also conducts analyses on related nuclear issues, particularly in South and Southeast Asia. The South Asian Strategic Stability Institute (SASSI) is an independent research institute based in London and dedicated to peace and stability in South Asia. SASSI's focus extends beyond nuclear stability, but it hosts and participates in a number of events related to South Asian nuclear issues. SASSI also releases research papers, conference reports, and occasional papers through its website and through the *Journal of South Asian Nonproliferation*. Papers infrequently cover issues outside of South Asia, such as the Iranian nuclear program. The Institute of Peace and Conflict Studies (IPCS) is an independent defense, foreign policy, and security studies think tank based in India and usually focused on South and Southeast Asia. IPCS maintains a significant nuclear issues program that releases a range of publications of various lengths and depths. IPCS also hosts international conferences and events.

Gauging the Success and Functions of the Nuclear Nonproliferation Regime

Although it is far from an exhaustive list, the preceding broad survey should have clarified that the scale and scope of the global regime, whose purpose is to prevent the proliferation of nuclear weapons, are truly staggering. Giving the lie to realist accounts of the difficulty of cooperation on matters of security, the NNP regime is truly global in reach, with many intersecting ties of collaboration between states, inter- and intrastate bodies, and a variety of other actors. If liberal IR gives us a narrative of progressive regime building, then one measure of the success of this regime is to gauge the extent to which its good intentions are materialized. In Tannenwald's account, the success of the nuclear taboo so far lies simply in the prevention of nuclear weapons use since the World War II use of the atomic bomb on Japan. Much has also been made of President Kennedy's now famous claim in 1962 that the United States was facing the prospect of fifteen to twenty-five nuclear powers by the 1970s, something that the NPT was seen to have averted. But consider this: although there have been reductions since the level of global nuclear weapons arsenals peaked in 1986, Robert Norris and Hans Kristensen estimate that in 2013, there were still approximately 17,200 intact nuclear warheads in the world.[32] More than 90 percent of existing warheads are in U.S. and Russian possession (see Figure 2). Nearly forty-four hundred warheads were operational to some degree and ready to launch on relatively short notice, and roughly eighteen hundred U.S. and Russian warheads were on high levels of alert. The United States possessed roughly 7,700 intact warheads, of which the

Pentagon had roughly 4,650 (2,150 operational) and another 3,000 retired warheads held by the Department of Energy (slated to be dismantled by 2022). In addition to Russia, which still had approximately 8,500 intact nuclear warheads, the United Kingdom had roughly 225, France another 300, and China about 250. Of the four NWS not party to the NPT, India was estimated to have 90 to 110 warheads, Pakistan another 100 to 120, and Israel approximately 80, and North Korea likely had enough fissile material for around 8 to 12 bombs. All four of these states, and China, continue to increase the size of their nuclear stockpiles. In other words, although the total number of nuclear weapons in the world is declining, largely because of reductions in the huge U.S. and Russian arsenals, this obscures the fact that all the current NWS continue to produce new or updated weapons, and all nine claim nuclear weapons to be essential to their security.[33] None of this includes the possible weapons that may be produced in the future by potential proliferators that generate so much concern, whether those be uranium-enriching states, such as Iran, or other "latent" or "breakout" states. Some, arguing that it is not the NPT but other factors that have inhibited proliferation, foresee the number of NWS in the future rising, perhaps at the rate of one or two additional ones every decade (Wesley 2005). A publication by the Brookings Institution suggests that with wide global dispersal for all the building blocks for a nuclear arsenal, including through the black market, the world stands at the brink of a "nuclear tipping point" (Reiss 2004). Even if one argues that these sorts of dire and dramatic predictions of upcoming instability are exaggerated, and at least partly a product of anxieties that surround the dispersal of weapons materials and technology to those outside of the "nuclear club," it is still the case that nuclear nonproliferation and disarmament efforts have failed to produce a sense of nuclear peace and security.

Yet every prominent agreement, such as the Final Document that emerged from the 2000 NPT Review Conference, which reiterated the commitment of the NWS to both existing arms control agreements[34] and to concrete steps toward disarmament (the "Thirteen Steps"); the New START signed and ratified recently by the United States and Russia; or declarations such as President Obama's 2010 Nuclear Posture Review or his April 2009 Prague speech calling for a nuclear-free world, is greeted by a flurry of excitement among commentators and arms control and disarmament activists, even leading the *Bulletin of the Atomic Scientists* at the University of Chicago to move the minute hand on the metaphoric

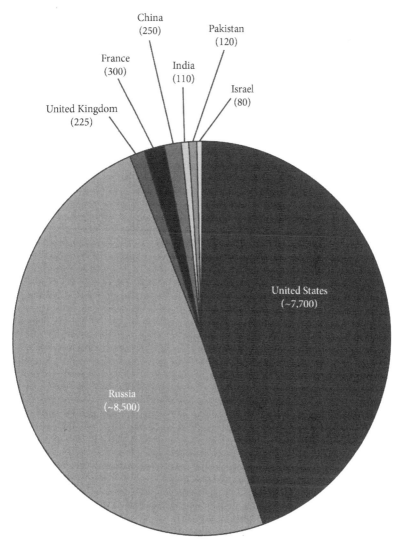

Figure 2. Distribution of global nuclear weapons. From Norris and Kristensen (2013, 76).

doomsday clock by a minute or two.[35] But that clock still stands at five minutes to midnight, having changed twenty times since its creation in 1947 and teetering between seventeen minutes to midnight in 1991, when the United States and the Soviet Union signed START and took some unilateral steps to remove ICBMs and bombers off hair-trigger alert, to as close to two minutes to midnight in 1953, when the United States and the Soviet Union tested the hydrogen bomb within nine months of each other. In this stark symbolic rendition of the dangers of nuclear weapons, the world always remains a few small minutes away from a nuclear catastrophe. People seem to wait with bated breath as the arms control community prepares for and engages in the five-year NPT review conferences, efforts that take up millions of dollars in resources only to stall over disagreements on particular phrases in the agenda—creating a "toothless review process, though established with the best of intentions in 1995 [that] has become another factor in the diminishing credibility of the NPT regime" (Johnson 2010, 436).

In discussing the emergence of an arms control epistemic community whose emergence and influence eventually led to successful negotiation of the ABM Treaty, Emanuel Adler (1992, 111) points out how the "analytical middle marginalists," who were essentially realists in their belief in the perennial clash of state interests, and the "moderate antiwar marginalists," who were largely liberal in their suspicion of armaments and preferred disarmament to arms control, eventually converged into a single epistemic community in agreement over the short-term advantages and necessity of arms control over disarmament. But any faith in nuclear disarmament, and there appears to be quite a good bit in the NNP regime outlined earlier, is constantly deferred for what in the larger scheme are largely marginal changes in levels of arsenals or doctrines. If the NNP regime is an attempt to suture the triad of deterrence, nonproliferation, and disarmament, the last leg of that triad is an always receding goal made marginal by the appearing necessity of the former two. In fact, in an updated op-ed in the *Wall Street Journal,* the recently converted abolitionists with whom this chapter started—the "gang of four"—clarified that despite their commitment to long-term universal disarmament, as long as nuclear weapons existed, the United States needed to "retain a safe, secure and reliable nuclear stockpile primarily to deter a nuclear attack and to reassure our allies through extended deterrence."[36] A research project undertaken by two graduate students and published by the James Martin CNS charted forty-two plans for disarmament since the unlimited extension of the NPT in 1995 and has articulated the danger of proliferation as the predominant rationale for disarmament in these proposals. Though these researchers end on the optimistic note that "the wheel of disarmament is not being reinvented, but the drivers are finally gaining momentum," there is nothing concrete to suggest why that is the case.[37] Indeed, the Arms Control Association report card assessing progress on nuclear nonproliferation and disarmament—grading on an A to F scale eleven states with current and suspected nuclear weapons programs on ten nuclear nonproliferation standards—comes to the much more accurate conclusion that current global institutions are "neither on the verge of crumbling nor on the cusp of success."[38] Instead, the regime appears to reproduce and sustain itself from year to year in and through its many interconnected nodes.

How, then, might one explain this sprawling and expanding complex of institutions, practices, and ideas that sustains itself through the hope, at its minimum, of preventing nuclear weapons use and, at its most ambitious, of ridding the world of nuclear weapons? Whereas progress on the latter can be considered an abysmal failure, any progress on the former always appears precarious and will undoubtedly remain precarious as weapons and weapons material proliferate, horizontally, vertically, and possibly diagonally, and the goal of disarmament always gets pushed to an indefinite future. Certainly the fact that nuclear weapons have not been used in any wars since World War II can be considered "success," as can the reductions in total numbers of weapons. Yet, the fact that we continue to live with so much fear of an impending nuclear catastrophe might give us some pause as to the level of success achieved. Indeed, it should be considered even more remarkable that so many resources, invested in so many redundant efforts, need to be invested in simply *preventing* from use weapons that require so much investment of resources to produce and maintain (the latter is the subject of chapter 4). Thus, if one contrasts this rate of success with the scale and scope of the NNP regime that was elaborated in the previous section, one is led to ask what function this massive regime serves that is not simply about the prevention of nuclear war and that cannot simply be evaluated on a success–failure template. In other words, what does this dizzying array of agreements, institutions, agencies, think tanks, publications, advocacy, and activities *do* that is not just the sum of the many good intentions for achieving nuclear peace?

Rather than judging the success of this regime in terms of its own purported intentions, perhaps one can turn to a different kind of regime analysis than that offered by liberal IR theorists, one that considers regimes through an analysis of their effects rather than their aims. There is now an established critical tradition, particularly influenced by poststructural and postcolonial analyses of power, of describing the "regime of development" as a vast discursive apparatus of institutions, norms, and practices that govern the behavior of, and relations between, scholars, policy makers, state leaders, functionaries of NGOs, local activists, and other stakeholders in "development."[39] Of these, one in particular that analyzes the persistence of this massive regime of development despite and through its "failures" stands out as exemplary for our purposes. Through an ethnographic analysis conducted in the very specific location of Lesotho, James Ferguson (1994) offers a brilliant account of the complex regime of development institutions, agencies, ideology, discourse, and experts that persistently reproduces itself despite a long history of failure in achieving its stated objectives.[40] Much like the NNP regime, it is not that the development industry does not occasionally alleviate particular problems and have some beneficial effects on the lives of those it claims to help, but most judgments of the massive scale and scope of this regime in terms of its overall objective of alleviating global poverty are usually pretty scathing. Rejecting both the liberal critiques that accept the beneficent impulses of a progressive development apparatus they would like to see redeemed through technical fixes of existing problems and the Marxist-inspired structural critiques that see the development industry as simply a conduit for the interests of capital and imperialism, Ferguson is more interested in tracing the "interventions of 'development' agencies not for what they don't do or might do, but for what they do" (13). From this perspective, the liberal explanations of an expanding NNP regime through the cumulative efforts of more and more parties interested in stopping all mechanisms of weapons proliferation (for instance, through tracking, securing, and stopping the transfers of fissile materials or weapons technology or through attempts to cut back on existing stockpiles via various treaties), all toward the common aim of decreasing the dangers of nuclear weapons proliferation and use, are simply inadequate. But also inadequate, in this approach, is the kind of structuralist critique of the liberal regimes literature offered by Susan Strange (1982), in which she sees regimes as epiphenomenal to the "real interests" that drive state behavior.[41] Indeed, Ferguson rejects neither the charitable intentions of development practitioners nor the actual workings of capitalist and imperialist interests in and through development institutions. He is, rather, more interested in seeing how a particular social institution operates in ways that exceed its original intentions to further historically specific economic and political interests. In making this argument, Ferguson draws from Foucault's conceptualization of "discourse," not as a set of utterances or rhetoric, as in Tannenwald's study of the nuclear taboo,[42] but as a set of historically and contextually specific practices that acquire a certain systematicity or political intelligibility through a recurrence of similar effects.

As a discourse, the NNP regime is a multiplicity of practices animated by the desire for nuclear peace, practices quite polyvalent in emphasis and sometimes even contradictory in logic, but each refers back to the other through a sense of common mission. Thus, whereas the NPT attempts to halt the horizontal proliferation of nuclear weapons based on dismissing any role these weapons might play as guarantors of security, the various START, SALT, and ABM treaty agreements were concrete attempts to curtail numbers and types of weapons, sometimes with the explicit aim of bolstering the security that deterrence provides. The enormous efforts involved in urging states, particularly the United States, to ratify the CTBT, or to successfully conclude the FMCT, are motivated by the sense that prohibiting all forms of testing or the proliferation of weapons materials will only fortify attempts like the NPT to prevent the development of new weapons by NNWS and are considered significant by even those disarmament activists who see the enormous nuclear stockpiles of existing NWS to be the more serious problems and who urge these states to undo their own weapons programs despite no treaty-based requirement for them to do so. Thus the massive resources deployed by so many think tanks and NGOs to track the circulation of nuclear weapons materials and programs, and monitor the possible development and upgrading of nuclear weapons capabilities in "problem areas" like Iran, North Korea, and Syria, work only partly in conjunction with the significantly fewer efforts to monitor ongoing efforts of existing NWS to reduce and/or eliminate their own weapons, but they all see themselves as engaged in a similar enterprise.

The NNP discourse is also dominated by "expert" articulations of the problems posed by nuclear weapons and mechanisms to rid the world of their dangers, whether they come from scientists, physicians, lawyers, or deterrence strategists. This expertise-guided discourse is not absent of active disagreements and debates—and a glance through any of the conference proceedings of major think tanks or publications on the subjects will provide ample evidence of hearty exchanges on a variety of subjects—but much of this happens within a language community that sets certain parameters on thinking about nuclear weapons and peace. Ferguson refers to the "standardization" of development interventions that stems from the work of a small, interlocked network of development experts who bring a very particular view of the problem of development and a particular kind of development expertise to bear on it. Using "devspeak," which is more than just jargon, these professionals subscribe to a "distinctive style of reasoning" or "devthink," that allows them to raise certain kinds of questions and provide particular answers, while delimiting others (Ferguson 1994, 258–60). Carol Cohn (1987) has described the level of abstraction in the "technostrategic" language and thinking practiced by "defense intellectuals" in which the primary referent is weapons and weapons systems rather than the human beings whose injury and death is what, ultimately, these weapons are about.[43] Cohn suggests that this sort of "expertise" not just defines the terrain of questions that can be asked about nuclear weapons possession and use and the options available to prevent their use, as well as evacuating certain kinds of concerns and fears from discussion, but it also serves as an important boundary marker so that those without access to it cannot be taken seriously.[44] Increasing differentiation of "arms control" from the perceived imprecise, utopian elements in the thinking of disarmament advocates by international security specialists in the 1960s happened through the adoption of a "technocratic or problem-solving orientation" that made it more politically acceptable (Krause 2011, 26). Adler's (1992) account of the arms control epistemic community that played a critical role in the successful negotiation of the ABM Treaty documents how certain modes of thinking about weapons and the world were developed at some of the important think tanks such as RAND and universities such as MIT and were transmitted through state agencies such as the ACDA. Indeed, the publications on nuclear proliferation provide considerable evidence of the extent to which this sort of technostrategic language and thinking is firmly and widely entrenched, even in the works of those advocating disarmament.

Like Foucault's analysis of the prison in *Discipline and Punish,* Ferguson seeks to understand the ways that "failures" are *productive.* In the case of the development industry, the multiple and persistent failures of development to alleviate poverty have two sets of effects—"side effects," which, according to Ferguson (1994, 225), are better thought of as "instrument-effects" of "what 'turns out' to be an exercise of power." On one hand is the expansion and entrenchment of state power and, on the other, the depoliticization of both poverty and the state by the relentless pursuit of "technical solutions" for the sufferings of powerless, exploited, and oppressed people. It is thus that we see the regime of development as an "anti-politics machine" through which practices of governmentality simultaneously expand and depoliticize the state. So even though there is no grand conspiracy at work here, it is "because 'failed' development projects can so successfully help to accomplish important strategic tasks behind the backs of the most sincere participants [that] it does become less mysterious why 'failed' development projects should end up being replicated again and again" (256).

How may we understand the replication and multiplication of the NNP regime despite its lackluster record in making the world safe from the persistent presence of nuclear weapons? Like the development industry, it is not the good intentions of the many different agents involved in the regime—policy makers, scientists, lawyers, researchers, scholars, activists, and so on—that is in question. Indeed, it is safe to say that the multiplicity of efforts aimed at tracking, monitoring, lobbying, raising public awareness, and in general working toward preventing the spread of nuclear weapons and associated materials and technology or the elimination of existing stockpiles and programs are all a product of these good intentions. But much as the development discourse often uses an unconscious form of backward reasoning from the conclusion that more development is needed to the premises required to generate that conclusion (Ferguson 1994, 259–60), the NNP regime reproduces and replicates itself from the genuine desire for nuclear peace to the endless and redundant articulations of the "problem of nuclear weapons." Thus it is that the much-anticipated peace dividend from the end of the Cold War was largely dissipated as massive and redundant weapons systems continued to exist and be modernized at the same time as some cuts were made, and more and more initiatives to curtail proliferation and urge disarmament emerge from many different quarters that largely regurgitate the same fears and same proposed actions, while little gets accomplished.

But even if these efforts may not have been particularly "effective" in making the world safe from nuclear weapons or "efficient" in the use of enormous redundant resources to produce constantly receding goals, it has had other and quite real effects. Albeit quite differently from the regime of development whose projects have a much more direct effect on people's everyday lives, the NNP regime, too, has extended the reach and power of the state in multiple ways. Arms control measures are, after all, a technology of the state, deployed by the state for particular ends.[45] Interstate treaties rely on and empower states in particular ways; the creation of a global inspections regime requires the cooperation of states in tracking and monitoring various societal conduits for the flow of goods and money and in enforcing the system of nuclear safeguards and helps extend the panopticon-like gaze of the state in all kinds of directions. Though at first the IAEA had much more limited access to only facilities declared by governments, with the Additional Protocol, NNWS in particular have had to accept much more extensive and intrusive inspections that could be imposed unannounced and in locations outside declared facilities. Required to cooperate with the IAEA, such states find their external sovereignty truncated even as their internal sovereignty is strengthened. The development of the nuclear weapons programs of Iraq, North Korea, Libya, and possibly Iran, especially since the discovery of the transnational clandestine operation run by A. Q. Khan, has made this question of monitoring even more urgent. A substantial revision of the Nuclear Suppliers' Guidelines in 1993 extended its reach from exports of primarily nuclear materials to regulations pertaining to a wide range of "dual-use" goods, which now required national permits and fortified export-licensing processes as well as tougher domestic laws and penalties for transgressors (Walker 2004, 36).

Post September 11, 2001, vulnerability of nuclear weapons and material to theft or sabotage by a terrorist group generated calls to increase interstate cooperation that would tighten materials protection, control, and accounting efforts (Busch 2002). In April 2010, President Obama hosted a Nuclear Security Summit attended by forty-seven international leaders, including representatives from recognized and unrecognized NWS as well as NNWS—the largest gathering of world leaders organized by an American president since the 1945 meeting that created the UN—whose purpose was securing nuclear materials from possible theft by terrorists. The UN Security Council Resolution 1540, adopted on April 28, 2004, implicitly recognizes that only states can be legitimate holders of WMD and explicitly calls on states to enact domestic controls that would prevent proliferation of WMD, related materials, and their delivery vehicles to non-state actors.[46] In the implementation of this massive apparatus of nonproliferation, overlapping state, interstate, and intrastate bureaucracies extend the practices of governmentality in all sorts of ways that reinforce the state's monopoly on the use of lethal force (Krause 2011). Furthermore, the very logic of governmentality as encoded in various arms control practices—meant to ensure strategic stability and balance through the governmental rationality of the modern state—militates against the goals of disarmament (Mutimer 2011; Krause 2011).[47] If this expansion of state power in the case of development happens in the name of national development (Ferguson 1994, 268), in the case of nonproliferation, it happens in the name of national security and hence acquires a certain sense of urgency that allows all kinds of intrusions into civil society and the realm of the private that might otherwise be considered problematic. The IAEA expects and depends on collaboration with national intelligence services, and the task of monitoring nuclear materials and technology diffusion in a rapidly globalizing world adds even more urgency to this collaboration. But in doing so, it also bolsters a state system within which states are positioned quite unequally, and hence empowered quite differently by the NNP regime. In other words, the NNP regime depends, builds on, and strengthens state power and does so by engaging states in a collaborative exercise within which some states will always remain marginal.

It is this question of the hierarchical global order kept in place through the NNP regime that is the subject of the following chapter. And as with development in which all political challenges to the system are effectively squashed "not only by enhancing the powers of administration and repression, but by insistently reposing political questions of land, resources, jobs, or wages as technical 'problems' responsive to the technical 'development' intervention" (Ferguson 1994, 270), political challenges that might call into question the conceptualization of security, or draw attention to the inefficient use of resources in arms control and disarmament proposals, or suggest inequality and justice to be issues more worthy than peace can be evacuated of their radical potential by making nonproliferation and disarmament technical issues that need urgent policy interventions for their successful resolution. As I argue later in the book, this depoliticization of nonproliferation can mask the underlying desires and the economic and political interests that drive the production and proliferation of nuclear weapons. Processes through which the desire for nuclear weapons is cultivated and the political economy through which their production is sustained are the subjects of chapters 3 and 4, respectively.

Conclusion: From Regimes to Order

This chapter described the enormous, sprawling global regime whose purpose is to curtail the possession and use of nuclear weapons that has been established in the last many decades. This is a multilayered and complex regime, composed of hundreds of substate, state, and interstate bodies, organizations, agencies, and activists who are driven toward cooperation with the knowledge that nuclear weapons are extremely dangerous and need to be controlled or eliminated. "Cooperation under anarchy" is the bailiwick of liberal IR theorists. For these theorists, this scale of cooperation against all odds can only be explained through the good intentions of experts and policy makers who can push otherwise self-interested states toward larger, collaborative, and more benign conceptions of their identities and interests. Yet, these accounts are inadequate to explain not just the scale of this massive global infrastructure but its ability to sustain and replicate itself despite its successive failures in making a world safe from the presence and spread of nuclear weapons. Using James Ferguson's Foucauldian analysis of the productive failures of the development regime, this chapter asked what is served by this enormous architecture of nonproliferation that is more than just the sum of liberal good intentions. The next three chapters turn to an examination of the global unequal order that sustains the desire for and production of nuclear weapons.

Earlier in this chapter, I suggested that explaining cooperation is generally a challenge for realist IR theorists. Yet Zachary Davis (1993) offers a description of the nuclear nonproliferation regime as a "realist regime"—a regime that exists not because of any benign transformation in state behavior, interests, or identities, as liberals suggest, but because of the mutual interests of great powers, particularly under U.S. leadership, to create a cooperative arrangement that can stop the spread of nuclear weapons and thus sustain the existing nuclear status quo. In other words, Davis argues that a highly discriminatory regime, centered on the NPT, exists, because it is based on and helps maintain a hierarchical global order. In the following chapter, I take up this debate between liberals and realists once again through an examination of this hierarchical global order both sustained and occluded by the NNP. Realists are able to account for power, I suggest, in ways that liberal IR theorists neglect or underappreciate. Yet both realist and liberal approaches to the NNP regime are premised on certain presuppositions about Europe's others. The NNP regime exists, not because it effectively solves the "problem of nuclear weapons," but because it also helps constitute a certain rendition of the problem of nuclear weapons that serves a global ordering function.

CHAPTER 2

Whose Nuclear Order?

A Postcolonial Critique of an Enlightenment Project

Whither the Nuclear Non-Proliferation Treaty (NPT)?

In the massive regime erected to stall and eliminate nuclear weapons possession that the previous chapter discussed, the NPT has had a certain pride of place. Signed in 1968 and going into effect in 1970, with all but four countries in the world as party to the treaty, the NPT has long been considered quite effective in preventing the horizontal spread of nuclear weapons. Among some of its strongest supporters on the left, it has also been celebrated for enshrining the principle of disarmament. However, there appears to be a fair bit of recent anxiety that the NPT may be in crisis. A series of events in the last decade—the nuclear tests conducted by India and Pakistan in 1998; the withdrawal of North Korea from the treaty in 2003, followed by its nuclear tests in 2006 and 2009; concerns about a nuclear weapons program under way in Iran (which remains a signatory of the treaty);[1] the discovery in 2003 of the vast reach of the nuclear smuggling network run by former Pakistani nuclear scientist A. Q. Khan; fears of nuclear proliferation to terrorist actors; and the negotiation of the 2003 Indian–U.S. nuclear treaty that effectively, even if not formally, recognizes India's nuclear status (something prohibited by the terms of the NPT)—have raised serious questions about the future viability of the NPT. In short, the NPT, once considered a stalwart treaty in its ability to halt the spread of nuclear weapons and perhaps provide a mechanism to move toward global disarmament sometime in the future, appears to be fraying from numerous loose strands. The unraveling of the 2005 NPT review conference only fortified this general feeling, exacerbated by the unilateralist thrust of the previous U.S. administration's interests in counterproliferation, missile defense, and even nuclear testing and the development of "useable" nuclear weapons. Some have hailed the recently signed and ratified New

START as restarting the momentum toward arms control and President Obama's April 2009 Prague speech and the U.S. administration's 2010 Nuclear Posture Review as changing direction toward one more conducive to nuclear disarmament. But not many appear to be particularly sanguine about the health of the NPT, at least in its current form, or put much faith in its ability to stop further proliferation or get us to "nuclear zero" anytime in the near future.[2] What, then, is the role of the NPT in holding together a regime whose overall commitment is to make the world safe from the terribly destructive power of nuclear weapons?

As the previous chapter suggested, studying the cooperative thrusts of international relations has been the bailiwick of liberal theorists in the field of international relations (IR). Much of this analysis of cooperation among states has happened through studies of international regimes, with emphasis on *why* and *how* states cooperate. In chapter 1, I suggested that an analysis of what the nuclear nonproliferation (NNP) regime *does*, especially in ways that exceed the reasons for its creation, may reveal more about the global dynamics kept in place through international institutions. Though very much in the camp of liberal IR, William Walker's quite innovative approach to the NPT is precisely a study in what the NPT-centered regime does—which, in his account, is to institutionalize a progressive global "nuclear order" embodying the Enlightenment values of reason and trust. Walker is attentive to the inequality institutionalized within the treaty, and in his impassioned call to resurrect and reform a flailing treaty, he pleads for a sincere renewal of the commitment to disarmament on the part of nuclear weapons states. Not surprisingly, Walker's account of a liberal international order has received its fair share of criticism, much of it attacking its unfounded and even dangerous optimism that gives short shrift to "political reality." This attack mostly comes from realists who draw attention to the centrality of power in international negotiations and make no apology for the inequality within a treaty that reflects the shape of an unequal world.

This chapter undertakes a critical analysis of this important debate, interrogating the *kind of order* kept in place by the NPT and its associated regime, with particular focus on the common presuppositions of the non-Western world undergirding the entire debate. After a very quick overview of the NPT, I spend some time detailing Walker's quite methodical and careful argument as it developed over the course of his writings before turning to a discussion of the various criticisms leveled against him by realists. Following that, I mount a postcolonial analysis of the global hierarchy that both sustains and is sustained by the NPT-centered security regime, beginning first with the conception of Enlightenment at play in the work of Walker's critics and then turning to examine the exclusionary logics through which order is conceptualized in formulations of the Enlightenment Order.

The NPT

The obvious backbone of the global nonproliferation regime, the NPT[3] distinguishes between two types of states: nuclear weapons states (NWS) and non–nuclear weapons states (NNWS). As defined by Article IX, the five NWS are those states that exploded a nuclear weapon prior to January 1, 1967: the United States, the United Kingdom, Russia, France, and China. The NNWS are all other parties (currently 184 countries). The four states that are not party to the NPT are India, Israel, Pakistan, and North Korea (formerly a member). All four nonsignatories possess nuclear weapons, but Israel has never publicly acknowledged its weapons program.

Significant Articles

Article I prohibits existing NWS from providing any nuclear material for use in explosives "to any recipient whatsoever."

Article II prohibits NNWS from receiving or manufacturing nuclear explosives.

Article III provides for safeguards and examination of all declared nuclear facilities in NNWS by the International Atomic Energy Agency (IAEA). NWS are not required to accept the safeguard agreements (though many voluntarily do so).

Article IV allows for the research and development of peaceful nuclear technologies by all treaty members. Significantly, the treaty commits NWS to sharing peaceful nuclear technology with NNWS.

Article VI commits NWS to the cessation of the nuclear arms race and continued efforts toward total nuclear disarmament.

Article X allows parties the right to withdraw from the treaty with three months' notice.

Brief History of the NPT

In the aftermath of failed postwar disarmament negotiations, a number of countries successfully proliferated (the USSR, 1949; the United Kingdom, 1952; France, 1960; China 1964), spurring concerns about global nuclear stability and security and disproving early assumptions regarding the difficulty in mastering nuclear technology. Amid estimates of two dozen nuclear weapons–possessing states by the end of the 1970s, the United Nations (UN) adopted a 1961 resolution (proposed by Ireland) calling on all states to conclude an international agreement on nuclear proliferation. On August 17, 1965, the United States submitted a draft nonproliferation treaty to the Eighteen Nation Committee on Disarmament (ENDC), which outlined the basic provisions of the future NPT. Despite significant disagreements over the nature of the United States' nuclear commitments in Europe, both the United States and the USSR submitted identical drafts of a nonproliferation treaty to the ENDC on August 24, 1967. Negotiations of the treaty proper then began.

These negotiations focused on several issues. First, they concerned the specific operations of the IAEA: though the USSR demanded all countries accept IAEA safeguards, many European nations sought to preserve their regional systems of control. The resulting compromise led to each country independently (or in groups) negotiating safeguards requirements with the IAEA. Second, NNWS maintained reservations about forswearing nuclear weapons without reciprocation from the existing nuclear powers. Article VI, negotiations on a Comprehensive Test Ban Treaty, and legally binding security assurances served to secure compromise on that. Finally, NNWS sought guarantees that nuclear renunciation would not place them at a significant military disadvantage. A UN resolution thus promised assistance from the NWS to NNWS in the event of nuclear threats (neither France nor China partook in this resolution). Likewise, the United States, the Soviet Union, and the United Kingdom adopted negative security assurances not to use nuclear weapons against any NNWS.

The NPT became open to signatures on July 1, 1968, and entered into force on March 5, 1970, after U.S. ratification (which was delayed because of a Soviet invasion of Czechoslovakia in August 1968). Article VII commits the parties to a review conference every five years, with the most recent taking place in May 2010. Originally negotiated for twenty-five years, the NPT was indefinitely and unconditionally extended when it came up for review in 1995.

The NPT's efforts at halting proliferation have received significant challenges. Two major challenges (the South African and Libyan nuclear programs) were successfully resolved,[4] but many remain. The refusal of India, Israel, and Pakistan (all nuclear weapons–possessing states) to sign has consistently been an issue of concern, particularly in light of the recent U.S.–Indian nuclear deal that enables civilian nuclear transfers from the United States to India (which violates the mandate of the NPT). Similarly, North Korea's withdrawal from the treaty in 2003 and subsequent announcement of its nuclear weapons program via a series of tests led many to question the effectiveness of the NPT, particularly given the ease with which countries can withdraw. Finally, questions remain as to the nature of the Iranian nuclear program, which has previously been found in violation of IAEA safeguards and has been repeatedly condemned in the UN.

The Liberal Enlightenment Order of the NPT

In one of the most celebratory defenses of the NPT offered recently, William Walker has famously suggested that the NPT helped instantiate a liberal Enlightenment Order based on progressive values of human reason and rationality. This order, he argued, was threatened by the counter-Enlightenment forces undergirding the George W. Bush administration's unilateralist aggressiveness. Walker's argument about the Enlightenment-inspired nuclear order was developed over a series of writings, which began with his distress at the possible fraying of the NPT and the ensuing disorder that that portends and then only later fully developed as an argument about liberal Enlightenment values. I begin by outlining the main contours of this argument as it developed over the course of his writings[5] before turning to its critique by several commentators, most of whom question the liberal optimism underlying his analysis and accuse him of giving short shrift to the realist power configurations that gave rise to, and will be necessary to sustain, an understandably imperfect but important treaty.

In an obvious precedent to his later work on the nuclear Enlightenment, William Walker began developing his influential thesis on the role of the NPT in creating a nuclear order in the journal *International Affairs* in 2000. Without really fleshing out the concept of an "international order" but concerned that the old nuclear order was crumbling, in this article Walker essentially describes the kind of nuclear order that emerged with the negotiation of the NPT and argues strenuously for its restoration and reform so as to avoid rampant proliferation and nuclear catastrophe. Written on the eve of the George W. Bush presidency, Walker emphasizes the centrality of the United States in the creation and maintenance of the NPT regime, even then seeing the impending disorder emergent from U.S. arrogance and unilateralism, and concludes with a ringing endorsement of the multilateralism and commitment to disarmament enshrined in the Final Document that emerged from the 2000 NPT Review Conference (Walker 2000). An oft-cited and significant text, it is only in his 2004 Adelphi paper that Walker further develops his previous thesis through a more sustained engagement with the conceptual question of international order, especially in light of what he sees as all the disorder-inducing actions of the Bush administration following the terrorist attacks of September 11, 2001, actions that had further eroded the NPT-centered regime since he wrote his 2000 article (Walker 2004). Though Walker elaborates and substantiates his previous argument in light of these changed circumstances, what is most interesting about this Adelphi paper is his more careful effort to conceptualize "order." In his Adelphi paper, Walker alludes to the Enlightenment values undergirding the NPT-centered order, but it is in his later 2007 article, also in *International Affairs,* that Walker fully develops the argument that the NPT-centered nuclear order embodied an Enlightenment project that combined faith in human rationality (deterrence) with efforts to prevent proliferation (abstinence) and accuses the Bush administration of following a counter-Enlightenment project imperiling a carefully crafted multilateral order.

To make his arguments, Walker presents a triumphalist narrative of historical progress, progress whose undoing is his grave concern. In this, a series of steps (Intermediate-Range Nuclear Forces Treaty, Strategic Arms Reduction Treaty [START] I and II, NPT Additional Protocols, Nuclear Weapons Free Zones, Missile Technology Control Regime) made the decade from 1986 to 1995 the "golden age" in the increasing marginalization of nuclear weapons, all of them culminating in the 1995 NPT review conference (at which the NPT was indefinitely extended), which seemed to offer a new dawn for nuclear reductions and nonproliferation. But these hopes were dashed as the NPT's project proved too optimistic, because it assumed nuclear weapons could be drained out of international politics, that U.S. and Russian commitments to disarmament had a solid domestic political backing, that Russian economic modernization would eventually make deterrence irrelevant, that the Middle East peace process could foster genuine solutions, and that India and Pakistan would exercise nuclear restraint. The failing of all of these things put the regime under stress, but the real crisis that unhinged the order was the U.S. Senate's decisive rejection of the Comprehensive Test Ban Treaty and its pursuit of a National Missile Defense that demonstrated a lack of faith in deterrence (Walker 2000).[6] The September 11, 2001, terrorist attacks further opened room for formerly fringe understandings of international order, encouraging U.S. primacy and unilateral counterproliferation efforts to dominate U.S. policy making. Though the events of September 11, 2001, ultimately brought these ideas to the fore, Walker traces them in his 2004 article to the 1991 Gulf War, when the United States realized its military preponderance, blurred distinctions between nuclear and other weapons through the language of weapons of mass destruction (WMDs),[7] grasped the ramifications of technological advancement on nuclear weapons procurement, and framed the Western relations with the Middle East in adversarial terms. Concurrent with the September 11, 2001, transformation of the international order, a series of other crises also shook the existing geopolitical framework: the Indian and Pakistani test explosions, the U.S. abrogation of the Anti-Ballistic Missile (ABM) Treaty, the breakdown of the United Nations Special Commission monitoring WMD production in Iraq, and the revelation of covert supply networks—all combining to portend the possible dissolution of a carefully crafted and quite effective global nuclear order. This piece concludes right on the eve of the 2005 NPT Review Conference, on the reiterated hope of a return to an international order founded on international legitimacy and multilateralism rather than U.S. unipolarity (Walker 2004).[8] Two central concepts underlie this historical analysis—order and Enlightenment values; let me turn to Walker's discussion of these.

A Nuclear Order

Three fundamental facts after the invention of nuclear weapons create an "ordering imperative" in international politics—nuclear weapons facilitate an extremely rapid and total war; new nuclear states threaten major instability; and technology will eventually diffuse (including through the development of civilian nuclear programs) to make proliferation possible in a range of new states (Walker 2000). Indeed, the preoccupation with international order that emerged from the experiences of twentieth-century wars became an "obsession" once the destructive power of nuclear weapons was recognized (Walker 2004). In his 2007 piece on Enlightenment values that engages the question of modernity, this ordering imperative emerges from the twin "paradoxes of modernity": on one hand, Hiroshima revealed the inescapable modern paradox that scientific and technological progress had inadvertently produced the possibility and fear of catastrophic destruction,[9] but on the other hand, the anarchy of international relations made political control over those forces quite difficult. The result of this was, Walker says, gesturing in slightly tongue-in-cheek fashion toward political realists, that if "states were left to their brutish ways," one could have a "lethal nuclear anarchy" (Walker 2007, 437). Thus, and recognizing the absence of any "satisfactory response" to the "profound questions of legitimacy" that any unequal nuclear order posed, Walker suggests that the NPT-centered order that began to be fashioned, especially after the 1962 scare of the Cuban Missile Crisis, relied on a two-pronged approach: "a managed system of deterrence" that held among existing nuclear states[10] and "a managed system of abstinence" for NNWS (Walker 2000, 706). This description of the nuclear order as a combination of managed systems of deterrence and abstinence continues to be central in all of Walker's writings.[11]

To conceptualize "order," which he does in his 2004 Adelphi piece, Walker draws on an odd mix of thinkers. On one hand, he uses John Ikenberry's three types of order to suggest that the Cold War was characterized by a combination of "power balance" and "constitutionalism," which subsequently gave way to the "hegemonic order" imposed by a triumphalist post–Cold War United States dominated by certain influential interests emboldened by the September 11, 2001, crisis. In the former period, constitutionalism helped stabilize the balance of power, creating a harmonious and symmetrical architecture of nuclear order based on "reciprocal obligations" that reconciled the asymmetry of interests between the nuclear haves and have-nots (Walker 2004, 12–13). Indeed, he goes to some length to emphasize, quoting from Ikenberry, that the system of deterrence and abstinence on which this order was based was "deeply constitutional insofar as it was 'organised around agreed-upon legal and political institutions that operated to allocate rights and limit the exercise of power' and held international law in the highest regard" (30). Counterposed to this expansive and celebratory account of a liberal international order, he also makes use of another articulation of international order as composed of potential friends and enemies, now drawing from Alexander Wendt's spectrum of self–other relations (in which enemies are distinct from rivals and friends) and Carl Schmitt's discussion of three kinds of enemies (conventional, true, and absolute) to elaborate this arrangement. Here he sees the primary objective of international ordering to, at the minimum, "reduce enmity to a more benign and contained rivalry," and more ambitiously, reduce "both enmity and rivalry to a sustained condition of forbearance or amity wherein states and other actors define their relations as intrinsically cooperative and strive to revise life and liberty by peaceful means alone" (10). However, argues Walker, although interstate enmity was effectively contained through previously deployed ordering strategies, the emergence of al-Qaeda as an absolute enemy in the Schmittian sense—an enemy, it must be pointed out, not just to particular states but effectively to the state system—has actually amplified the need for this sort of order, because "without durable and cooperative relations among states, and especially among great powers, there can be no solution to the problem of enmity in either dimension" (17). So he takes some care to remind readers that despite his criticisms of the Bush administration's unilateralist thrust, the primary transatlantic divide, as he sees it, is over the question of *how* to order, not over the desirability and necessity of order—the choice being between "the establishment of a condominium of great powers, or a shift to a more naked form of hegemony" (49).

It is helpful to point out here that although Walker lauds the creation of this NPT-centered normative order with a truly global reach, he is insistent that the legitimacy of the order rested on "mutual obligation and reciprocity" and that the inequality institutionalized within the treaty was based on a "temporary trust" extended to the existing NWS on the understanding that they would progress toward nuclear disarmament (Walker 2000, 708). But, despite its flaws, the NPT order is decidedly the triumph of liberalism over realism. The multilateralism and commitment to disarmament enshrined in the Final Document that emerged from the 2000 NPT Review Conference were, in his view, a clear assertion of "the inherent superiority of a security politics that placed the achievement of a cooperative order-through-law above a unilateralist order-through-power" (722). Very much in the liberal vein, this, for Walker, is an affirmation of faith in the better judgment of "the community of NPT Parties" over that of the selfish, narrow interests of "individual nation-states" (724). This is what he, in the Adelphi paper, drawing from Hedley Bull this time, calls a "society of states"—starting as the project of a select group of states, the NPT by the time of the 1995 Extension Conference was "reaffirmed by both greater and lesser powers alike" to become "the property and manifestation of a true international society—even a global society—of states" (Walker 2004, 37).[12] This characterization of the NPT-centered international order as an inclusive, democratic, and reciprocal arrangement, despite its inherent inequalities, is crucial to Walker's liberal conceptualization of international cooperation.

An Enlightenment Order

In his 2007 article, Walker's triumphalist narrative of the NPT order becomes even more expansive as he looks for the inspiration of its liberal values in the European Enlightenment. Thus, if "the exceptional nature of nuclear weapons calls for an exceptional kind of cooperative politics," a politics that can, in liberal fashion, "draw states into a rule-based order that could moderate the power play that nuclear weapons encouraged" (433), it can do so only "by enveloping the international politics of nuclear weapons in progressive enlightenment values" (433), giving rise to a grand Enlightenment project that is

> permeated by assumptions of—and expressions of faith in—
> a ubiquitous *rationality* and commitment to *reason*; the attainability of *justice* in the face of obvious inequalities of power and opportunity; the possibility of *trust* among states on the basis of international *law*; the ability of organizations to exercise *control* over complex technological activities; and the feasibility of *progress* in escaping a nuclear-armed chaos and realizing nuclear energy's economic potential. (431; emphasis added)

Rational control over complex technological forces exercised through a reasoned, just, and lawful arrangement based on trust is what makes this regime a progressive Enlightenment project. But equally important is the faith placed in "the project's intrinsic universalism"—that "the dangers and opportunities with . . . nuclear technology confronted *all* humankind, the rights and responsibilities . . . fell upon *all* institutions and peoples, and the subsequent need [was] for the engagement of *all* states in the task of providing a secure foundation for order" (436; emphasis original). The Enlightenment, in this rendition, may be of European genesis, but is

universalist in reach and significance. It is against this grand vision that
Walker charges the Bush administration of pursuing a "nuclear counter-
Enlightenment" that relies on threats of an encroaching disorder to abandon traditional concepts of justice and reverse long-standing norms against
nuclear use. He accuses the administration of discarding the use of "public
reason" and unilaterally abandoning the constitutionalism of the NPT
and the related multilateral treaty regime. Despite its problems, Walker
reminds us, the order based on Enlightenment values has an "inherent
superiority," because without it, we would be left with "a degraded international politics, a more frequent recourse to violence and a perpetual vulnerability to catastrophe" (433).

Most of this 2007 article consists of a history of nuclear weapons policy
and the nonproliferation regime to explain the origins of the Enlightenment rationality that came to characterize the NPT-centered progressive
nuclear order and how that treaty eventually began regressing. Reminding readers of the early calls for radical changes in the organization of the
international system to deal with the destructive power of nuclear weapons,
such as in the Acheson–Lilienthal Report and the Baruch Plan, he points
out how Bernard Brodie's articulation of deterrence as a mechanism to in-
ject rationality into an irrational process and NSC-68's strategy of con-
tainment came to dominate superpower relations. These, in combination
with the Cuban Missile Crisis some years later, fostered a profound faith
in the rationality of humankind to limit the dangers of nuclear warfare. It
is in the early 1960s, then, that one sees "the replacement of the hitherto
non-negotiable demand for complete nuclear disarmament by a pragmatic demand for a halt to nuclear proliferation and the arms race prior to
elimination" (Walker 2007, 435). Walker recognizes that establishing the
universalism of the NPT required resolving the sheer inequality of status
the treaty contains, and he understands this resolution as incumbent on
the unambiguous significance of the norm of disarmament, even though
vaguely expressed through Article XI. It is clear that he understands nonproliferation only as a "provisional norm"—as against the "eternal norm"
of disarmament—and this is what makes the possession of nuclear weapons by existing NWS a "temporary trust" (436).

He now argues that the 1995 indefinite extension and the achievement
of near-universal ratification transformed the treaty from a "dynamic instrument of cooperative engagement" into a "static instrument of disci-
plinary confinement" (Walker 2007, 439). As such, the international belief in progress transformed into a fear of regress that necessitated a new

ordering strategy. This provided the basis for the Bush administration's aggressive posture toward rogue states that rested on questioning the rationality of deterrence against irrational actors. Bush thus began a program of counterproliferation and counterterrorism that threatened the multilateral enlightenment basis of the NPT. The WMD deception in the war on Iraq followed by the legitimization of India's nuclear program served further blows to the nuclear order—destabilizing the unequal relationship between the nuclear haves (now expanded to include India) no longer expected to disarm and the nuclear have-nots that must never proliferate. "This was a dagger that sank deep into the heart of the NPT," says Walker, "given its basic principle that nuclear weapons are intrinsically illegitimate everywhere and for all time," thus evacuating "the issues of justice and the principle of reciprocal obligation" of their relevance (448). He concludes that this logic is particularly dangerous in that it begins to deny the possibility of imagining an international politics shaped by the cooperative ideas of the original nuclear Enlightenment, and so he ends by renewing the call for disarmament—"the pursuit of nuclear disarmament has a security logic that is stronger than ever" (451). Yet it is interesting that even though he suggests that such disarmament is not just a utopian ideal, it turns out to be simply "a direction of travel—towards an increased political and instrumental restraint, now serving the avoidance of both nuclear war and catastrophic terrorism. It neither requires nor necessarily welcomes a precipitous abandonment of deterrence" (451).

Or Could It Be Just Unenlightened Power Politics?

Walker's arguments have received some fairly energetic critiques, many included in a 2007 special issue of the journal *International Affairs*. All of Walker's critics join him in applauding the role of the NPT in sustaining a nuclear order and appear to share his concerns about the fraying of the treaty. None of them welcome the dissolution of the treaty, and some offer suggestions to reform and fortify it. In other words, there is no disagreement in this entire debate about the usefulness, necessity, or even primacy of order in a nuclear world. The primary disagreement is over Walker's understanding of *how* the NPT creates and sustains global order and what would be required for its continued efficacy. The thrust of the critiques leveled against Walker's arguments can be divided into two related themes. On one hand are those who accuse Walker and liberal arms control proponents more generally of being unenlightened idealogues, doing more damage than good in their earnest idealism. On the other hand, and in an effort to demystify this harmful ideology, is what may be considered the "reality-check" form of critiques that attempt to correct Walker's misunderstanding of the historical record and of current political realities. These two critiques frequently work in conjunction with each other, urging Walker and liberal arms control proponents like him to forgo their misplaced and harmful optimism and embrace a realistic appraisal of international politics more likely to create and sustain international order in a nuclear world.

Joachim Krause and Michael Rühle levy the sharpest attacks on Walker's alleged "ideological biases" disguised as Enlightenment reason. Krause (2007) charges liberal arms control proponents generally, of whom he sees Walker as representative, of blatant "hypocrisy" in that they accuse the Bush administration of ideological bias, while refusing to see their own ideological blinders. Rühle (2007), like Krause, also questions the use of "enlightened reason" in Walker's analysis, suggesting that his celebratory, maximalist, and ultimately ideological claims about the NPT are based on "faith," not scientific facts, and far overstate the importance of the NPT. It is, ultimately, this "myth-making oversimplification of a complex historical reality" that Yost (2007), summarizing the thoughts of these other critics, suggests results in a polemical exercise designed to "sell" a particular interpretation of nuclear history while discrediting other perspectives. Seeing the huge ideological influence of this "liberal arms control epistemic community" in the creation of the nuclear nonproliferation regime, both Krause and Rühle set themselves the task of exposing and debunking the "myths" that have dominated the pursuit of nuclear nonproliferation. In this they see themselves as bringing Enlightenment reason to bear on the wishful thinking and historical distortions of a community that has immunized itself from outside criticism, thus replacing ideological polemics with enlightened dialogue. For these commentators, this ideological bias in Walker's writings is not just problematic but dangerous. But before we get to that, it may be useful to discuss the most central "myth" that Walker's critics aim to expose.

In pretty hard-nosed realist terms, all of Walker's critics point to the power-laden political realities out of which the NPT and its associated regime emerged and which have sustained it so far. The NPT, reminds Pierre Hassner (2007, 456), was "an uneasy and fragile compromise based on existing power relations more than a project based on a coherent long-term vision." This is a key point that every single one of Walker's critics asserts again and again. Rejecting the idea of a grand Enlightenment project, Rühle (2007) sees the NPT as a mundane treaty with various structural flaws[13] emergent from hard bargaining among states with divergent interests and capacities, all of whom were engaged in fairly crude cost–benefit calculus.[14] Some critics draw attention to the actual negotiations, which, in Krause's (2007) analysis, reveals that the NPT is not and was never a product of an enlightened consensus but rather a *bargain* in a realist world of substantial power differentials. And, as many of these critics point out, that bargain was to freeze the status quo by preventing horizontal proliferation, *not to achieve disarmament.*[15] Indeed, most of these critics recognize that this is an unequal and perhaps even unfair treaty, but rather than apologize for that inequality, they defend it as a realist product of a realist world. Krause emphasizes that it emerged in that explicitly unequal form from various compromises in the original negotiations process, a process that demonstrated clear fractures within the ranks of both existing NWS and NNWS.[16] Indeed, the final agreement (as well as the indefinite extension in 1995) was a bargain largely between the United States and the silent majority of NNWS who could not build programs of their own and so had an interest in seeing further proliferation stopped; all the other NWS and the vocal NNWS who eventually joined the treaty had to be brought in on a case-by-case basis through various inducements (Krause 2007). States, such as Israel, India, and Pakistan, that wanted to have a nuclear option stayed out of the treaty, and others, such as Iran and Iraq, calculated that they could develop that option while parties to the treaty, hardly evidence of any greatly successful norm-setting trend (Rühle 2007). Thus, these critics suggest, the "system of abstention" was more a product of strategic cost–benefit calculations than of the normative force of the NPT—and in that sense the NPT may well be considered an "epiphenomenon" or, even worse, "a mask behind which nuclear proliferation activities may proceed" (Yost 2007, 558). The weakness of this imperfect treaty—both in terms of legitimacy because of its discriminatory character and in terms of its efficacy because of the absence of any viable punishment for noncompliance—is thus reflective of this imperfect process of bargaining in an unequal world with different state interests at play (Hassner 2007, 460).

But, and more importantly, argue Walker's critics, forgetting this background of hard bargaining and compromise and treating the NPT as a grand liberal project is dangerous. This is especially so with respect to the question of disarmament. Many of these critics dismiss the significance of disarmament in the overall bargain of the treaty. Rühle (2007) is perhaps the most forthright in presenting the treaty as an obvious attempt to institutionalize inequality in which the weakly worded Article VI was simply a way to make that inequality more palatable. But to treat the NPT as a disarmament treaty, these critics caution, is dangerous enticement to those states that can cynically manipulate the lack of progress on the purposely vaguely worded Article VI to pursue their own proliferation goals (Krause 2007; Hassner 2007; Schulte 2007). Arguing that there is no causal connection between disarmament and proliferation, and that the nonfulfillment of Article VI commitments by the P-5 has never been a driver of proliferation, some of these commentators suggest that the overemphasis on Article VI by the "liberal arms control community" has aided potential proliferators from having a ready justification for pursuing nuclear weapons (Hassner 2007; Rühle 2007; Krause 2007; Yost 2007). The nuclear ambitions of no proliferator would be curtailed by the disarming of existing nuclear powers, and indeed, "some of them might even be encouraged or reinforced in their decision to go nuclear by the removal of the threat of nuclear retaliation by one of the existing nuclear powers" (Hassner 2007, 463). Thus unrealistic calls for nuclear disarmament ultimately weaken the treaty. Deriding Walker's idealistic enthusiasm, Schulte (2007, 509–10) says,

> It would be unfortunate, therefore, if [Walker's] passion for abstract systemic perfection led to further undermining of regime legitimacy and credibility. In nuclear matters, as in others, we should not exalt a universal vision of the best by destructively deprecating the actually existing, though contingent, good.

If we remember, in addition, that the bargain in question was not just one between the nuclear haves and have-nots, as Walker contends, but indeed part of a larger and more important bargain in which the P-5 commit to using their power, including force, to secure a stable international order, then it is their unwillingness to do that more than their unwillingness to disarm that is imperiling the current nuclear order (Roberts 2007, 527). Thus order, for all these commentators, is necessary, but it occurs not through liberal optimism in the good practices of all states; rather, it occurs through the willingness to exert power to maintain the status quo. To think otherwise is dangerous precisely because it imperils that order.

It is this sense of misplaced optimism that also leads Walker, charge some of his critics, to misunderstand the place of nuclear weapons in strategic doctrine. Here Krause (2007) points out that despite the misplaced belief among liberal arms control ideologues, such as Walker, mutually assured destruction (MAD)—as in Walker's "managed deterrence"—was never at the heart of nuclear strategic doctrine in the United States or Soviet Union; indeed, nuclear weapons were always considered usable in certain contexts within particular war-fighting doctrines. Yost (2007) claims that although the United States demonstrated some commitment to deterrence, the Soviet Union's behavior suggests that it never did. Contrary to Walker's belief, the Soviets sought to minimize their vulnerability by hardening targets, putting up robust defenses, and creating a strong offensive capability, none of which actions demonstrate an Enlightenment-like faith in human rationality.[17] In suggesting the existence of a "managed system of deterrence," then, Walker underplays the enormous level of fear and distrust that characterized the U.S.–Soviet relationship (Yost 2007). Drawing a larger conclusion here, this myth of rationality, according to Krause, emerges from the mistaken liberal pacifist premise that arms and arms racing are dangerous and cause wars, premises that can be destabilizing and dangerous. There is, of course, considerable realist scholarship in the area of security that has argued that liberal pacifism breeds complacency, and at times, arms control can be destabilizing, whereas arms racing is stabilizing.[18] Hence some of these critics urge a discarding of the knee-jerk negative attitude toward nuclear weapons as inherently illegitimate and dangerous, Krause even reminding Walker that these were the weapons that helped vanquish the counter-Enlightenment of Nazi Germany and Imperial Japan as well as the totalitarian Soviet Union: "without US nuclear weapons, the political breathing space for enlightenment would have vanished in Europe some 50 years ago" (Krause 2007, 495).

Having performed a "reality check" on the NPT as both a "managed system of abstinence" and a "managed system of deterrence" by examining more closely the political conditions that gave rise to the NPT, Walker's critics also point to the changed political reality of the contemporary period, which needs to be accounted for in any proposal to reform and fortify the NPT-centered arms control regime. While agreeing with Walker that the NPT may be in jeopardy, many of them accuse Walker of exaggerating the role of the United States in its emerging fractures and its future redemption. Walker would likely agree with Krause that most of the Bush administration's nuclear policies can be traced to President Clinton,[19] but rather than blaming this change on empowered domestic constituencies within the United States, as Walker does, Krause (2007) argues that these reflect a changed international environment that necessitated a different approach to proliferation. Similarly, Rühle (2007) notes that the changes in U.S. policy that Walker characterizes as a "counter-Enlightenment project" occurred as a reaction to changes in the proliferation environment, not as the cause of those changes. In particular, he points to the events of September 11, 2001, as lowering U.S. tolerance of proliferation and the uncovering of nuclear smuggling networks as posing new challenges to stopping proliferation. Like realists generally, he criticizes liberal arms control proponents like Walker of clinging to defunct arrangements negotiated under different political conditions, without attending to the significant ways that the global security situation had changed. Thus many of his critics contend that Walker is wrong in holding the Bush administration and American neoconservatives as solely culpable for the fraying of the NPT-centered arms control and disarmament regime (Roberts 2007; Schulte 2007; Hassner 2007). Yost (2007) holds Russia and the European Union as equally culpable in emerging problems with this regime and even suggests that, rather than abandoning the NPT, President Bush actually made some genuine moves to committing the United States to nuclear reductions. Hassner reminds Walker of the hypocrisy among *all* nuclear powers and even NWS about their own weapons programs and commitment to universal nuclear disarmament (Hassner 2007, 462).

Furthermore, these authors question the strength of the United States in determining the success or failure of the nonproliferation regime in the future (Hassner 2007; Yost 2007). Against Walker's idealistic hope in U.S. power, Schulte (2007) points toward the limits of U.S. power, particularly in compelling states like India to disarm; the limited effects of U.S. posture and arsenal size on other states'—notably the Democratic People's Republic of Korea's and Iran's—decision calculus; and the backlash against possible U.S. leadership in any strengthened verification and safeguards regimes. The authority of the West has declined in light of the rise of new powers (China, India, powerful nonstate transnational groups), and the policies of the Bush administration (Iraq and Afghanistan wars, acceptance of Israeli and Indian nuclearization) have created strong trends of anti-Americanism as well as suspicion and mistrust of the West's intentions—creating the kind of skepticism that renders even proposals like that by Shultz, Perry, Kissinger, and Nunn[20] unlikely to receive favorable reception (Hassner 2007). Finally, among the changes in the global political environment with which many of these critics say any future nuclear order will have to contend, the emergence of "undeterrable actors"—rogue states and terrorists—occupies a prominent place. I turn to that discussion in the next section.

The Real Threat of Unenlightened Others

There are ample suggestions among Walker's critics that any "rational" nuclear order can only collapse in the face of the abundant "irrationality" that exists out there, where the "out there" is always the unenlightened non-West. Drawing attention to the changed political conditions that now confront the NPT, Rühle lays out in an alarmist tone that terrorists, lacking the instinct of national survival that even rogue states have, are essentially undeterrable, and the proliferation that occurs outside the "classical interstate system" is harder to manage through the current nonproliferation regime. Of course, Walker, too, thinks of terrorists as the "absolute enemy," to protect against which an interstate NPT needs to be fortified, and even echoes the dramatic language of his critics when he refers to them as the "irredeemable forces of darkness" carrying a "lethally armed unreason" (Walker 2007, 444). But it is not just terrorists that are the problem here. Deterrence may still be valid in *most* interstate rivalries, argues Hassner, but in jeopardy, when confronted with irrational, suicidal adversaries who define their cultural or religious opposition in absolutist terms (Hassner 2007, 465). These may be terrorists, but also states like Iran. Indeed, the tone of Hassner's entire piece—of all of Walker's critics, Hassner is the most sensitive to the inequality of the NPT order—goes from pointing to the hypocrisy of the NPT regime, which made the legitimacy of the nuclear order always suspect, to a real suspicion and fear of rising threats from the non-West that require protection, even through missile defense, if that were affordable and effective (Hassner 2007, 465–66). Yost agrees and concludes his piece by bemoaning the low level of commitment to a "common moral obligation" that would permit the building of a more enduring international society: here "the most serious obstacles to the realization of [Walker's] vision" comes, not from the United States, as Walker suggests, but from "the rise of new power centres, particularly in Eurasia, and the emergence of violent and highly capable non-state actors," a precipitous decline in the international order in a "direction unfavorable to the West" (Yost 2007, 574). Roberts, too, focuses on the changed international environment that makes it quite difficult to resurrect a new nuclear order, arguing that there is no compelling analytical conceptualization of what such an order might look like in today's world, especially given little understanding of how deterrence might function against newly emerging threats. In particular, verging on quite fantastical language here, Roberts worries about a potential "nuclear armed caliphate" that would constitute the most fundamental challenge to nuclear order (Roberts 2007, 526). The frequent slippage between terrorists and terrorist-like states in the preceding accounts comes from certain presuppositions about "rationality," where the presumed willingness to risk suicide is often the marker of irrationality.

All of these, then, become occasions to allude to the real abode of Enlightenment rationality, which, in many of these accounts, is firmly in the West. Troubled by the abstract universalism of Walker's position, and his casting of American neoconservatives as the counterenlightened, Schulte urges Walker to consider the "unscrupulous, fanatical or radically revisionist regimes" outside of the American ruling elite: *By definition, the most troublesome, risk-taking and zero-sum decision-makers will not be persuaded into a simple direction deriving from benign eighteenth-century European rationality*" (Schulte 2007, 501–2; emphasis added). Not the universalist project involving the good intentions of *all* states that Walker believes, Yost insists that "the establishment of the NPT was a 'grand enlightenment project' only in the hopes and aspirations of a certain school of thought in western societies" (Yost 2007, 556).

> Walker overstates the extent to which western (to say nothing of non-western) nations were in the 1960s and 1970s committed to a "grand enlightenment project" and believe in "a ubiquitous rationality and commitment to reason." In other words, he idealizes the dominant school of thought in the United States (and among the "policy elites" in several like-minded western nations) in those decades and then projects it onto other nations. (552)

From the premise that reason and rationality are primarily the province of the West, it is a short step to the argument that nuclear weapons more legitimately belong in some places than others. Thus Rühle argues that the NPT should not fade away and die but rather adopt new measures for countering proliferation. Among these changes is the need for a global acceptance of discriminatory nonproliferation efforts (i.e., targeting Iran and North Korea more than states like India) and an increased reliance on coercive counterproliferation and sanctions measures. He insists that discriminatory nonproliferation efforts have to consider the nature of political regimes, something he accuses the liberal arms control community of ignoring: "Simply, if irreverently, put: a nuclear-armed democracy is preferable to a nuclear-armed dictatorship" (Rühle 2007, 520). But democracy almost always stands in for the West and its allies, and if others outside of that sphere are, by definition, inscrutable, unreasonable, and threatening, then nuclear weapons may well be needed by these democracies to keep these others at bay. Thus Krause ends his piece on this note, which is worth quoting at some length:

> The possession and non-possession of nuclear weapons cannot be dissociated from the issue of democracy and freedom. Nuclear weapons in the hands of long-established democratic governments with a tradition of restraint and responsibility concerning international order are usually not a problem—except for rogue actors, ambitious non-democratic rulers and surprisingly, liberal arms controllers. *One might even argue that international order—defined as the rule of non-use of force—is possible only when a small number of responsible states possess nuclear weapons.* The issue is, however, how to keep problematic actors from getting control over nuclear weapons. There is no golden key available to solve this dilemma, but the 1968 NPT was at least a very successful instrument in striking such a deal. It should not be given up for the pursuit of nuclear disarmament, which would spell much more insecurity as long as the world remains as is. The nuclear non-proliferation regime certainly needs to be adapted to the changed circumstances of the new world, but there is no need to destroy it by turning it into a disarmament treaty. (Krause 2007, 498–99; emphasis added)

In other words, the role of the NPT, from this perspective, should be to keep in place an unequal order. In a world of widespread irrationality, this order is a mechanism to keep in check those barbaric, threatening others who mostly reside outside of the rational, enlightened West. It is thus that while many of Walker's critics question his suggestion of the NPT as an Enlightenment project, they have no hesitation claiming that if there is any enlightenment to be had, it is in the West, and chafe against the suggestion that counter-Enlightenment forces may well reside in the West (i.e., in U.S. right-wing articulations, according to Walker), because their place is quite clearly elsewhere. The NPT does not represent a grand Enlightenment normative project, in their view, not just because its creation reflected power politics and crude materialist cost–benefit calculus at work, but also because Enlightenment rationality and values reach their limits against the various others who need to be accounted for in any global nuclear order.[21]

Whose Nuclear Order?

In one of the most potent and famous critiques of Benedict Anderson's (1991) classic study of nationalism, Partha Chatterjee (1993b) asks the pointed question, "Whose imagined community?" to refer to the Eurocentricity of Anderson's approach to the universalism of the modular form of the nation. In that vein, and in light of the discussion in the previous section, it may be useful to query a little more deeply what assumptions underlie an "Enlightenment nuclear order" as conceptualized in the debate between Walker and his critics. Order has been a guiding imperative for both realists and liberals in IR, arising from the "anarchy" that, ontologically given, preformed states face. It may be useful to remember that Walker begins his ruminations on the NPT with the question of order. Neither Walker nor his critics disagree on the need for order, and in fact, they underscore how much the presence of nuclear weapons absolutely necessitates a global order. But who has the power to order, and with what effects?

In a brilliant exposition on the colonizing of Egypt, Timothy Mitchell (2000) examines the "power to order" as a particular kind of colonizing power. In vivid detail, he describes the epistemology through which a colonial order established itself in the modern consciousness—or rather an "appearance of order," very much a product of the Enlightenment "curiosity" unleashed by the breaking of theological bonds, organized itself through the fiction of a Cartesian gaze in which the West occupies the center and *only through which* "disorder" (i.e., Egypt in his analysis) becomes visible. In other words, as Mitchell explains, order and disorder are not ontologically given and plainly visible but come into being through particular technologies that orient our view of the world. This order, which then confronts us metaphysically as something that precedes and exists apart from the materiality of the objects ordered, helps us to apprehend the world as a whole and the proper place of the objects within that whole. It is this ordering imperative, when it reaches a global scale, that helps mark the cultural and historical break between the West as the site of reason, rationality, propriety, and civilization, in opposition to the barbarian and irrational outside of itself—the process that Edward Said (1979) has called "Orientalism."

The NPT, from this perspective, may be seen as one technology that helps us grasp and shape the world through its mechanisms of hierarchical ordering. Rather than help make friends out of rivals and enemies, as Walker suggests, it helps us to recognize our friends, rivals, and enemies through their location within its architecture. In Mitchell's analysis, the third world, or the Orient, is a creation of that colonial order, its truth and identity revealed by its place within that order, defined vis-à-vis the West. In this rendition, NWS and NNWS as, respectively, responsible or untrustworthy possessors of nuclear weapons don't exist ontologically prior to the NPT,[22] but it is through the representational technology of the NPT that we come to recognize them as such. The point is not that this is a misrepresentation per se, but that the NPT, in effect, provides us one among other mechanisms to apprehend and make sense of the world, of the very reality that so many of Walker's critics urge him to consider. In this reality, certain actors have always already been interpellated as certain *kinds* of actors.

If Walker's critics question his characterization of the nuclear order as one inspired by liberal Enlightenment values, it is in particular Walker's suggestion of the *universalism* of those values by which they are most troubled. But in doing so, and somewhat ironically, this puts them very much in the camp of those postcolonial critics who have also questioned the extent to which the purported universalism of the Enlightenment rested on a series of exclusions of Europe's others. Uday Mehta (1990) has attempted to make sense of the contradictions between the celebrated universalist and inclusionary pretentions of liberal theory and its systematic and sustained exclusionary history and practices.[23] In many ways, this contradiction is very much like the universalist NPT that Walker lauds and its exclusionary dimensions that he laments. But rather than suggesting that such exclusions are a symptom of inadequate or incomplete implementation of liberalism's universalism (as Walker does) or an expression of some hidden motive within liberal theories (as some critics might suggest),[24] Mehta identifies the exclusionary basis of liberalism within its very theoretical core: "it is so not because the ideals are theoretically disingenuous or concretely impractical, but rather because behind the capacities ascribed to all human beings, there exist a thicker set of social credentials that constitute the real bases of political inclusion" (429). Such exclusions are effected when the universal capacities ascribed to all humans in liberal theory require "specific cultural and psychological preconditions woven in as preconditions for the actualization of these capacities," or when qualities ascribed in the abstract have to be filled in with the "content" of historical practice, a filling in that requires the mobilizing of particular "exclusionary strategies" (430). If particular states have already been deemed as deficient to the task of responsibly handling nuclear weapons within the terms of the treaty, then it makes sense to see the NPT as a way to freeze the status quo and permit only some states the access that others are denied.

Mehta makes his argument through a study of the writings of some key Enlightenment thinkers who helped articulate the universalist arc of liberalism's values—freedom, equality, and rationality—values that find their limits against "undeveloped" or "inscrutable" races, cultures, and peoples whose inferior position within an evolutionary schema always renders them unprepared for the privileges of liberal institutions (contract, rule of law, representation, self-government).[25] The particular strategies of exclusion that are at work are quite different in the work of the different thinkers whom Mehta studies,[26] but in the final accounting, they all end up, to use Dipesh Chakrabarty's famous words regarding John Stuart Mill's historicist arguments, "consign[ing] Indians, Africans, and other 'rude' nations to an imaginary waiting room of history" (Chakrabarty 2000, 8). To the extent that disarmament by existing NWS remains a forever deferred goal, NNWS always remain in the waiting room of history, never quite ready to handle the nuclear weapons that existing NWS deem necessary for their own security yet unavailable to NNWS regardless of their actual felt insecurities. As a liberal institution, the NPT not only denies these less than fully rational actors the means to practice the deterrence that NWS claim is necessary for their own security but, more importantly, allows existing NWS to hold on to their own weapons against a threat that is never quite vanquished as superpower Cold War rivalries give way to rogue states and terrorists. Walker's critics suggest that NWS may need to hold on to their weapons to keep at bay those new threatening others whose rationality is always in question. Indeed, if nuclear weapons helped defeat the counter-Enlightenment forces of fascism and totalitarianism and in that sense kept European Enlightenment alive, as Krause (2007) argues, then it may well be reasonable to keep nuclear weapons in the hands of those who can exercise reason. Claiming to be the true bearers of enlightened reasoned thinking in this sense, Walker's critics are thus much more open and explicit about the exclusions of the Enlightenment than Walker is. Although they do not appreciate the full force of this, they recognize the profoundly hierarchical world out of which the NPT emerged and which in turn it helped shape and consolidate.[27] In this world, the infinite interim of the realist present that is never quite ready to yield to the future utopic achievement of nuclear zero is where the NNWS must wait in history.

Instead of subscribing to the dualistic structure of a hierarchical "reality" juxtaposed against a democratic "utopia," one could, indeed, agree with Walker that the NPT very much reflects a progressive, utopian Enlightenment project, but as many postcolonial theorists argue, the Enlightenment was *in reality* also a profoundly hierarchical project premised on a series of exclusions of Europe's (colonial) others. The "cosmopolitan hope that had accompanied the liberal promotion of modernity" (Walker 2007, 444) was thoroughly saturated with racist premises about cultural and civilizational difference. The journey from Fukuyama's liberal assimilationism through Huntington's clash of civilizations to Kagan's easy imperialism that Walker notes with respect to the Bush administration's policies (Walker 2004, 52), rather than being a radical break in epistemological orientation, is quite consistent with this history of prejudice that undergirds many Enlightenment-inspired narratives of modernity.[28] Postcolonial scholars have pointed to the deep and abiding traces of the colonial encounter in the shaping of modernity and in the existing institutions of contemporary international relations (Grovogui 1996; Mitchell 2000; Krishna 2001; Jones 2006b). Antony Anghie (2006) points to the deep racist and colonial traces in contemporary international law and "good governance" initiatives that, on the surface, explicitly abjure racism and function in the name of sovereign equality, but nevertheless serve to "manage" third world countries and peoples. Arturo Escobar (1994) has studied the production and management of the third world through a racist and colonialist discourse of development that also serves as an apparatus of discipline. It should come as no surprise, then, that progressive arms control regimes and institutions acting in the name of peace and security, too, should reflect these deeply held presuppositions about the (post)colonial world.

There is no question here that Walker is genuinely interested in saving the NPT to get to disarmament; deterrence, for him, is only a temporary placeholder to prevent backsliding (Walker 2004, 35). In this, he is in the good company of many other scholars and activists who urge the United States to cut its arsenal size as a step toward complete disarmament, which, in their view, was always the original purpose or "grand bargain" of the treaty (Carranza 2006; Cortright and Väyrynen 2009; Perkovich and Acton 2008; Daley 2010; Johnson 2010). But this position fails to understand how easy it is to defer disarmament to an indefinite future when the world always confronts us through an ultimately exclusionary framework. As the previous chapter pointed out, there has been no dearth of disarmament plans and proposals since the NPT came into existence, and these continue to this day; many of these are carefully crafted and well elaborated and lay out very specific and concrete steps. Yet year after year, there is some marginal success in achieving nuclear reductions but little real traction on actual disarmament. Walker himself suggests that the "idealism" of disarmament had to yield to the "pragmatism" of arms control to get to the NPT. Furthermore, even when he actually believes that disarmament is not just a utopian ideal, it turns out to be simply "a direction of travel" as he himself cautions against a hasty abandonment of deterrence (Walker 2007, 451).[29] But disarmament always remains *asymptotic,* a constantly receding future never quite at hand and hardly invoking much political anxiety (even as existing NWS continue to expand and/or update their arsenals), while proliferation and developing nuclear weapons programs elsewhere cause not just dismay but frequently panic. Indeed, though Walker alludes to justice as an Enlightenment value that structures the NPT, justice always gets pushed in the interest of orderly security and peace.[30] It then becomes hard not to ask to what extent the spirit of mutual trust and cooperation through which the NPT emerges in Walker's laudatory narrative was simultaneously premised on the deep suspicion and fear of those who could not be trusted to have nuclear weapons. Indeed, one may argue that the rationality embedded in the doctrine of deterrence was meant to apply to those select few considered capable of behaving rationally, and the fears of proliferation arose largely from the premise of irrationality that plagued Europe's barbaric others.

Arguments that a far too complacent United States needs to rethink and rework the concept of deterrence in an effort to maintain and project its dominance have also come from some of the writings on the "second nuclear age" (Gray 1999b; Payne 1996; Bracken 1999; 2012). Proliferation is yielding a much more multipolar "second nuclear age" of unpredictable, inscrutable, and potentially undeterrable rogues who are no longer disciplined by the superpower confrontation of the first nuclear age (Payne 1996; Bracken 2012).[31] The paradigm of deterrence may be attractive and an "expression of centuries of enlightened Western thinking and hope about war and its prevention," but it is "hubris," suggests Payne, to believe that one knows one's foes so well as to rely so utterly on their judgment and rest on the "Assured Vulnerability" of deterrence in this age; indeed, "humility" requires one to be militarily prepared (Payne 1996, 78). Thus a cautionary call for humility in one's ability to comprehend "the other" resolves itself through fortifying the boundaries of "the self" by deploying the instruments of death more effectively. Bracken's earlier book, predictably titled *Fire in the East,* suggests that the United States needs to adapt to the "post–Vasco da Gama world"—a world in which the great civilizations of the East, which could not be so entirely decimated by the Europeans as the American Indians had been, were now reenergized as atomic powers in a globalized McWorld (Bracken 1999). But by 2012, Bracken is expressly concerned that a complacent United States that had "projected its antinuclear ethos onto the world" had been putting all its efforts into nonproliferation initiatives, such as the NPT, that were bound to fail in a world where "not everyone shared these values," thus leaving itself strategically unprepared (Bracken 2012, 5). Arguing strenuously against abolition, Bracken suggests that a nuclear-free world order in which the United States could be preponderant would, of course, be preferable, but in the absence of that possibility, the United States needs to figure out a longer-term (fifty-year) strategy to manage a world of multiple nuclear weapons–possessing states with much more effective proactive nuclear strategizing (Bracken 2012). In the end, it appears that in a world where assumptions about non-Western inscrutability and unpredictability run so deep, the case for U.S.–Western nuclear weapons possession will always remain compelling, and disarmament can forever be postponed.

Providing an abundance of examples, Hugh Gusterson (1999) demon-

strates how widely shared the general perception of third world, and especially Islamic, nuclear irrationality is vis-à-vis the perceptions of the safe
and reliable possession of nuclear weapons by Western nuclear democracies.[32] This rarely questioned, taken-for-granted "common sense" pervades
media coverage; exists among politicians, policy makers, and even nuclear
scientists; occurs in respected journals; frequently spans the political spectrum; and exists despite all the evidence of safety mishaps, close calls, and
aggressive nuclear behavior among existing NWS. The interpellation of
"suppliers," "recipients," and "rogues" in the area of nuclear export controls
constructs a division between the legitimate insiders and the always potentially dangerous outsiders in a way that both justifies inequalities and
reinforces the connection between status and nuclear weapons (Mutimer
2000). Public policy arguments for erecting a ballistic missile defense system in the post–Cold War world have frequently relied on racist and sexist
discourse about proliferators to make a case for strengthening U.S. hegemony (Bjork 1995). Rejecting the "nuclear alarmism" that exaggerates the
threat of contemporary nuclear proliferation while downplaying the dangers of the Cold War security environment, others have suggested that current rogue states, such as Iran and North Korea, may be no more dangerous than the Soviet Union or the People's Republic of China were during
the Cold War and, seen in terms of local imperatives, may be facing quite
similar security issues to those faced by France or Israel at the time of their
nuclearization, yet they generate very different kinds of anxieties (Gavin
2009–10; Mueller 2010).[33] This colonial discourse, or what Gustersen calls
"nuclear Orientalism," casts an infantilized third world given to impulse,
passion, and fanaticism as untrustworthy custodians of nuclear weapons
within a Western geopolitical imaginary that positions the West as policing
agent of any proliferation transgressions (cast as "crime" and "theft"). It is,
of course, useful to remember here that it is precisely such nuclear policing
that many of Walker's critics suggest any stable order in a nuclear world
demands, because order is functional, as Roberts (2007) reminds us, only
when the strong are willing to exercise necessary force. If the nuclear order
is a "society of states," as Walker suggests, then it is, as Hedley Bull (1977)
would have no trouble recognizing, a quite unequal society in which power
and force have a normative binding function.[34] It is thus that the NPT "has
become the legal anchor for a global nuclear regime that is increasingly
legitimated in Western public discourse in racialized terms" (Gustersen
1999, 113), a "nuclear order" no doubt, but not necessarily one in which *all*

"peoples and states could place their hopes and trust, and through which conflicting norms and interests could be reconciled" (Walker 2007, 433).[35] So "trust" may, indeed, need to replace fear and force in the move to disarmament, as Nicholas Wheeler (2009) suggests, but that will need working through the deep-seated historical mistrust sewn into the very fabric of a hierarchical international order.[36]

The Empire Talks Back

That the preceding exclusions can then refract back through the charge of "nuclear apartheid," wielded (albeit strategically) in the guise of postcolonial resistance, should not be entirely surprising and should certainly give us some pause about the progressiveness of the kind of nuclear order established through cooperative treaties such as the NPT. States that see themselves as excluded from the "privileges" of the NPT have often invoked the exclusionary framework of the treaty and its associated regime to justify their own programs, a point that Walker's critics see as cynical manipulation of the treaty enabled by liberal arms control advocates such as Walker, who voice concern about the institutionalized hypocrisy of the NPT. But while scholars may disagree on the extent to which the NPT was serious in its commitment to disarming the existing NWS, it is hard to dispute the fact that the inequity inscribed within the treaty—recognizing and legitimizing the nuclear weapons of the five states that had exploded a nuclear device prior to 1967 practically in perpetuity (given the indefinite extension in 1995), while prohibiting all other states from acquiring any nuclear weapons—has become a political weapon wielded by some states to point to the hypocrisy of the nuclear five (coincidentally also the Permanent Five of the Security Council) and occasionally to pursue their own weapons programs.

Thus India was able to wield the charge of "nuclear apartheid" as it declared itself a nuclear power in 1998, followed shortly by Pakistan. Indian state leaders framed "the US-led non-proliferation regime as a racist, colonial project" meant to deny India's hard-won achievements (Perkovich 1999, 7).[37] Indian external affairs minister during those nuclear tests Jaswant Singh stated quite explicitly that the division between nuclear haves and nuclear have-nots within a discriminatory and flawed nonproliferation regime that sets "differentiated standards of national security" creates "a sort of international nuclear apartheid" (Singh 1998, 48). To use the word *apartheid* is clearly to use a racial signifier, and one that carries with it a certain contemporary political resonance, given the very recent shameful history of the complicity of many first world states with the racist regime in South Africa. Under very different circumstances no doubt, the nuclear apartheid argument is in one sense an attempt to point to the continuing exclusions and marginalizations faced by people of color in third world countries in a global order dominated and controlled by privileged whites in first world countries. Now it is clear that this black–white distinction is problematic. Not only can China, as one of the nuclear five, clearly not be categorized in the latter category, but it is also problematic to conflate state boundaries with racial boundaries, despite the racial implications of all boundary-making exercises. However, the articulation of "whiteness" with power is deep and compelling for many and draws on a particular postcolonial logic. Let us, for instance, hear the words of a scholar on Indian security writing just before the Indian tests:

> There continues to exist three "White" nuclear weapons states as part of the Western alliance to which in all likelihood a fourth one, Russia, may be added when its "Partnership for Peace" merges into NATO. It may be recalled that following the Indian atomic test of 1974, President Zulfikar Ali Bhutto of Pakistan had reportedly said that there was a Christian bomb (US, Britain and France), a Marxist bomb (Soviet Union and China), a Jewish bomb (Israel's bombs-in-the-basement) and now a Hindu bomb (India), but no Muslim bomb. Likewise, India could possibly complain now that there were four White bombs, one Yellow or Beige bomb, but no Brown or Black bombs, an unfair and unacceptable situation. While China may continue to show some defiance against the policies of the West on occasion, the nuclear distribution indicated the continuing domination of the traditional White imperialists in an overwhelmingly non-White world. (Thomas 1998, 285)

Similarly, J. Mohan Malik (1998, 201), in reference to the nuclear apartheid position, says that "an unstated reason behind India's nuclear ambivalence had been the belief that the possession of nuclear weapons by 'white' nations implied their racial and technological superiority that could not go unchallenged." It is this sense of racial discrimination in a postcolonial world that was invoked by a spokesman for the Bharatiya Janata Party

(BJP), the Hindu nationalist party in power in 1993, at the time of the tests, when he said, "We don't want to be blackmailed and treated as oriental blackies" (as quoted in Perkovich 1998, 16).

The de facto legitimization of the Indian nuclear program through the 2008 U.S.–Indian nuclear fuel deal has only made the stature of the treaty even more suspect for those signatories who had committed to a de jure nonweapons status and has renewed charges of nuclear apartheid from those, such as Pakistan, not similarly recognized as "legitimate nuclear states."[38] Pakistan's National Command Authority recently charged that thanks to three recent developments, a "neo-nuclear apartheid" had emerged. The U.S.–Indian civil nuclear energy deal, U.S. support of India's permanent Security Council seat, and promised membership to India in export-control cartels such as the Wassener Arrangement and the Nuclear Suppliers Group, it was suggested, were all efforts to welcome India into an exclusive nuclear club that India itself had previously critiqued (Kazmi 2010). The Indian government's support of a U.S.-led resolution against Iran at a 2005 IAEA Board of Governors meeting, reversing its earlier position on the question of Iran's production of its own nuclear fuel, had been read by others, as well, as the sort of capitulation that comes with the eagerness to join the nuclear club (Boese 2005). It may be useful here to invoke Tzvetan Todorov's (1999) two figures of alterity—the "noble savage," whose location within the primitive end of the evolutionary–developmental scale renders him potentially assimilable, and the "dirty dog," whose utter inscrutability and radical otherness renders him always threatening and hence only eradicable through violence. Or as Mehta (1990, 441) says with respect to liberalism, "the putative perimeter of its sympathies is marked by the expansive range of the differences it tolerates. The limiting point of this perimeter is a form of alterity beyond which differences can no longer be accommodated." In this rendition, India may well be assimilated within a somewhat expanded "nuclear club," while others remain forever outside the ambit of Enlightenment rationality and its associated liberal institutions. Claiming outrage over the U.S.–Indian nuclear deal, which they suggest now frees up India's domestic output of nuclear fuel for weapons production, Pakistani officials have used that charge to shore up their own weapons production (Sanger and Schmitt 2001).

Resentment toward the discrimination of the NPT-centered nonproliferation regime, expressed as a form of postcolonial grievance against global inequality, has emerged from other places as well. In a scathing and compelling critique of U.S. policy toward Iran, Ogultarhan (2010) concludes that U.S. policies on Iran are rooted in Orientalist perceptions of Iranian irrationality and stem from deep-seated Orientalist understandings of East versus West that see the Iranian state as incompatible with Western de-mocracies. It is not surprising for Iran itself to invoke its place within a global hierarchy of states to justify its nuclear weapons program. A mili-tary official, unveiling the construction of underground missile silos, situ-ated it in the context of its ongoing confrontation with the West, saying, "With these installations . . . we are certain that we can confront unequal enemies and defend the Islamic Republic of Iran" (Broad 2011). Reacting to an initiative to create a global nuclear fuel bank that would arguably re-duce the need for countries interested in nuclear energy to produce their own fuel,[39] the Iranian ambassador to the IAEA even charged that this, as an attempt to monopolize technology and science, was another form of nuclear apartheid.[40] Similarly, according to North Korea's state media, the North Korean representative to the UN, during a conference on nuclear disarmament, charged the United States with seeking "absolute nuclear superiority" and suggested that it had "no moral justification . . . to lecture other countries about proliferation" (Sang-Hun and Myers 2011).

The point here is *not* that "nuclear apartheid" causes proliferation, and India, Pakistan, Iran, and North Korea should in no way be seen as at-tempting to rectify global hierarchies of class and race.[41] Indeed, numerous scholars have spent considerable time studying the multiple causes, motiva-tions, and factors that drive proliferation (Sagan 1996–97; Khan 2002; Singh and Way 2004; Hymans 2006; Jo and Gartzke 2007; Solingen 2007). These often include, in addition to whatever security rationales there may be and the interests of various military–industrial complexes, a good bit of do-mestic nationalist posturing and global status seeking, both of which are well served by the nuclear apartheid argument. It may be worthwhile to remember here that at one time, French and British leaders, too, looked to the atomic bomb not only as a substitute for their declining colonial power but also as a means to guard against their own possible colonization by the superpowers (Hecht 2012b, 23). It should not surprise us that the charge of nuclear apartheid has muscle in legitimizing proliferation to both do-mestic and foreign audiences. Walker's critics are correct in pointing to the cynical manipulation of the hypocrisy argument by self-serving statist in-terests, but the manipulation can happen not because liberal arms control-lers call attention to it (as though NNWS would miss it in the absence of these interventions!) but because the hypocrisy exists. Not only is Article VI weakly worded and frequently ignored, but the entire focus of the treaty is on "horizontal proliferation" (preventing NNWS from acquiring weapons), while "vertical proliferation" (expanding and/or updating the nuclear weapons of existing NWS) continues apace.[42] Rühle (2007, 515) berates the "liberal arms control community": "by giving vertical and horizontal proliferation equal weight, it has postulated a kind of moral equivalence between NWS that retain their status and NNWS that are cheating," thus reiterating the different statuses of the different parties to the NPT.[43] Setting aside the question of how one assesses moral equivalence here, the fact is that vertical proliferation gets very little attention (not even Walker talks about it), and horizontal proliferation causes great anxiety. Arguing against some of the criticisms of Walker's nuclear Enlightenment thesis made by Michael Rühle, Rebecca Johnson agrees that the official disarmament commitments of the NPT are weak, a weakening that was a product of Cold War power politics at the time, but emphasizes that this wasn't simply a "sweetener to make the NPT more palatable"; from the perspective of the world's NNWS, the commitment to disarmament in the treaty was key to their ascension, and this demand was fortified when the treaty was indefinitely extended by consensus agreement in 1995 and reiterated during the 2000 review conference (Johnson 2010, 440). Yet, to the extent that Article VI has been generally and repeatedly seen as so marginal to the overall project of the NPT, it puts into relief the unequal structure of the NPT, and that may well have helped justify proliferation and hampered progress toward universal disarmament.

Conclusion: Order and Inequality

Many scholars have pointed out that despite all the hype and fears, the rate of nuclear proliferation, at least since the creation of the NPT, has been quite slow (Potter and Mukhatzhanova 2010a; 2010b; Hymans 2006). *Cascadology* is the term Mueller (2010) uses to characterize this sort of unwarranted obsession with proliferation. For those who believe that the NPT had something to do with halting or at least dampening the speed of proliferation, the possible unraveling of the treaty naturally generates concerns. In this chapter, I have suggested that at least some of these underlying anxieties have to do with the dissolution of the global order the NPT helped sustain, and from which the nuclear nonproliferation regime effectively deflected. What is the role of the NPT in holding together this regime, whose overall commitment is to make the world safe from the terribly destructive power of nuclear weapons?

In the important and influential work of William Walker, the NPT has been celebrated as a universalist progressive global "Enlightenment project" that has helped avert nuclear catastrophe and can, if pursued in earnest and without hypocrisy, lead to a world without nuclear weapons. Walker's work has been vigorously contested for its dangerous idealism that emerges from its neglect of "real" political conditions in the past and the future. Among those real conditions are the threats that emerge from various "unenlightened others"—terrorists and terrorist-like rogue states—whose utter irrationality makes nuclear weapons in the custody of responsible NWS, who can actually wield Enlightenment rationality, a continuing necessity. One could, of course, question the very conceptualization of rationality as it works with respect to nuclear weapons and deterrence, an issue that is taken up in the following chapter. This chapter has argued that the political order the NPT both represents and instantiates has always incorporated these deep prejudices about others, prejudices that have a long history in Enlightenment thought, and the many anxieties that attend the NPT's possible unraveling are at least partially a product of that kind of thinking. Walker's critics are open about their prejudices about who can or cannot be trusted with nuclear weapons in a way for which most liberal universalist accounts of international order simply cannot account. Yet, what has always undergirded the NPT and its associated regime is a set of preconceptions about the geography of Enlightenment rationality and the borders of its limits. If we do feel relatively safe in a world with an NPT that makes so few demands on NWS to eliminate their massive arsenals of weapons, especially given the fact that one of those NWS is the only state in the world to have ever used those weapons, and even as these NWS continue to update and expand their arsenals, that in itself is evidence of deeply and profoundly internalized prejudices about the global distribution of reason and trust.

Much of the advocacy for the abolition of nuclear weapons happens with a sense of dire urgency. In that discussion, the potency of nuclear weapons, their unique ability to destroy humankind, their catastrophic powers, acquire a certain currency whose purpose is to shake the consciousness of political leaders, policy makers, and the general public. The antinuclear peace activists on the left were often dismissed as emotional and irrational, but the new voices of authority arguing for disarmament, individuals with strong credentials in "rational" strategic thinking, have similarly invoked such alarmism to make their case. Although the dangers posed by nuclear weapons are certainly immediate and pressing, the sense of catastrophic urgency invoked in the calls for abolition have the effect of making arguments regarding inequality appear trivial. In other words, to suggest that the NPT is not accidentally, or incidentally, but foundationally unequal in its very presuppositions, and that it is sustained by an unequal economic order, seems marginal to the "real" need to minimize and eventually abolish the possession of those weapons for all. This chapter suggests that there is a false sense of presumed equality invoked in these calls for abolition—"we are *all* better off in a world without nuclear weapons"—that gives short shrift to the actual inequality that currently sustains proliferation and will follow any future abolition.

The universalist and progressive impulses of the NPT give it its prominence, but it is precisely that universalism and liberal progressiveness that mask the exclusions that have shaped the nuclear order the NPT has created and portend some of the frayings we are witnessing at present. To think productively and in a way that can engender genuine consensus about a nuclear-free world, we need to tackle the profound challenges of global structural inequality that currently sustains the nuclear order. This requires the pursuit of universal disarmament, but for reasons of both peace and social justice. Indeed, all the elaborate plans created for getting us to "nuclear zero" to which the previous chapter referred will be unsuccessful if they fail to recognize the larger structural imperatives that make nuclear weapons desirable. It is to that question that the next chapter turns.

CHAPTER 3

Unusable, Dangerous, and Desirable

Nuclear Weapons as Fetish Commodities

From Energy to Weapons: The Ontology of Danger

The previous chapter discussed what is considered one of the two grand bargains in the negotiation of the Nuclear Non-Proliferation Treaty (NPT)—the permission that existing nuclear weapons states (NWS) had to retain their possession of their nuclear stockpiles in return for a (weakly worded) commitment to nuclear disarmament sometime in the indeterminate future. Much has also been made of the second of those bargains, considered to be a serious loophole in a treaty that aims to prevent the horizontal spread of nuclear weapons—permitting states to house the entire nuclear fuel cycle within their countries for the purposes of civilian uses of nuclear energy, even though the enriched uranium or plutonium produced through that process may eventually, with some extra effort, be turned toward nuclear weapons production. Indeed, this is precisely what happened in North Korea, which continued its clandestine weapons program while a signatory to the NPT, before withdrawing from it to test its own nuclear device, and is the current concern about the Iranian nuclear program that Iran claims is for civilian purposes, while others remain suspicious that the enriched uranium produced by Iran will soon be turned toward weapons use. Implicit in the treaty, then, is the assumption that there is a clear ontological distinction between nuclear weapons and nuclear energy and that it is the former that is far more dangerous and worthy of extensive preventive efforts, while the latter is benign or even vital to economic development. It bears reminding here that much of the current controversy regarding Iran has to do with uncertainty about how one tells, short of a declared state intention to weaponize (as with India, Pakistan, and North Korea), when and how the break from nuclear energy to nuclear weapons occurs.[1]

The NPT, thus, is a treaty that is quite firmly about *weapons* proliferation, not nuclear proliferation more generally. But also implicit in this
institutional recognition of the dangers posed by nuclear weapons is an
assumption about the deep *desire* for nuclear weapons among states.[2] As
chapter 1 discussed, Nina Tannenwald (2007) has argued that one beneficial result of the nuclear nonproliferation regime is that there is now in
place a "nuclear taboo"—that is, a strong (but not completely inviolable)
normative constraint against the use of nuclear weapons. In other words,
the enormous investment of resources in arms control institutions and by
antinuclear activists has made nuclear weapons so abhorrent that no state
is likely to use them without facing what to most would appear unacceptable international approbation. Even those who don't entirely subscribe
to the stronger version of the taboo argument have suggested how an informal "tradition" of nuclear nonuse is now fairly well established (Paul
2009). Yet it appears to be the case that states continue to desire nuclear
weapons, not just the NWS that are so reluctant to disarm, as chapter 2
discussed, and states that acquired weapons after the NPT came into effect but also all the potential proliferator states that need to be restrained
through strengthening faltering treaties such as the NPT. Indeed, undergirding all the anxiety about the possible unraveling of the NPT and the
worldwide proliferation that that may unleash[3] is this premise of a deep
state desire for the acquisition of nuclear weapons. Herein lies a puzzle—
why would states desire weapons that require enormous investment of
resources, are considered deeply abhorrent, and most importantly, cannot
be used, or that even arguably make state security more precarious?[4]

This chapter asks how supposedly tabooed and unusable nuclear weapons have emerged as fetishized objects of state desire, especially in a postcolonial context. I begin by discussing some of the explanations provided
for *why* states proliferate. Although the route from nuclear energy pursuit
to nuclear weapons acquisition turns on the supply of bomb-grade fissile
materials made possible through nuclear power projects, I start by focusing on the decisional moment in weapons proliferation by discussing
what are called the demand-side variables. I argue that most of the discussion of state motivations for nuclear weapons acquisition—national
security, domestic bureaucratic or nationalist interests, normative status
and prestige—fail to adequately theorize the allure of nuclear weapons,
an allure that deduces from, but is not reducible to, their lethal potential.
I then turn to an analysis of how commodities acquire social value, draw-

ing from Marxist political economy, critically examining two different but connected logics of exchange through which nuclear weapons have emerged as "fetish commodities." On one hand, the logic and language of deterrence tames the "unimaginably" destructive powers of nuclear weapons to enhance their exchange-value via a negation of their use-value, thus making them both useful and attractive. On the other hand, as a very particular class of fetish commodities—"luxury goods"—nuclear weapons come to be seen as markers of status and rank, thus enhancing their exchange-value even further. I conclude by suggesting that it is this fetishization of nuclear weapons that helps maintain that clear ontological distinction between energy and weapons and impairs our ability to think of them as emergent from a process of production. It is from this analysis that I turn in the following chapter to examine the larger political economy that is rendered invisible when nuclear weapons become so fetishized, bringing back the so-called supply side of nuclear proliferation and its material entailments.

Why Do States Seek Nuclear Weapons?

In search of the magic key to solving the so-called proliferation puzzle,[5] there is perhaps no question that has exercised proliferation scholars more than the following: why do states seek nuclear weapons?[6] Although supply-side variables have received renewed attention in recent years, many explanations for proliferation focus on the demand-side question.[7] Of these, Scott Sagan's three-pronged approach that identifies "national security," "domestic politics," and "norms" as possible causes of proliferation (or restraint) was a seminal piece that has informed many other studies (Sagan 1996–97).[8] Indeed, in that piece, Sagan emphasizes the policy importance of understanding demand in addition to all the efforts at restricting the supply of nuclear materials and technology.[9]

Sagan's essay was an attempt to supplement the underlying realist assumption in proliferation studies that states seek nuclear weapons when they face a significant military threat that cannot be met through other means—widely used to explain the nuclearization of the Soviet Union (as well as Cold War arms races more generally) and Britain, France, China, India, and Pakistan, as well as to explain the eventual nuclear disavowal of South Africa and the nuclear restraint of Argentina and Brazil. From this realist perspective, as Sagan points out, the NPT is simply a mechanism to help resolve the "collective action" problem of anarchic insecurity through which states can enhance their security by exercising mutual nuclear restraint (Sagan 1996–97, 62).[10] In a somewhat modified version of the realist thesis, T. V. Paul's (2000) "prudential realism" keeps in place the focus on national security, while recognizing that nuclear forbearance may well be in the self-interests of technologically capable states in particular contexts in which the pursuit of nuclear weapons may imperil their security situations. In other words, states forsake nuclear weapons not necessarily because their security situation is nonthreatening or ameliorated but because nuclear weapons may make them more vulnerable.

In contrast to this national security model, Sagan's domestic politics model is an attempt to open the black box of the unitary realist state to reveal the various bureaucratic and political interests—nuclear scientists, military planners, politicians—that drive nuclear weapons acquisition for sometimes entirely parochial organizational ends that may have little to do with enhancing national security.[11] Domestic political contests among competing factions, claims Sagan, can provide a fuller explanation for India's decision to nuclearize,[12] South Africa's decision to denuclearize, and Argentina's decision to forsake the nuclear weapons option. From this perspective, the NPT regime helps empower antinuclear domestic coalitions who then develop a further stake in nuclear restraint (Sagan 1996–97, 72). There have been other interesting versions of this domestic politics model. For instance, Etel Solingen has been one of the most prolific discussants of the political economy of nuclearization, suggesting how liberalizing coalitions within states interested in integration into the global economy can drive nuclear restraint in a post-NPT globalizing world. In short, Solingen argues that regime type (internationalist, inward oriented, or compromise-hybrid) matters, both for the likelihood of proliferation and for the efficacy of economic sanctions or inducements (Solingen 1994b; 2007; 2012).[13] In a different version, emphasizing the centrality of "beliefs" in foreign policy making, Peter Lavoy (1993) has made the very interesting argument that it is less the actual security situation facing a state than the ability of an influential national elite group of political and military leaders to create a "nuclear myth" about the security (or insecurity) that would result from nuclear acquisition that helps explain a country's decision to acquire or forsake the nuclear weapons option.

Though the domestic politics explanation is useful for moving away from an abstract concept of nuclear security and toward restoring the importance of the practice and politics of nuclear decision making, it still does not account for the enormous *allure* of nuclear weapons, especially among politicians and nationalist elites, or for their ability to mobilize such great enthusiasm or such great fear among the electorate. That allure is partially explained in Sagan's third model—the "norms model"—that turns to the symbology of nuclear weapons and the role that plays in shaping a state's national identity. Here Sagan turns to some of the norms literature discussed in chapter 1 to explain both the French decision to pursue nuclear weapons to bolster its declining prestige as a world power in a postcolonial world and the Ukrainian decision to give up its nuclear inheritance to position itself as a responsible—that is, not rogue—state.[14] The NPT, according to Sagan, could be seen to have played an auspicious role in both enabling Ukraine to take a bold disarmament stand and for the international community to coordinate collective sanctions and inducements for its disarmament (Sagan 1996–97, 81–82). This norms model, of course, underlies some of the realist as well as domestic politics explanations, both of which recognize that nuclear weapons can bestow a certain kind of prestige or attract moral condemnation in ways that can either enhance or hinder security in certain situations (Paul 2000) or bolster particular domestic coalitions or kinds of regimes (Solingen 2007). However, those who might be placed in the norms camp more firmly place their primary focus on the norms themselves and their impact on nuclear decision making (without necessarily rejecting realism or liberal domestic politics explanations). Of these, Jacques Hymans's and Maria Rublee's norms-based explanations for nuclear acquisition and restraint—both drawing from psychology—have received a fair bit of recent attention.

Placing "emotion" at the center of his analysis, Hymans (2006) uses the test cases of France, Australia, Argentina, and India (two acquirers and two abstainers) to construct a model of proliferation that relates to individual leaders' "conception of national identity." He argues that "oppositional nationalist" leaders, who possess a unique combination of fear and pride, are far and away the most motivated to proliferate, although domestic political conditions (as was the case with Australia and Argentina) might inhibit them from doing so.[15] Using social psychology theory as applied to the nuclear abstentions of Japan, Sweden, Germany, Libya, and Egypt, Rublee (2009) tries to explain how nuclear norms and the international social environment shape nuclear decisions not to proliferate. An "antinuclear norm" as created and established via the development of a nuclear nonproliferation regime helped link legitimacy to nonproliferation, thus changing the security benefits versus financial costs calculus for policy makers in important ways.[16] In these norms-based accounts, ideational elements—whether those are the articulation of a certain normative conception of the national self or the strong normative influence of certain values about security and nuclear weapons—matter in the actual decision making with respect to proliferation.

Although norms-based explanations help establish that the status attached to nuclear weapons and/or nonproliferation matters, what they don't explain fully is *why* it matters. Why does the decision to acquire nuclear weapons appear "a revolutionary one," in the words of one of the scholars discussed earlier, an important threshold that states plunge across or abstain from crossing (Hymans 2006, 9)? The decision by any particular state to develop sources of nuclear energy is certainly taken note of but hardly appears remarkable enough for the kind of global status enhancement or moral approbation that the move to nuclear weapons clearly is. Indeed, the widely used terms—"nuclear *restraint*" and "nuclear *abstinence*"—so important for many of the preceding scholars to understand to help create the conditions for them, presume a deep and abiding desire to possess and consume nuclear weapons despite whatever ill effects those weapons might actually bring. To put it differently, what most of the studies on the demand for proliferation largely undertheorize is *how* nuclear weapons have acquired the kind of *value* that makes them such vivid markers of the ultimate kind of security and status, such desirous objects that one must be restrained to, or abstain from, acquiring, if one does not already have them and that are so difficult to give up, if one already has them.

There is no question, as Sagan as well as many of the other authors discussed previously recognizes, that normative constructions can cut both ways. On one hand, the possession of nuclear weapons may bestow a certain kind of national prestige or function as the sign of global status. For states positioned disadvantageously within the global developmental hierarchy, they may well signify a coming-into-modernity—a kind of postcolonial mimicry that may hold a very particular set of meanings for third world states.[17] On the other hand, signing on to a global normative taboo against the possession of nuclear weapons, such as by joining the NPT as a non–nuclear weapons state that has explicitly forsaken (in some cases a previously considered) nuclear option, may also signal a certain kind of modern and progressive sensibility.[18] In other words, nuclear weapons can acquire meaning as a particular kind of object and marker of status, either in their possession *or* their rejection.

But what is it about nuclear weapons that bestow on them such enormous power? What makes these weapons the kinds of objects capable of creating certain kinds of desiring subjects? Why do so many authors, as stated earlier, who are so exercised by trying to understand why states want to proliferate or have refrained from doing so, rarely discuss this enormous and awesome allure of nuclear weapons? Indeed, it appears that that allure is taken for granted, assumed as derivative of their massively lethal capacity, despite the wide acceptance of the premise that such weapons are very unlikely to be used. In other words, it appears that much more attention has been paid to understanding the conditions under which nuclear weapons proliferate or nuclear restraint practiced and very little on theorizing why they have become so desirable to pursue or restrain from pursuing. I turn next to a discussion of nuclear weapons as particular kinds of desirable and valuable objects.

The Value of a Nuclear Commodity

How do nuclear weapons acquire the enormous symbolic value that makes them such a marker of modernity? To understand how we recognize nuclear weapons as the kinds of objects that confer such high security and status, I want to turn, in this part of the chapter, to a theory of commodity fetishism to explain the generation of nuclear desire. But before I turn to a discussion of the desire for nuclear weapons, let me say a few words about what kinds of objects nuclear weapons are. To do so, I begin with a conceptualization of a "commodity" in Marxist political economy, an object produced through labor but whose value accrues through the process of exchange. I then turn in the following section to the doctrine of deterrence as a particular kind of exchange economy—an economy of signs—that simultaneously confers value on the weapons and domesticates their threat, discussing here also the technocratic and sanitized language through which nuclear weapons and strategy are articulated and apprehended. In the final section of the chapter, I theorize how this economy of exchange generates nuclear weapons as a fetishized commodity of a very particular kind—a "luxury commodity"—that demarcates global status and power and generates the nuclear desire that is generally taken for granted in the previously discussed studies of nuclear proliferation.

A central aspect of his critique of bourgeois political economy in volume 1, part 1 of *Capital*, Karl Marx (1977) analyzes the "commodity" as a very particular kind of object that emerges in the context of capitalism.

Always a product of socially organized human labor, a commodity, says Marx, is "an external object, a thing which through its qualities satisfies human needs of whatever kind" (125). Distinguishing between "use-value," which arises from the direct or indirect use of a thing, and "exchange-value," which is not an intrinsic property of an object but a relation between use-values that emerges from exchange, Marx discusses the circulation of money in this process of exchange at length in this section of *Capital*. What makes an object a commodity is this exchange, the production of not just use-values but "social use-values" that are exchanged through a medium of exchange, that is, money (131). Money, which helps extend the process of exchange, aids in the conversion of objects into commodities by providing a medium through which products of labor become commensurate with each other in exchange, coming to serve as "the form of appearance of the value of commodities" (184).

Marx's motive is to reveal the "strange" or "mysterious" character of the "commodity-form" in capitalism, in which "exchange-value manifests itself as something totally independent of their use-value" (128), occurring through a process of "reification" that leads to what he calls "the fetishism of the commodity":

> The mysterious character of the commodity-form consists therefore simply in the fact that the commodity reflects the social characteristics of men's own labour as objective characteristics of the products of labour themselves, as the socio-natural properties of these things. . . . The products of labour become commodities, sensuous things which are at the same time supra-sensible or social. . . . It is nothing but the definite social relation between men themselves which assumes here, for them, the fantastic form of a relation between things. (164–65)

In other words, commodities become fetishized when they come to be seen as valuable in and of themselves, their value as intrinsic to their properties, and independent of the social relations and the human labor through which they emerge and acquire value. Money—as "the finished form of the world of commodities" (168)—only serves to conceal these social relations further, becoming, in a sense, the ultimate fetish object, "the commodity which functions as a measure of value" (227)—such as when we think of the value of a commodity in terms of its money-price.

Money thus becomes the "universal commodity" (235), so that the accumulation of money in the form of wealth comes to be an end in itself.

As Slavoj Žižek (2008) points out quite eloquently, Marx's great contribution is to show how the fetishism of interpersonal relations—such as when the power of the king is "misrecognized" as intrinsic to the king's natural properties rather than bestowed by his subjects—is replaced in capitalism by the fetishism of the commodity (18–22). Indeed, Marx's brilliance is in showing how the superstitions of primitive religions—attributed at the time of Marx's writings (and now) to the exotic, barbaric, irrational non-Western cultures to be saved by enlightened Christian capitalism—are replaced within a rational, capitalist modernity with the magical powers attributed to commodities as the new "idols of the marketplace" (Mitchell 1986).[19] Marx's project in this first part of *Capital* is very much one of demystification—revealing the social relations of production that are concealed in this continuing process of "misrecognition."[20]

But capitalism, as many cultural theorists have pointed out, is not just an economic system but a complex cultural one. Arjun Appadurai (1986) argues that while in Marx (and in most subsequent economic analyses), the commodity remains quite firmly tied to capitalist forms of production, it is the exchange aspect and dynamics of commodities (also found in pre- or noncapitalist economies) that has remained undertheorized and needs more attention. Appadurai suggests breaking with "the production-dominated Marxian view of the commodity and focusing on its *total* trajectory from production, through exchange/distribution, to consumption" (13). Drawing from Jean Baudrillard, Appadurai makes the case here for theorizing utility (and demand) itself as social and relational—tracing the commodity's "social life" in the sphere of exchange—thus treating the process through which economic exchange generates value as *political* and the product of shared cultural meanings. So the question becomes one of examining "the conditions under which economic objects circulate in different *regimes of value* in space and time . . . the ways in which desire and demand, reciprocal sacrifice and power interact to create economic value in specific social situations" (4; emphasis original).

What kind of commodity is a nuclear weapon, and how does it acquire value? While manufactured much like other commodities under capitalist production relations that help realize enormous profits for private capital (as the following chapter demonstrates in detail), nuclear weapons are a very particular kind of commodity with some peculiar characteristics that distinguish it from other commodities. On one hand, they are very much seen as "political commodities," produced in great secrecy with very limited access to knowledge of how they work, and for a single consumer—the state—rather than in a larger commercial marketplace. Hence nuclear-corporate interests have a stake in the economic and political health and orientation of a state on which it is also often heavily reliant for both buying their products and subsidizing their production, insulating them, in ways similar to many conventional weapons, from normal capitalist production (Rosow 1989; Kaldor 1982; Luckham 1984; Masco 2006). This form of "military Keynesianism" can take different forms in different historical and global contexts but shows the tight connection between military power and the capitalist political economy, a connection often occluded when the significance of weapons is refracted primarily through the lens of state security (Rosow 1989). I discuss the entailments of the pursuit of nuclear power for the neoliberal security state in the following chapter.

But there is another manner in which nuclear commodities are distinct, and in this respect, also from conventional weapons. Though there is a sense in which the utility of nuclear weapons is taken for granted in articulations of state security, its actual use-value appears much more complicated. Ever since the actual use of the two atomic bombs in Hiroshima and Nagasaki, the use-value of nuclear weapons has acquired a curious meaning. I have already referred to the nuclear nonuse norm—the suggestion among scholars that nuclear weapons are unlikely to be used. But in addition, the doctrine of deterrence—which became the strategic framework and grounds for accumulating nuclear weapons—was formulated also to *prevent* the use of nuclear weapons (Masco 2006). If nuclear weapons have remained valuable despite this focus on their nonuse, one must examine the ways they accrue value through processes of exchange. What, in other words, are the kinds of exchanges that generate nuclear value? In the next section, I turn to nuclear deterrence as one kind of exchange economy through which nuclear weapons emerge as fetishized objects of security. In the following section, I discuss another economy of signs through which nuclear weapons emerge as fetishized objects of status and ranking. It is through these exchanges that nuclear weapons acquire meaning and value as very particular kinds of fetish objects, but as I suggest in the concluding section of the chapter, like commodities more generally, these processes of fetishization conceal their origins in production and their valuing through social relations.

Deterrence as a Semiotic Economy:
Nuclear Weapons as Security Fetish

Poststructural analyses of security have quite compellingly argued that "danger"—whose ontological status in the state of nature (i.e., anarchy) as given is a central aspect of political realism—is itself a product of social relations (Campbell 1992; Weldes et al. 1999). In realism, weapons, which constitute the "high politics" of military power, are necessary to contain, placate, or destroy this danger. Certainly more sophisticated realists understood how the arms themselves could become threats (Jervis 1976; Walt 1985), but it is to critical security theorists that we owe the insight that weapons, armies, and military maneuvers only signify something within a discourse of shared meanings (Campbell 1993; McCanles 1984). What is interesting about the doctrine of deterrence, as a particular structure of strategic knowledge, is that it comes to rely almost entirely on such intersubjectively shared meanings, interpretive claims, and modes of communication.

Distinguished from *defense,* which has to do with withstanding an attack, and *coercion* or *compellence,* which involves using force to attain some objective, deterrence is about *preventing* a potential attack through the *threat* of visiting unacceptable retaliatory damage. Not entirely unknown in the prenuclear era, Bernard Brodie (1965), widely regarded as the author of the strategy as employed in the post–World War II period, considered its operation to be qualitatively different in the nuclear age, when the risks of breakdown in deterrent threats are too severe. The understanding of nuclear (non-) use on which the doctrine of deterrence relies is based on the severity of a nuclear threat. But as Thomas Schelling (1966) elaborated so brilliantly, nuclear deterrence rested not just on the threat to use nuclear weapons but also on the "credibility" that one was willing to actually use them. The Cold War doctrines that created the conditions of mutually assured destruction (MAD) and the post–Cold War postures of various nuclear powers have never been static, elaborating complicated possible scenarios and conditions under which nuclear weapons could and/or would be used against different kinds of targets and enemies. But the purpose of deterrence, of course, was precisely to prevent such use, and the elaborate systems of command, control, and communications that were developed in conjunction with the doctrine were done so at least partially to ensure that such weapons were not used by "accident."[21] It is thus that "the 'use' of nuclear weapons . . . took the form of speech, backed up by doctrine and deployment, but hedged all about with hypotheticals and conditionals" (Lipschutz 1995, 11). As speech, its purpose was to persuade others of one's capability and will.

The doctrines underlying MAD—generally regarded as the architect of Cold War peace between the two superpowers—were predicated on the ability of *both* sides to make the nuclear threat credibly. Indeed, deterrence only holds when all opponents *understand* and *believe* in the seriousness of the threat. Though still ostensibly about the requisite military capability and the willingness to use it, deterrence, then, is primarily about *communication*—about communicating the presence of weapons one is willing to use to visit damage that would be considered unacceptable (McCanles 1984; Taylor 2007). For deterrence to work, communication must be understandable, which requires a common universe of meanings. This is what makes deterrence "the diplomacy of violence" (Schelling 1966). Indeed, many of the fears of proliferation to states and actors outside the nuclear club often stem from a concern about what may be called "communication failures," sometimes articulated as the inability of immature new nuclear states to create effective infrastructures of control and practice rational deterrence, but often presuming the limits of the community within which certain values and communication are and can be shared.[22]

In other words, the success of deterrence is reliant on an effective exchange of signs—the ability to convey, credibly, the right kind of message—and its stability as a doctrine is further reliant on the reciprocation of that signal. This is what makes MAD a "semiotic regime constituted by signs" (Taylor and Hendry 2008), underwritten by the unusability of weapons whose power is too lethal to contemplate yet whose acquisition is necessary precisely because of such power. Though this economy of signs constantly refers to objects outside of itself—to the nuclear weapons themselves—to signify both capability and willingness, the value of the weapons themselves is to communicate this intention *so that they may not be used*. It is an odd system, as Brodie (1965, 273) himself recognized, in which "we expect the system to be always ready to spring while going permanently unused."

This is the sense in which Jacques Derrida talks about deterrence as "fabulously textual" and Jean Baudrillard as "simulation." Derrida (1984, 24–29) theorizes the strategy of deterrence as primarily rhetorical—

reliant on dissuasion or negative persuasion—a "performative apparatus" based on the anticipation of a phantasmatic nuclear war forever deferred (see also Taylor 2003).[23] Functioning through the management of improbabilities, deterrence, suggests Baudrillard, makes nuclear weapons a "hyperreal form," because its logic rests on the fact that "*the real atomic clash is precluded*—precluded like the eventuality of the real in a system of signs. . . . The whole originality lies in the improbability of destruction" (Baudrillard 1994, 32; emphasis original). Certainly both Derrida and Baudrillard recognize, even if underemphasize, the materiality of the massive stockpile of actual weapons, and even draw attention to the ways that the communicative logic of deterrence generates an ever-escalating level of arms accumulation with real societal effects, but their aim is to argue that deterrence itself functions as a semiotic economy, the exchange of signs that make up its logic is directed at the deferral of the actual use of nuclear weapons because "the referent of nuclear narratives can never be realized without the erasure of narration itself" (Taylor 2003, 2). Ever since the United States extracted what Baudrillard calls the only "use value" or made "real" use of the bomb in Hiroshima, the whole point of acquiring nuclear weapons is now to preclude their use, to pacify "any inclination toward violent intervention" (Baudrillard 1994, 39).[24] It is thus that deterrence effectively erases the distinction between war and peace, putting in place a continuous simulated war whose purpose is to preclude a "real" war (Baudrillard 1994). Never actually used, its power insinuates and permeates society, and as an object of exchange, it engages most social, political, and cultural institutions (Chaloupka 1992; Masco 2006).

It is within this economy of exchange that nuclear weapons become *valued*. The value of the nuclear threat emerges not so much from the weapons themselves but from the communicative exchange about those weapons.[25] In other words, the weapons become comprehensible as threats through deterrent communication. Using the concept of the Derridean supplement, McCanles argues that whereas the communicative text (threat) and the weapons themselves are inextricably linked within the strategy of deterrence, the verbal text of the threat is a "supplement," not just in that it is "needed to articulate the mute threat of military capability" but also in that "it is necessary to complete an otherwise incomplete—and in regard to nuclear hardware, paradoxically impotent—weapons system." As a supplement, deterrent communication comes to "speak for" what are, in effect, mute weapons, "thereby allowing force to threaten" (McCanles 1984,

14).[26] The weapons themselves are mute because their destructive power is too lethal to contemplate—thus the tendency of many commentators to speak of the dangers of nuclear weapons as "unimaginable," "unthinkable," and "unspeakable"—but they can be made to speak through the language of strategy, games, and simulation.[27] And the vocabulary of nonuse is central to this language. Communication that underwrites deterrence as a strategy is no doubt predicated on, and signals, the grave material dangers posed by nuclear weapons—their ability to visit unacceptable retaliatory damage of a kind not possible by other weapons—yet the doctrine itself helps evacuate this danger by simultaneously communicating that these (massive and growing number of weapons) are not to be used. Deterrence, in other words, is the language through which nuclear weapons speak to communicate their potency, but by suggesting their unusability.

The use of highly technical and abstract language to describe deterrence and nuclear weapons also helps transcend the limits of speech that nuclear weapons seemingly impose and further contributes to the evacuation of nuclear danger (Chilton 1982; Hook 1984; Cohn 1987; 1993; Schiappa 1989; Kauffman 1989; Gusterson 2004). The language and imagery[28] of what has been termed *nukespeak*—the wide use of abstractions, technical jargon, acronyms, metaphors, playful euphemisms, meaning-laden weapons names and titles, and the wide use of passive voice—has been likened to a form of propaganda that makes nuclear weapons more acceptable, thus acculturating a society to their presence while linguistically domesticating their dangers (Chilton 1982; Schiappa 1989). If deterrence allows otherwise mute weapons to speak, nukespeak makes it possible to speak of nuclear weapons, including of their possible uses, albeit in ways that make utter light of their actual dangers. Nukespeak, however, is not just the use of euphemism, whose replacement with more "appropriate language" would simply make the dangers of nuclear weapons transparent. Instead, it produces and shapes a reality, a set of discursive truths about what is possible or rendered unlikely by nuclear weapons and strategy. Cohn's brilliant analyses demonstrate how the "technostrategic language" of nuclear deterrence drains out the real flesh-and-gore consequences of possible nuclear use through the use of high abstractions and masculine playfulness in which the implicit referents of strategy are weapons and not people (Cohn 1987; 1993). As the kind of language that suggests mastery and control, nukespeak suppresses contingencies and contradictions, contains dangers, and normalizes the possession and potential uses of nuclear weapons, in effect obscuring human agency and accountability in nuclear policy and inhibiting ethical reflections on nuclear weapons development and possession. It is thus that the semiotic economy of deterrence, in combination with the language used to describe it, tames the otherwise unimaginable risk of nuclear weapons; the weapons are able to provide security without being used, and their possession is necessary for deterrence to work.

We can now see how nuclear weapons emerge as a fetishized object of security in this economy of signs. A *fetish* is an object to which is ascribed certain powers that are seen to emerge from its essential qualities rather than the social relations and networks that bestow power on that object. In a capitalist economy, as we have already seen, the "commodity"—and money as the ultimate kind of commodity—comes to be the fetish object, ascribed with a certain value and power of its own, independent of the conditions and relations of its making and valuing. De Santana, also drawing from a Marxist analysis of commodity fetishism, suggests thinking of nuclear weapons as "fetish objects" that result from the "fetishism of force." If the entire logic of nuclear deterrence, she argues, rests not on the use-value of nuclear weapons but on their "threat-value," which emerges from an economy of exchange, then much like the material form of money has no use-value apart from its exchange-value, the material form of nuclear weapons is "nothing but a carrier of their social function" (de Santana 2009, 331). Baudrillard, too, draws this connection to money as a medium of exchange and, in particular, the speculative trade in money that so characterizes contemporary capitalism:

> Deterrence is not a strategy, it circulates and is exchanged between nuclear protagonists exactly as is international capital in the orbital zone of monetary speculation whose fluctuations suffice to control all global exchanges. Thus the *money of destruction* (without any reference to real destruction, any more than floating capital has a real referent of production) that circulates in nuclear orbit suffices to control all the violence and potential conflicts around the world. (Baudrillard 1994, 33; emphasis original)

Similar to the pursuit of wealth in the form of money, the accumulation of nuclear weapons generates "power" (de Santana 2009, 331). Marx (1977, 177) reminds us that "no chemist has ever discovered exchange-value either in a pearl or a diamond," so it is not the massively destructive explosive capacity of the weapons—a characteristic of their physical properties—that makes them so valuable but rather

> a process of reification through which their social form of value
> (properly attributable to the network of social relations between
> states) is treated as if it were a natural feature of the physical substance of the weapon. . . . The process of fetishistic reification
> means that states act as if the threat of a nuclear attack . . . were
> inherently valuable, as if the ability to deter military aggression . . .
> were a feature of the physical characteristics of nuclear destruction,
> rather than a feature of the social process through which actions
> are interpreted as meaningful with respect to one another. In other
> words, we act as if being threatening (and therefore powerful) were
> an inherent trait of the substance of nuclear weapons in the same
> sense that the quality of being explosive is inherent in their physical embodiment. (de Santana 2009, 339–40)

What makes nuclear weapons so valuable are the social and political processes through which they have been endowed with certain meanings: "nuclear weapons are powerful because we treat them as powerful" (de Santana 2009, 327). Indeed, de Santana emphasizes the role of "belief" in this process of fetishism, comparing the security that nuclear weapons ostensibly provide to the healing powers of African fetish objects.[29] Much like these fetish objects, the weapons themselves don't provide material protection or security; indeed, the weapons may make one more vulnerable and insecure, as scholars who study proliferation restraint have suggested. But "to be effective, nuclear deterrence requires that an opponent believe in the credibility of a retaliatory threat. The security that nuclear weapons provide operates at the level of belief that may or may not correspond to the level of reality" (337). However, even if this structure of belief is in itself textual, it works only if people believe that there is a "transtextual domain of actual military power. People will respond to the power textualized in discourse only as long as they believe that such an entity as power distinct from discourse really exists, and remain ignorant that the prince, being always an emperor with no clothes on, becomes powerful only when they dress him in that power" (McCanles 1984, 13). This is what makes it necessary to possess stockpiles of nuclear weapons, even if the aim is to prevent their use. Here we see the "misrecognition" to which Žižek (2008) points at play in the process of fetishization—the nuclear objects come to stand in for a security that is provided through the shared social understandings and relations that constitute the structure of mutually comprehensible deterrence.

"Money is the alienated essence of man's work and existence; this essence dominates him and he worships it," says Marx (1978, 50). And so it is that nuclear weapons emerge as objects of veneration or sacred objects, where "faith" in the awe-inspiring power of nuclear weapons becomes a way of "nuclear forgetting": "a concerted attempt to forget, ignore, or suppress, by whatever means necessary, nuclear fears" (Ungar 1992, 136). Forgetting, as W. J. T. Mitchell points out, is central to the Marxist concept of commodity fetishism—a forgetting not just of the projection of value in the commodity but also of its historicity, its emergence as powerful at a time and in a context, and out of a certain dynamic (of security and deterrence), that endowed it with meaning. Forgetting makes objects appear "immutable" (Mitchell 1986, 192–93). This is the kind of forgetting that results in the "paradox of indispensability"—nuclear weapons, which are not even best understood as weapons (but rather instruments of mass extinction) because they are "politically prostate," paralyzing their possessors from being able to use them, are nevertheless considered indispensable, and in arms races induced by panics, they are accumulated in ever-increasing numbers to provide a magical sense of impossible omnipotence that can overcome the paralysis: "it is a case of the virtually useless being regarded as utterly vital" (Ungar 1992, 85). It is thus that on both sides of the Cold War, the escalating reliance on nuclear technology as the fix to an ideological conflict meant that the "technofetishistic appeal of nuclear weapons enabled a social relation between nations to be mystified as a strategic orientation between machines" (Masco 2006, 21).

It is this process of fetishism that creates what Lifton calls "nuclearism"—which is not just a political but also a psychological dependence on nuclear weapons to provide an impossible security (Lifton and Falk 1982). One might think of nuclearism as a particular kind of ideology, subscription to which makes nuclear weapons desirable.[30] But it is also clear that leaders, policy makers, and citizens more generally understand nuclear weapons as dangerous and even as ultimately imperiling one's security. So instead of a theory of "false consciousness" in the Marxian sense, it may be more useful to think of nuclear fetishism as working through a structure of beliefs that confronts nuclear decision makers as a "reality" to which they need to respond. It is possible, as Žižek (2008, 28) points out, to be "fetishists in practice, but not in theory," that is, to understand the fetish object as a product of social reification and yet confront it, at the individual level, as a reified object that structures social reality and the ability of individuals to navigate it in particular ways. As Žižek explains, people may well know and understand money as not valuable in and of itself but rather as an expression of social or market relations, but to the extent that their life choices are affected by the ways that social relations are structured through money, they act in accordance and hence reproduce that reified social reality in which money is fetishized.

In a similar vein, it is entirely reasonable to think that nuclear policy makers understand the "irrationality of rationality"[31] within the logic of deterrence, but to the extent that the doctrine of deterrence structures a certain social reality in which nuclear weapons as unusable objects have acquired a certain fetish status, they are led to behave in accordance with it. Indeed, as people may occasionally reject the accumulation of money as wealth as an end in itself, so leaders may occasionally reject the magic of a nuclear weapon's alleged powers and practice nuclear restraint.[32] But this acceptance of the magical powers of nuclear weapons may explain what Lifton and Falk (1982, 14) describe as the "helplessness" that people in nuclear states feel in relation to "the bomb's infinite, mysterious killing power . . . unable to break out of the death-trap we know to be of our own making," or what he, later in the book, articulates as the psychological state of "nuclear numbing."[33] Or, as Luckham (1984, 5) argued, also drawing from an analysis of commodity fetishism,

> Through these transformations social relations between living human beings have come to be experienced as relationships between abstract qualities or things; between commodities; between (and among the branches of) those abstractions we call states; and between stockpiles of weapons. Ordinary men and women are apparently confronted with social forces which operate according to laws (those of the market place, of politics and of the arms race) which neither they nor even their leaders can control.

Drawing on Walter Benjamin's discussion of the phantasmagoria as an illustration of the technological distractions of modern life, Masco (2006,

16–17) suggests that the "hypnotic focus on nuclear annihilation during the Cold War provided a sensory distraction . . . that displaced the consequences of life within a nuclear economy." The fetish status of nuclear weapons provides just such a distraction from the social relations underlying "(in)security." But if, in addition to their claimed ability to produce security, nuclear weapons as fetish objects have other powers as well, then they may well be even more desirable to possess. So let us examine a little more closely what kind of a fetish commodity a nuclear weapon is by turning to another economy of exchange through which nuclear weapons acquire value.

The Semiotic Economy of Desire:
Nuclear Weapons as Luxury Fetish

Appadurai (1986), as discussed earlier, argues for the need to theorize the ways that demand and desire for commodities themselves emerge from the process of exchange and generate value for a commodity. In his discussion of how commodities acquire value through economies of exchange, Appadurai distinguishes the category of "luxury goods" as "goods whose principal use is *rhetorical* and *social,* goods that are simply *incarnated signs,*" and suggests the following five as attributes of these sorts of goods:

(1) restriction, either by price or by law, to elites; (2) complexity of acquisition, which may or may not be a function of real "scarcity"; (3) semiotic virtuosity, that is, the capacity to signal fairly complex social messages (as do pepper in cuisine, silk in dress, jewels in adornment, and relics in worship); (4) specialized knowledge as a prerequisite for their "appropriate" consumption, that is regulation by fashion; and (5) a high degree of linkage of their consumption to body, person, and personality. (38; emphasis original)

Drawing heavily on Appadurai's work, Sankaran Krishna (2009b, 71) suggests that nuclear weapons become exemplars of a "special class of luxury goods in an international symbolic and security economy." Each of the five characteristics enumerated by Appadurai appears to apply quite well to nuclear weapons.[34] First, their circulation is "restricted," no less because of the NPT's prohibitions on their movements but also because they are expensive to acquire;[35] second, their "complexity of acquisition" is determined by the many kinds of restrictions on the supply of the materials and technology required to produce them—all artificial restrictions placed to control the dissemination of fissile materials and scientific knowledge now several decades old; third, their "semiotic virtuosity" lies in communicating not just security, as argued in the previous section, but also status, power, and modernity, as I argue more fully shortly; fourth, the "specialized knowledge" of sophisticated technostrategies of deterrence and associated infrastructures of control and communication that are necessary for their "appropriate" consumption makes them accessible only to supposedly highly rational and complex societies, as suggested in the previous section; and fifth, their "linkage" is seen in the ways they come to stand in for, and signify, the very body and personhood of the state, making them spectacular national monuments, as I discuss further later (Krishna 2009b). Thus nuclear weapons are the kinds of goods that have what Appadurai calls "high discriminatory value," and that value emerges, again, not from their use-value as weapons but from a different kind of consumption within an economy of exchange that endows them with power and prestige (Appadurai 1986, 38). Unlike, for instance, landmines, whose political visibility is predicated on the dangers of their actual and viscerally felt use-value, the fetishization of nuclear weapons has meant that their political visibility resides much more on this symbolic value in an economy of exchange. This makes nuclear weapons objects of deep desire, no less by states who seek status and recognition within an unequal international order, and both their acquisition and their repudiation are articulated through an implicit recognition of that symbolic economy of meanings.

Let us attend a little more closely to the logic through which restriction generates desire. In the domain of elite or luxury goods, "we have the politics of fashion, of sumptuary law, and of taboo, all of which regulate demand" (Appadurai 1986, 57). Here one may see the mundane operation of market economics as the restriction of supply via the legal and institutional controls on who can possess nuclear weapons, and the specialized knowledge for their manufacture and consumption, only available and accessible to a select few, raises their price. This, in turn, increases demand for the weapons, that is, makes them even more desirable. What makes the link between value and exchange *political,* according to Appadurai, are the shared understandings of what is desirable and reasonable and how and who determines that—always a contested process that sets up social relations of order and privilege between parties with different interests: "It is in the interests of those in power to completely freeze the flow of commodities by creating a closed universe of commodities and rigid set of regulations about how they are to move. Yet the very nature of contests between those in power (or those who aspire to great power) tends to invite a loosening of these rules and an expansion of the pool of commodities" (Appadurai 1986, 57).

Just as wealth via money determines individual opportunities and social rank, "access to power in the form of nuclear weapons determines a state's opportunities and place in the international order. In both cases, the physical form of the fetish object is valuable because it serves as a carrier of social value" (de Santana 2009, 327). Furthermore, if, "like money, it is the 'scarcity' of nuclear weapons that makes them an appropriate carrier of social value" (333), then all the attempts to halt or prevent proliferation also serve to enhance value. Indeed, much-discussed taboos against nuclear *use*, which are not taboos against possession, only reinforce this fetishism.[36] As de Santana points out, "there is no better way to produce desire than through prohibition" (341). It is in this sense that nuclear fetishism also both helps maintain international hierarchy and provides the impetus to acquire the nuclear value that would enhance a state's global status. Thus

> deterrence is not just a strategy. It also functions as a myth that serves to keep a series of submerged or covert goals on the major powers' political agenda. . . . Nuclear weapons have thus become the privileged instruments of the internationally dominant states and ruling classes; and deterrence, arms control, non-proliferation and national security their ideology. (Luckham 1984, 8–10)

The hierarchical nuclear order that the previous chapter discussed is very much kept in place through the fetishization of deeply desirable nuclear weaponry.[37] When those who consider themselves lower in that ranking, that is, countries such as Iran and North Korea, seek "equality" through nuclearization, it is largely "equality among global consumers to appropriate a global product" (Sanadjian 2008, 87). I consider the substantive content of that kind of equality more fully in the next two chapters.

It is important to point out here that the distinction sometimes made between symbolic and real power is moot here. Fetish commodities are not merely symbols in that their role is not primarily representational, but certain kinds of fetish objects can take on a symbolic significance, such as through conferring status and power. Even though she recognizes the "real power" that accrues through nuclear acquisition, de Santana differentiates fetish objects from symbolic objects because the latter are primarily referential, their intention is communicative, and their physical existence is not essential to the functioning of its accompanying social context (de Santana 2009, 330). It is true that nuclear weapons, as fetish idols, are not worshipped because they are seen to symbolize something else; rather, they are really seen as powerful in and of themselves, or to put it differently, from within the logic of security and deterrence, "they are magical objects that contain within themselves the principle of their value" (Mitchell 1986, 192). Distinguishing between fetishism, idolatory, and totemism, Mitchell (2005) points out that even though each of these signify different kinds of relations to things, the same object can function as a fetish, idol, or totem, depending on its accompanying narratives and social practices (see Mitchell 2005, chapter 9). In other words, fetishized nuclear weapons can also serve as idols or totems of the nation or modernity. Fetish objects can acquire symbolic value, but that symbolic value also serves to make power "real." It is precisely because nuclear weapons have emerged as symbols of power and status that their acquisition (as well as rejection) confers "real" power.

Taylor and Hendry (2008, 314) point out that the ontological status of nukes has long "oscillated between arms and monuments," but it is the reification of nuclear weapons that has turned them from arms *into* monuments, their fantastical (unusable and omnipotent) powers making them into objects of deep desire by those who want to possess them and by those who want to abolish them (Taylor and Hendry 2008, 314). In a sense, Cold War deterrence effectively "*fused* nuclear arms and monuments" when the second strike capability of the two superpowers meant that "nuclear weapons could *only* be used as symbols of national capability and intention," thus functioning as signs (Taylor 2003, 2; emphasis original). Here they become signs of national power, the "preeminent national fetish" designated as not just the "ultimate arbiter" of state security but also as "the one true sign of 'superpower' status" (Masco 2006, 8). If, in the case of the superpowers, nuclear power functioned as a "techno-aesthetic whose primary importance in the global order is one of appearance" (Masco 2006, 22), the process was no different for a third world state such as India, whose nuclear reactors and tests (and eventually weapons) became aesthetic monuments of its postcolonial promise of modernity (Abraham 1998, chapter 5), or in Iran, where nuclear power has become a currency of cosmopolitan global identity (Sanadjian 2008).[38] Thus it is that the allure of the bomb itself has now emerged as a fetish object with the potential to generate enormous exchange-value, as different kinds of "atomic consumption" and different forms of "atomic tourism"—such as the museumization of missiles and bombs, national day parades that display weapons in prominent ways, national stories and narratives conveyed through the names that are conferred on weapons, commercial tours of reactor and test sites, and so on—generate revenues and help consolidate state power.

Even if the power that is conferred on nuclear weapons might emerge through the linguistic tricks of deterrence and imposed restrictions on their supply and consumption, these are what have designated nuclear weapons with the status of a qualitatively different kind of object—to be distinguished from the category of "normal," that is, "conventional weapons"— and as part of the "abnormal" or "supernormal" category of "weapons of mass destruction." That these categories are somewhat fictive is beside the point here.[39] The point, rather, is that the "normalization" and the "abnormalization" of these two categories are part of the same logic, making one kind of weapon eminently useable,[40] while reifying the other through imbuing it with fantastical powers.[41] Even those who explicitly reject nuclear weapons on the grounds of their immorality or their evil character accept the distinctiveness of the status—as a deeply desirable object— that nuclear weapons have acquired through an economy of exchange, even as they point to the dangers of nuclear weapons' possible future use. Calls for the destruction of "idols," after all, implicitly assume the power that the idols embody. Indeed, whenever the rejection of nuclear weapons is articulated as a moral imperative—and celebration of the NPT often takes that form—that rejection contributes to the fetishism of nuclear weapons. This supranormal status of nuclear weapons is affirmed when nuclear opponents and activists (in a fashion not unlike deterrence strategists) continue to depict these weapons as connoting the limits of both imagination and speech, the "unimaginable" consequences of their possible use delivering us into the realm of the "unspeakable."[42] In that sense, when Derrida finds a nuclear war to be a "nonevent," contrasting it to the many more real conventional wars that have occurred and are occurring, he accepts this ontological distinction between nuclear and conventional weapons and war, reinforcing the phantasmatic status of the former even as he draws attention to the logic through which that phantasm is generated. How, then, may we imagine, think, and speak the dangers of nuclear weapons in ways that make them real and eventful? I turn to that question in the following chapter.

Conclusion: From Fetishism to Materiality

This chapter has argued that the vast literature that attempts to explain the demand for nuclear weapons has undertheorized the enormous allure of, and deep desire for, nuclear weapons. The bulk of this chapter, then, has attempted to attend to the ways that demand for nuclear weapons is generated, not through a rationalist examination of the process of state decision making, but through theorizing nuclear exchange as an economy of signs that endows nuclear weapons with certain kinds of cultural meanings. I have argued that the semiotic economy of deterrence, in conjunction with the technostrategic language of nuclear policy making, has produced nuclear weapons as a fetish commodity—too dangerous to use yet necessary to possess to prevent their use. As fetish objects, these powers are seen to reside within the weapons themselves rather than in the social relations that have endowed them with certain capacities to produce the ultimate kind of "security" against otherwise implacable enemies. Or even when these powers and capacities are seen as suspect, they can confront policy makers as powerful in ways that make them seemingly irresistible to acquire. That these commodities have acquired the status of "luxury commodities" should be no surprise, then, keeping their pursuit highly regulated and helping sustain a deeply unequal and violent world through the generation of unachievable ambitions for status and power.

Unlike the vast literature that examines why states seek nuclear weapons, I have tried to demonstrate how the pursuit of nuclear weapons has been depoliticized, the weapons as fetish objects serving as solutions to the problem of security and enmity, while concealing a remarkable set of institutions, interests, and practices that sustain this problem-solving exercise and that themselves profit from that exercise. Part of my aim here has been to reveal the *politics* of nuclear decision making, a politics that involves the making of nuclear meanings and values. This is not simply a matter of revealing the hidden meaning or reality that fetishization conceals but revealing fetishization—including the textuality of deterrence—as itself political, as making and shaping a nuclear reality that matters for the organization of our sociopoliticoeconomic lives. In other words, examining fetishization as political is to restore the "nuclear referent"—not just in the sheer materiality of nuclear stockpiles and their continuing (sometimes rather mundane) dangers but in the social, cultural, political relations that help produce, sustain, consume, and live with nuclear weapons on a daily basis and that are themselves shaped in profound ways through the existence of those weapons. To politicize nuclear desire, then, is to show how the fetishization of nuclear weapons does its own cultural work, sustaining various national projects as well as a massive political economy of weapons (Masco 2006). Or to put it differently, to restore the nuclear referent is to examine "the bomb as a social institution, with wide-ranging cultural, environmental, and psychosocial, as well as geostrategic effects" (17).

I have already discussed how the ideology of deterrence helps secure consent to the logic of nuclear security, so that nuclear policy makers desire the nuclear fetish even when they understand the obvious dangers of nuclear possession. But ideology also functions to mask or deflect from the larger social, political, and economic relations that sustain the pursuit of nuclear weaponry:

> The domination of weapons over man is part of that set of processes under which living human labor and the fruits of scientific progress have been subordinated to capital, to the "dead" human labour and knowledge materialised in the form of machines, organizations and weapons, Armament culture thus functions as an ideology, a set of symbols, ideas, myths and practices which arises from but conceals these transformations from those whose very existence they endanger. (Luckham 1984, 4)

The fetishism of the weapon enhances and obscures the larger capitalist political economy within which strategic doctrine is embedded—what Rosow (1989) calls the "political economy of nuclear violence"—the sociopolitical institutions and relations that sustain nuclear war preparation and that are usually occluded in the strategic language of the deterrence debate, despite their real consequences for the material well-being of people in nuclear states.[43] This is what may be called the supply side of nuclear proliferation, the forces that make it possible to pursue and acquire these most desirable weapons and, indeed, profit from that acquisition. Here we return to the clear ontological divide often drawn between nuclear energy and weapons with which this chapter began, and we ask where and how, in that larger political economy, that break gets made. There may be no automatic move from civilian nuclear programs to nuclear weapons, and indeed the decision to weaponize may well depend on domestic conditions, or coalitions, or leaders, or incentives and sanctions, but if nuclear weapons have become so fetishized as desirable objects of state security, then the road from latent capability to breakout is always a precarious one. But, moreover, the effects of a nuclear economy—*whether or not weapons are used or even acquired*—are already multiple, complex, and widespread. I turn to an examination of those effects in the next chapter.

CHAPTER 4

Costly Weapons

The Political Economy of Nuclear Power

From Accidents to Costs

I have already referred to the provocative "more may be better" argument made by well-known neorealist international relations scholar Kenneth Waltz (1981)—that the proliferation of nuclear weapons induces cautious deterrent practices among rational states, thus enhancing global security and stability. In his also well-known rebuttal of what is called the "nuclear optimism" argument, Scott Sagan (1994) paints a rather bleak image of alleged state rationality, pointing to the myriad instances of near-misses and close mishaps induced by the less than fully rational dynamics of the organizational systems and cultures responsible for administering nuclear weapons. The category of "accident" or "mistakes" is central to Sagan's quite compelling critique, as well as to "nuclear pessimism" accounts more generally, and indeed, it carries quite a heavy weight in antinuclear activism. This is true both for nuclear weapons abolitionists, such as Jonathan Schell (2000), and in the characterization of nuclear energy disasters of the sort that occurred at Three Mile Island, Chernobyl, and Fukushima Daiichi.[1] Suggestive of a lack of malignant cause or responsibility in nuclear politics, the reified status of "accidents" in a sense partakes in the fetishization of nuclear weapons, suggesting the possibility of managerial control exercised through the rationalist strategizing of deterrence (Chaloupka 1992, 12–16). Furthermore, this sort of characterization presumes the impossibility of foreseeing the consequences of investment in nuclear resources and in a sense evacuates any institutional or structural responsibility from the disasters that may follow such investment, although much public effort will be expended after any such "accident" in deciphering its cause or apportioning appropriate blame on particular actors (Thompson 1982, 20).[2] In addition, "accidents" focus one's attention on the dangers of

nuclear power as they are represented in their most spectacular forms—
the massive radioactive fallout following the misfiring of a weapon or the
malfunction of a reactor—mimicking the spectacularity of nuclear weapons as fetish objects. In other words, I am suggesting here that the trope of
"nuclear accidents" carries such weight in fears of nuclear power because
the fetishism of "unusable" nuclear weapons has distracted us from the
very real but much more mundane and widespread "effects" of the crude
materiality of nuclear power, in the different forms that already exist.[3] As
may be apparent, this brings us back to the connection between nuclear
energy and nuclear weapons.

These mundane and widespread effects that unusable fetishized nuclear
weapons occlude can be seen in a number of ways. First, our focus on the
enormous brutality of Hiroshima and Nagasaki as the *only* historical moment in the "use" of nuclear weapons makes it possible to divert attention away from the 2,051 other nuclear "test" explosions that might well
be considered to be "used mini-bombs."[4] The point here is not to diminish
the scale of destruction wrought in Hiroshima and Nagasaki but to draw
attention to the longer history of damage caused by nuclear weapons if we
were not to isolate one instance of weapons use. Second, much like the
debate on the category of "weapons of mass destruction," the status of depleted uranium munitions, used, for instance, in the 1991 Persian Gulf War
and in the Balkans, and that cause lingering radioactive effects on civil-
ians, raises important questions about the boundaries of what constitutes
atomic or nuclear weapons. Third, the fetishism of nuclear "weapons"
helps to keep alive what most nuclear security scholars recognize is the
ontologically false distinction between a "peaceful nuclear explosion" and
a "weapons explosion" and in that way contributes to keeping the question of nuclear energy distinct from the question of nuclear weapons. The
question here is not simply of the dangers of a complete nuclear fuel cycle
stationed in a country eventually yielding weapons, as mentioned in the
previous chapter, but also of the material dangers of investment in what
is considered "controllable" nuclear energy (radiation leaks, waste disposal), which are then thought to be different from the dangers of potentially "uncontrollable" nuclear weapons. It is in that sense that the Nuclear
Non-Proliferation Treaty (NPT), created to halt the spread of weapons
and encourage the spread of energy, has enabled and even normalized "nuclear proliferation," while attempting to restrain "weapons proliferation."
Finally, this kind of commodity fetishism impairs our ability to think of

nuclear weapons as emergent from a process of production that requires vast investment of resources and subsists on the exploitation of workers in the mining of nuclear materials and in the nuclear industry more generally, and serves enormous corporate interests with various kinds of stakes in nuclear energy and weapons. This last category of effects is the primary subject of this chapter.

Demystifying the fetishization of nuclear weapons, in very much a Marxist vein here, exposes the larger political economy through which nuclear weapons emerge as fetishized weapons and which often gets short shrift in the prominence given to the institutional form of treaties like the NPT as mechanisms for preventing weapons proliferation. These costs span the entire production cycle of a nuclear weapon—from uranium mining, conversion, and enrichment; to plutonium production and separation; to the fabrication of fuel rods and other weapons components; to (explosive and nonexplosive) nuclear testing; to warhead and missile production and maintenance; and to storage and waste treatment and disposal (Makhijani and Saleska 1995). Gabrielle Hecht (2006; 2012a; 2012b) has suggested that the "nuclearity" of an object—whether that be a nation, a technology, particular materials or processes, or a workplace—is not given in nature as a stable ontological fact but is rather established through a process of contestation with different interests at play. This shifting designation of nuclearity, especially to aspects of the nuclear production process furthest removed from actual weapons production (such as uranium mining), has profound consequences for what kinds of nuclear effects become legible, what kinds of regulatory apparatuses can be created, and who can claim protections from harms (Hecht 2012a; 2012b). It is unfortunate that most of the academic discussions of nuclear proliferation happen largely within the subfield of security studies, with relatively minimal intersections with the subfield of international political economy, thus drawing attention away from the larger economic forces at play in, and the broader effects of, the proliferation of nuclear power. Conjoining "security" to "political economy" brings attention to the ways in which state interests in nuclear weapons connect with capitalist interests in nuclear power and the lived insecurities that result from those intersections.

A postcolonial approach attentive to historical materialism also considers the ways that nuclear power—as a driver of "development" as well as a symbol of modernity—has become closely connected to the loss of economic sovereignty in a globalized world (Varadarajan 2004; Mathai

2013). For instance, China and India, in that order, are the two countries most rapidly expanding their nuclear energy programs to keep their expanding economies growing. This demand for nuclear energy from these two non-Western nuclear weapons states (NWS) often comes couched in language that suggests a (postcolonial) desire to rectify the North–South economic imbalance. In a similar vein, Sanadjian (2008) has shown how nuclear energy in Iran becomes fetishized as a currency of cosmopolitan global identity that masks internal relations of authoritarian oppression. In response, there are those in the United States who are arguing that the U.S. moratorium on building new nuclear reactors after the Three Mile accident imperils U.S. hegemony. In any case, advocating for nuclear energy as a "green solution" to economic development will continue to drive nuclear proliferation and, with it, all the attendant fears of future weapons proliferation.[5] Accounting for the production of nuclear weapons, then, requires some level of sensitivity to the costs of nuclear power more generally. Sketching out and analyzing the resource and human costs invested in the nuclear production process once again brings attention back to the continuities between nuclear weapons and nuclear energy that the NPT's focus on fetishized weapons largely glosses over. To attend to the political economy of nuclear weapons is, thus, to make visible their sheer materiality, the amount of resources invested in producing and reproducing that materiality, and its disparate effects on different bodies and states.

The analysis of this chapter rests on an examination of the larger global political economy of nuclear power (which will include a discussion of both nuclear weapons and energy pursuits) as well as a closer look at three very different kinds of nuclear states, all of which have significant programs in nuclear energy but are at different stages in their weapons programs: (1) the United States, the longest-established NWS and the most prominent driver of the NPT; (2) India, a relatively newer NWS that is not a member of the NPT and has been openly critical of it; and (3) Japan, a state long considered to be a breakout state that is now in the midst of public debates on the future of nuclear energy and has had a strong public abhorrence to a nuclear weapons program, despite the occasional debates among politicians on breaking out.[6] Throughout the chapter, the analysis draws from these case studies, in addition to the larger global political economy of nuclear power within which these cases are situated, to examine the costs of nuclear power. The analysis itself relies on three related mechanisms of calculating nuclear costs. Beginning at the most obvious level, the first section examines the massive material resources invested in the production of nuclear weapons—that is, the actual costs of nuclear weapons development, production, and maintenance—contrasting those with the opportunity costs of such investments. Relying primarily on studies of nuclear weapons costs in the United States and India, this examination foregrounds the stakes of very expensive nuclear weapons programs whose purpose is to produce ostensibly unusable weapons. Turning next to the connections between the nuclear weapons and nuclear energy industries, the second section examines the extent to which the presence of global and national corporate interests in the nuclear industry compromise various regulatory mechanisms. In other words, this section analyzes how the intersections of military Keynesianism with neoliberal corporate interests has costly environmental and safety effects, disproportionately borne by the most vulnerable peoples of the world. The third section continues this analysis of nuclear costs by examining the working conditions in the nuclear power industry, including uranium mining, siting of nuclear power plants, nuclear weapons testing, and waste disposal sites. This examination is an attempt at measuring nuclear costs in exploitation and human vulnerability.

The chapter concludes by suggesting that if nuclear weapons are indeed "unusable," then the massive resources invested in producing them should, quite literally, be considered "waste." Yet the understanding of these weapons as essential in their very unusability has rendered them "necessary" for national security. Add to this the "necessary" costs of nuclear energy, considered vital for national development but having considerable safety and waste disposal costs, posing weapons proliferation risks, and involving vast human and resource exploitation. Ultimately, this waste-versus-necessity debate obscures the capitalist interests that drive proliferation and the layers of exploitation that undergird it. It is thus that the "neoliberal security state" both fortifies itself and aids the fortification of global hierarchy. The following chapter, then, turns to a study of the hierarchical nation-state system produced and sustained through nuclear power and the nuclear nonproliferation regime.

Nuclear Weapons Costs: Current, Future, and Forgone

That nuclear weapons are costly would be an uncontroversial point to make. But even the most basic estimates of the costs of investing in nuclear weapons are quite complicated to establish, partly because of the many different dimensions of these costs, as enumerated further later (Bailey 1994), but also because of the odd character of the nuclear market (Kaldor 1982). Pointing to the inefficiencies of weapons production in the absence of an open market for the determination of value, Kaldor argues that it is collusion between the state and arms manufacturers that determines the utility of nuclear weapons, so that technological improvement entails enhancing the utility of the product to the customer (i.e., the state) rather than cheapening it. Utility determined through such collusion leads to ever-increasing dedication of resources to weapons production, even when the products may decrease actual utility as far as security is concerned, that is, weapons that require more maintenance, create more vulnerability, or endlessly enhance overkill capacity.[7] Most important, because these weapons don't reenter the production process, their entire costs, which include the costs of production and the mark-ups in sale, are a deduction from the surplus value earned elsewhere in the economy (Kaldor 1982, 270–74).[8] What this means, then, is that the costs of nuclear investment require attention not just to the resources dedicated to producing and maintaining the weapons but also some estimate of what alternative "use" could be made of this deduction from surplus value (i.e., opportunity costs) if it were not invested in the production of what may be considered "use-less" weapons. This section attempts to provide some estimates for both these kinds of costs.

Despite the difficulties of gathering sensitive data in an extremely protected industry, some attempts have been made to calculate the enormous costs of nuclear weapons, which give a sense of the enormity of expenditures as well as the multifaceted nature of such expenditures. At the global level, a recent report released by an arm of the World Security Institute, a Washington, D.C.–based think tank that emerged from the Center for Defense Information and that is headed by nuclear weapons specialist Bruce Blair, found that world spending on nuclear weapons has surpassed $1 trillion per decade (Blair and Brown 2011). According to this report, in 2010, a total $91 billion was spent on nuclear weapons globally, and 2011 had an estimated cost of $104 billion. The United States continues to spend the largest amount, spending $55.6 billion on nuclear weapons in 2010 and having been expected to spend $61.3 billion in 2011. Despite the shrinking nuclear arsenal that gets much attention every time a treaty such as the recent New Strategic Arms Reduction Treaty (START) is successfully negotiated and ratified, the report indicates that the United States plans to increase its investment in nuclear weapons infrastructure by 21 percent, at a cost of $85 billion over the next decade, and to spend an additional $100 billion on upgrading strategic nuclear forces during this period. Indeed, it is important to point out here that much of the celebrations of successful arms control negotiations, such as New START, and the focus on the importance of treaties like the NPT in halting future proliferation obscure the enormous investments in updating, upgrading, and modernizing the existing nuclear weapons of states that already possess them, belying the actual materialization of any "peace dividend" that was expected to follow the end of the Cold War.[9] States other than the United States also continue to invest massive amounts of resources in nuclear weapons. Of these other states, the Blair and Brown report indicated that India spent the sixth largest amount in 2010, at $4.1 billion, and was expected to spend $4.9 billion in 2011, one conservative estimate suggesting that that cost 0.5 percent of its annual gross domestic product (GDP) and almost 22 percent of its overall defense budget. This section examines a little more closely the enormous resources spent by these nuclear weapons states on a weapons program to produce weapons not meant to be used and the kinds of investments such expenditures preclude.

The U.S. Nuclear Weapons Program

Ever since the Manhattan Project, nuclear weapons production has been one of the leading industries in the United States. One of the most comprehensive studies of any nuclear weapons program done to date, a 1998 study of U.S. nuclear weapons conducted by the Brookings Institution, attempted to calculate the nuclear costs of a Cold War whose expenses spill far beyond the formal end of that rivalry.[10] Between 1940 and 1998, Stephen Schwartz calculated that the United States spent almost $5.3 trillion (in constant 1996 dollars) on nuclear weapons and weapons-related programs to produce nearly seventy thousand nuclear weapons, those costs exceeding $5.8 trillion if projected radioactive waste storage and weapons dismantlement expenses were to be included. Essentially, the military was written a blank check during the Cold War to ensure that the United States maintained its competitive edge over the Soviet Union in nuclear weapons development. Nuclear weapons spending exceeded all other government expenditures during this time period, with the exception of nonnuclear defense spending and Social Security, and if distributed equally across the population in 1998, costs totaled $21,646 per person. These costs include not just nuclear weapons procurement but also the costs of deployment, the costs of maintaining production facilities and command and control systems, decommissioning costs, environmental costs, and operational costs. On the basis of discussions with Stephen Schwartz and updating the estimates of this 1998 study, Joseph Cirincione calculated that between 1940 and 2005, the United States spent nearly $7.5 trillion on nuclear weapons. This amounts to roughly $115 billion spent on nuclear armaments per year over a period of sixty-five years (Cirincione 2005).

Stephen Schwartz coauthored an updated study on nuclear spending commissioned by the Carnegie Endowment for International Peace in 2009 (Schwartz and Choubey 2009). This report uses publicly available government documents to assemble a reasonably accurate—although not comprehensive—picture of most nuclear weapons and weapons-related spending. To assess such expenditures, this study allocates them to one of five categories: nuclear forces and operational support, deferred environmental and health costs, missile defense, nuclear threat reduction, and nuclear incident management. The report found that in fiscal year 2008, the U.S. federal government spent at least $52.4 billion on nuclear weapons and weapons-related programs, of which $29.093 billion was spent on nuclear forces and operational support, $9.188 billion on missile defense, $8.299 billion on deferred environmental and health costs, $5.165 billion on nuclear threat reduction, and $.700 billion on nuclear incident management. What these studies pioneered by Schwartz document so well are that the costs of nuclear weapons far exceed the actual production of the weapons, and indeed, considerable resources need to be spent on keeping safe the very weapons whose purpose is to produce safety. Indeed, the costs of storing and treating the nuclear waste and environmental contamination (whose radioactive effects will be felt for hundreds of thousands of years) caused by nuclear weapons production and testing (e.g., at extremely contaminated sites, such as at Hanford in Washington State and over vast stretches of Nevada) are literally incalculable because they exceed so massively the finitude of most cost estimates.

With the passage of the New START and growing concern over ballooning debt owing to the recession, the U.S. nuclear weapons program has seen some changes. New START, as discussed in chapter 1, stipulates a 10 percent reduction in the number of warheads that either country could have operational at any one time. While some members of the U.S. Congress and the military hoped to supplement the reductions imposed by New START with some form of "modernization" program, some of these programs were put on hold because of the climate of austerity that arose out of the 2008 financial crisis.[11] Although neither the treaty nor the push toward balanced budgets has altered the fundamental nuclear posture of the United States, both have engendered significant changes and reductions in expenditures. The term *reduction* may be a misnomer, however, given that it ignores both the historical and long-term costs of nuclear weapons discussed earlier and the fact that current spending is still increasing. When put into the context of the trillions of dollars that the United States (and the Soviet Union) has spent on nuclear weapons over the years, the postponement of a couple of projects hardly looks like a significant reduction in spending. Moreover, at the same time as the United States is cutting costs in specific areas, the government is also increasing nuclear weapons spending more generally. As Kristensen and Norris report, for its fiscal 2013 budget, the Obama administration requested a $500 million increase in funding for the National Nuclear Security Administration (NNSA), which amounts to a 5 percent increase from 2012 levels. This budget did not even specify out-year costs for the next three years, nor did it capture the full costs of long-term programs that are not set to be completed for decades. These programs include the navy's plans to replace twelve Ohio-class ship-submersible ballistic nuclear submarines, which would cost $80 billion at a minimum, and the air force's plan to replace its current bomber fleet, which would cost between $38 billion and $55 billion. The Obama administration's budget request for fiscal year 2013 only reflected $300 million of the air force's plan for new bombers and did not include any of the costs of the navy's submarine program (Kristensen and Norris 2012).[12] So while delaying specific programs has made it seem as if U.S. nuclear weapons spending is slowing, it appears that the United States is still spending billions of dollars maintaining and upgrading its nuclear arsenal every year. Indeed, the enormous costs of modernizing existing delivery systems and refurbishing warheads are considered a critical aspect of maintaining the safety and reliability of U.S. nuclear weapons.[13]

Beyond the monetary costs of nuclear weapons lies a much more tangible cost in the form of what that money might have otherwise been spent on. Just a simple cost comparison between the nuclear security budget and other government spending puts the high price of nuclear weapons in perspective. In 2008, the federal government spent at least $52.4 billion on nuclear weapons, not including the costs of classified programs.

In contrast, the United States spent only $39.5 billion on "international diplomacy and foreign assistance," $33 billion on "natural resources and the environment," and $27.4 billion on "general science, space and technology" (Schwartz and Choubey 2009). This type of "opportunity cost" can be made even clearer through an examination of the ways in which $55 billion could be used to better and save millions of lives. For instance, a nuclear peace advocacy group titled Nuclear Age Peace Foundation calculates that if the United States diverted the money it spends annually on nuclear weapons toward more humanitarian programs, the country could end the state of poverty of 500 million people. A portion of that same money could also prevent 2 million maternal deaths, provide 350 million people with clean drinking water, and grant 140 million children access to basic nutrition (Wolaver 2010). Another global disarmament advocacy group has created an interactive site for calculating the opportunity costs for the nuclear weapons programs of different countries and suggests that if U.S. nuclear spending during a time of economic downturn in 2011 were directed elsewhere, there would be 1.6 million fewer Americans unemployed, 3.2 million more college educations funded, and health care coverage for 288 million low-income Americans.[14] Although it may be unreasonable to assume that this money would be fully reallocated to these types of life-saving and life-enhancing programs should the United States decide to end its nuclear weapons programs, it is still important to understand what more than $50 billion can achieve if one is to comprehend the true cost of U.S. nuclear weapons.

The Indian Nuclear Weapons Program

At the same time as the United States has been expanding its nuclear weapons program, India has been creating a program of its own. Since its first test of a nuclear device in 1974—termed a "peaceful nuclear explosion" by the Indian government at the time—India has rapidly expanded its program, eventually declaring its intention to weaponize with five nuclear tests in 1998. In 2010, researchers at the *Bulletin of the Atomic Scientists* estimated that India possessed roughly sixty to eighty nuclear warheads, of which they believed fifty were fully operational (Norris and Kristensen 2010). A more recent 2011 report released by the Federation of American Scientists estimated that India possessed between eighty and one hundred nuclear warheads.[15] Whether the difference between the reports signifies a rapid expansion in India's stockpile is difficult to tell, but the two reports certainly indicate that India's nuclear weapons force has grown significantly since its beginnings in the 1970s.

To make its stockpile strategically viable, India has begun to develop a nuclear triad of aircraft, land-based missiles, and submarines capable of delivering the warheads that the country has created. The primary leg of this triad is India's fighter bomber aircraft, but India also has five land-based, nuclear-capable ballistic missile types, with two under development: the long-range Agni III and the near-intercontinental ballistic missile Agni V, and on July 26, 2009, India launched its first nuclear-powered ballistic missile submarine (Norris and Kristensen 2010). Financing the nuclear weapons program that India envisions is expected to cost the country an inordinate amount of money. Unfortunately, determining such a cost is difficult because India will not publicly release documents detailing either the previous costs incurred by India's nuclear weapons program or the estimated cost for the program's future development. However, there have been attempts to provide the cost estimates that the Indian government will not. One of the most comprehensive assessments of the future costs of India's nuclear weapons program was done in 2003 by C. Rammanohar Reddy, journalist with the Indian newspaper *The Hindu.* By first extrapolating what various purchases would need to be made for India to fulfill its current nuclear policy of "minimal deterrence," Reddy arrived at his estimate by then using the costs of similar purchases made by other countries as the basis for his predictions, including costs for the three components of fissile materials, delivery systems, and command and control infrastructure. Reddy estimated that at 1998–99 prices, India's nuclear program would cost the country between $7.7 billion and $8 billion dollars during the first decade of the twentieth century (Reddy 2003, 390). However, if one includes the additional costs incurred by investments in submarines and protective fleets, and the costs of the future development of intermediate-range ballistic missiles, submarine-launched ballistic missiles, and intercontinental ballistic missiles, the total cost of the program is closer to $16 billion to $19 billion over a decade (Reddy 2003, 391–92). The two most expensive parts of India's nuclear doctrine were estimated to be its command and control systems, including the costs of satellites for early warning purposes, and the country's delivery systems. In all, the program was estimated to cost India more than 0.5 percent of its GDP *per year* (Reddy 2003, 395). Needless to say, accounting for some of the longer-term costs of nuclear waste management and environmental remediation as the Schwartz study attempts to do would only spike these figures further.

Like investments in the U.S. nuclear weapons program, the financial investments in India's nuclear weapons program impose significant opportunity costs. Again, a cost comparison between India's nuclear weapons expenditures and other programs that it funds provides insight into these opportunity costs. As Reddy calculated—and his study is aptly titled "Nuclear Weapons versus Schools for Children" to make this point—the estimated annual outlay for the nuclear weapons program is roughly equal to what India spends on all forms of education, including "school and university education, technical and medical education, as well as teaching and research," every single year (393–94). Indeed, as Reddy points out, the commitment that the Indian government has made to universal elementary education could well be within budgetary reach if India were to decide to divert this money from nuclear weapons to education. In addition, the cost of India's command and control system over the next decade would be more than what India spent on health, education, rural development, drinking water, sanitation, and other social programs in the 1998–99 fiscal year (Reddy 2003, 394). Reddy summarizes this opportunity cost well when he writes, "While an annual outlay that is equivalent to 0.5 per cent of GDP may seem like a small price to pay for nuclear weaponisation, it is not so—since the costs involved will impose a considerable burden on the Indian government and could result in diversion of funds from priority social and economic programmes" (394).

Given the extreme importance of these various programs in India specifically, these additional costs are even greater than they may seem. Despite the increases in India's overall growth rates since the liberalization of the Indian economy in the 1990s, India's poverty levels remain very high, and government spending on social welfare programs, especially in rural areas, has been declining. If India's nuclear weapons program truly did cut into these types of government spending, then weaponization could have much higher costs than the numbers would seem to indicate.

What are the stakes of these massive investments in nuclear weapons? Who benefits from such investments? The following section begins by theorizing the relationship between the state (the consumer of nuclear weapons) and the nuclear industry (the producer of nuclear weapons), before elaborating on the costly consequences of these complex entanglements.

The Military Keynesianism of the Neoliberal State

In my discussion of the nuclear fetish in the previous chapter, I already alluded to the "military Keynesianism" through which nuclear weapons emerge as a very particular kind of commodity, a commodity whose sole consumer is the state, so that the nuclear weapons industry comes to have an enormous stake in the political and economic health of the state. But Mark Neocleous has argued that under conditions of modern capitalism, security itself has become a fetish commodity, and the security industry the agents of an ideology and culture of (in)security to which their products are tailored to provide a (depoliticized) solution (Neocleous 2007; 2008). Given the amorphous nature of what appears on the face of it to be such a basic human need for security, the capacity of the security industry to commodify the means of protection and safety is virtually limitless, suggests Neocleous, and the apparent urgency of the demand for security appears to inoculate the security industry from scrutiny.

There has been a long debate in Marxist scholarship about the extent to which the state is a direct agent of capitalist interests.[16] Literature on the extent and reach of the military–industrial complex has studied the close and vast connections between the state and military corporations.[17] Recent work on globalization has pushed these discussions much further by interrogating the extent to which the logic of neoliberalism has penetrated the very "core" of the state as security becomes more and more privatized (Singer 2007; Klein 2007). Neocleous points out that much of this discussion and many critiques of privatized security presume that security is "naturally" or "essentially" a public good, and it is the "hollowed-out" state that results from a growing reliance on private and corporate interests for the delivery of one of the state's core functions that is problematic (Neocleous 2007; 2008). But although *privatization* as a descriptive term may be useful for capturing some of the current changes afoot in the contemporary neoliberal world, Neocleous argues that a reliance on the liberal private–public distinction as an analytical device occludes the fact that rather than a transformation of state power, "the changes taking place help to reinforce part of Marxism's insight into the *unity* of state and capital" (Neocleous 2007, 349). Indeed, even as the neoliberal state has appeared to retract from the provision of many public goods, "one of the few aspects of the capitalist state actually reinforced under neoliberalism is the security apparatus" (Neocleous 2007, 354). Thus, at least in the case of security, a Keynesian state has not yielded to a neoliberal state, as most accounts of globalization suggest, but rather military Keynesianism now has a neoliberal character, as the connections between state and corporate interests have not just tightened but have also taken new forms. A focus on the security fetish in Neocleous's account helps in drawing attention to this "partnership" of capital and state, which, despite their differences and antagonisms, collude in sustaining capital accumulation *and* fortifying the state. This partnership, suggests Neocleous, is "increasingly organized around the ideology of security," and understanding security as a fetish helps us see security itself as "ideologically generated and developed as an interest of *both* capital and state" (Neocleous 2007, 349; emphasis original). This section takes a closer look at how these connections are sustained and the effects of this mutuality by examining three dynamics— the influence of the nuclear corporate lobby on state regulatory mechanisms in the United States, the influence of this lobby in lifting the economic sanctions imposed on India in the wake of its 1998 tests via the 2008 U.S.–Indian nuclear deal, and the close connections between the nuclear industry and state-level decision makers in Japan's nuclear industry. As will become clear, these connections make it difficult to keep the question of nuclear weapons proliferation distinct from the pursuit of nuclear energy.

Corporate Lobby in the Nuclear Weapons and Nuclear Energy Industries in the United States

The massive structure of the U.S. nuclear weapons industry is matched by a massive network of corporate lobbies whose purpose is to ensure continued funding and support from the federal government. A recent report authored by William D. Hartung (with Christine Anderson) for the Center for International Policy elaborates on the reach and intensity of this lobbying exercise.[18] Not a monolith, this network is composed of many different groups and organizations that both collaborate and compete at different times but that work closely with different representatives and organs of the state, often relying on military–strategic arguments to make the case for the production or extension of some particular class or component of nuclear weapons. But much of what drives these efforts are the overlapping and intersecting interests between corporations that design and build nuclear delivery vehicles, corporations that operate nuclear warhead–related facilities, and members of the U.S. Congress with nuclear weapons–related facilities or deployments in their districts or states (Hartung 2012a, 4).

Hartung's report documents the activities of the small group of major corporations, each backed by an extensive set of subcontractors, that are the primary beneficiaries of nuclear weapons spending. These corporations are involved in various areas related to weapons design, production, upgrades, and upkeep (including cleanup)—bomber production, submarine production, the nuclear-capable F-35 Joint Strike Fighter, cruise and ballistic missiles, plutonium pits, uranium processing, mixed oxide, nonnuclear components of nuclear weapons, and life extension programs (to refurbish and upgrade existing nuclear warheads). Some companies, such as Babcock and Wilcox, Bechtel, Honeywell, Northrup Grumman, and Lockheed Martin, are involved in multiple major nuclear weapons–related projects; each of these companies is heavily (in some cases, such as Northrup Grumman, exclusively) reliant on massive government contracts, and the companies' interests are pursued by an enormous network of lobbies. The network itself consists of three subsets matching the three parts of the nuclear triad: the air force, the navy, and land-based nuclear missiles. Although there is some overlap between lobbies because companies such as General Electric profit from the construction of both nuclear-capable aircraft and submarines, the lobbying groups and coalitions in Congress surrounding various legs of the triad remain separate. The multiple and overlapping groups that work together to push for nuclear weapons pursuit consist of active members of the U.S. Congress organized into specific caucuses designed to exert leverage on particular aspects of nuclear weapons production for each leg of the triad;[19] retired military personnel hired by lobby groups related to each leg of the triad, who are sponsored and funded by weapons corporations;[20] and the weapons-producing companies themselves, as mentioned earlier.

All of these organizations share the same basic goal of maintaining high profits for the companies they represent through a steady supply of government funds. Hartung documents the different activities engaged in by lobby groups, including "congressional packets" of relevant facts, quotes, and articles; "supplier days," which bring together representatives of lobby groups and corporations in contact with members of Congress; and annual symposia, publications, and so on. One of the most common ways of achieving leverage, however, is by influencing congressional leaders via campaign contributions. Over the course of their careers, the current influential congressmen and women with the power to make decisions regarding nuclear weapons spending had been given roughly $18.7 million by the top fourteen nuclear weapons contractors (Hartung 2012a, 14). During the 2012 election cycle alone, these same individuals were given $2.9 million by major firms (Hartung 2012a, 14). This spending is generally targeted toward members of four key subcommittees with jurisdiction over nuclear weapons spending: the Strategic Forces Subcommittees of the Armed Services Committees (which deal with nuclear delivery vehicles) in both houses and the Energy and Water Subcommittees of the Appropriations Committees (which deal with the larger nuclear weapons complex and have jurisdiction over the NNSA) in both houses. In 2012, more than $1.6 million was given to individuals who resided on one of these subcommittees (Hartung 2012a, 14). In general, contributions are concentrated around members of key subcommittees or members with nuclear weapons–related facilities in their states or districts, with these categories often overlapping. Whether or not campaign contributions directly translate into policy outcomes, there is no question that these sorts of efforts help create a space for the presence of corporate groups to articulate their interests and participate in shaping the contours and substance of policy debates.[21]

One of the keys to success for the nuclear weapons industry in terms of gaining influence on Capitol Hill has been the use of the "revolving door"—that is, the circulation of individuals between organs of the state (Congress and the military) and private industry (including corporate lobbies). For the nuclear weapons lobby in particular, there are a very large number of revolving-door lobbyists. Of the lobbyists employed by the fourteen largest nuclear weapons contractors, 137 formerly worked for "key nuclear weapons decision makers" (Hartung 2012a, 19). Of these lobbyists, ninety-six had worked for key congressional committees or influential members of Congress, twenty-six had worked for one of the military services, and twenty-four had worked for either the Department of Energy or the Department of Defense. These revolving-door lobbyists were often extremely important individuals in their previous congressional work; for instance, around a dozen of the revolving-door lobbyists that are a part of the nuclear weapons complex were chiefs of staff for key members of Congress (Hartung 2012a, 19). Besides becoming lobbyists, individuals formerly involved with Congress and the military have also become executives at major weapons corporations (Hartung 2012a, 19). The intimate connections between congressional decision makers and those trying to influence those decision makers have certainly attracted occasional criticism by concerned public groups but are generally tolerated as the way business is conducted in the U.S. capital.[22]

Like many accounts that are critical of excessive corporate influence on governmental policy making, Hartung suggests that the national security interests of the United States, which he suggests can be served by a much smaller number (three hundred) of nuclear weapons, should take priority over the narrower interests of nuclear weapons corporations that frequently push not just for particular weapons systems but also for expanded nuclear spending generally (Hartung 2012a, 21). In his words, "there is too much at stake to let narrow special interests trump the national interests when it comes to making decisions on nuclear weapons spending and policy" (21). But this presumes that the "national security interests" of the United States are transparent and exist apart from and outside of the forces that bring it into being. Indeed, Hartung's own report documents the strategic arguments frequently made (and publicized) by weapons lobbies and contractors—arguments that explain why a particular weapons system would provide effective deterrence or stability. Many of these arguments made by revolving-door experts both inform and help produce the security interests of the United States. Such arguments frequently become part of the strategic commonsense on which both proponents and opponents of increased nuclear spending rely, and it is through that process that national interests are produced.

The close imbrication of state and corporate interests is also quite evident in the nuclear energy industry, which is heavily dependent on government subsidies and loan guarantees for the building of reactors and coverage of liabilities.[23] Here, too, corporate lobbies wield considerable resources and influence,[24] and "regulatory capture" via campaign contributions and revolving-door industry interests are fairly well documented.[25] Although no new reactors have been built in the United States since 1977, there has been an extensive lobbying effort by the industry to secure subsidies and loan guarantees. It is no surprise that the nuclear energy lobby started fortifying its case almost immediately after the Fukushima Daiichi reactor meltdowns, anticipating the enormous worldwide resistance to nuclear power unleashed in the wake of that disaster.[26] These concerns about nuclear power have much to do with the ways in which the close connections between state and corporate interests compromise governmental regulatory oversight of reactor operations and storage of nuclear fuel.

The long history of U.S. governmental regulation of the nuclear energy industry began when Congress established the U.S. Atomic Energy Commission (AEC) in 1946 and Harry S. Truman signed the McMahon–Atomic Energy Act on August 1 of that year, which handed over atomic energy control to civilian hands.[27] This act opened the floodgates for future legislation that would spell out regulations on nuclear activity in the United States, nuclear trade with other countries, weapons testing, and nuclear fuel allocation. In 1954, Congress passed the Atomic Energy Act, which gave the AEC the authority to regulate and license commercial economic activities. At the time, the process of distributing a license included technical reviews, public hearings, and an independent evaluation of safety by the Advisory Committee on Reactor Safeguards. On August 26, 1964, President Johnson signed the Private Ownership of Special Nuclear Materials Act, which allowed for private ownership of reactor fuel. This legislation furthered the evolution of the U.S. regulatory environment, for although it relinquished government control over the sale of reactor fuel, it gave the AEC authority to regulate a new private market. By 1973, the commission was exercising in full the powers of regulation that it had been given, as it announced new requirements for emergency core cooling systems in light-water-cooled power reactors. In 1974, the Nuclear Regulatory Commission (NRC) was created to take on the regulatory duties of the AEC (Buck 1983). Since its inception, the NRC has pursued regulations on nuclear waste as controversy surrounding waste disposal has increased, and the NRC has also been regulating the producers of nuclear materials. Owing to the attacks on September 11, 2001, the NRC has also had to drastically increase its security requirements for nuclear fuel in any stage. The organization has had to exercise its licensing authority for nuclear reactors sparingly, however, as construction of new reactors has largely halted since 1977, but new projects are expected to resume.

Over its forty-year life-span, the NRC has been strongly criticized for being an example of "regulatory capture" and for promoting the commercial interests of the nuclear energy sector rather than ensuring safety. Critics have pointed to many instances of failed or overlooked regulation, the progressive lowering of safety standards because of industry pressure, the mild penalties for violations that are acknowledged, and the hesitance to reject license renewals. These criticisms became especially sharp after the Fukushima Daiichi disaster in Japan. It is important to point out here that the creation of the NRC (replacing the AEC) was an attempt to make the nuclear regulatory body an organization independent of the governmental organ involved with the promotion and pursuit of nuclear energy.[28] But this means that, now, 90 percent of the NRC's funding comes from fee billing, that is, from industry, which, though not unusual, compromises the independence of the regulatory body.

A recent Associated Press (AP) yearlong investigation found that federal regulators had been colluding with industry officials to keep unsafe aging reactors operating by either lowering those standards or not enforcing them.[29] In fact, no application for license renewal has been rejected since the first one was approved in 2000, and since the more stringent relicensing rules that did lead to rejections were relaxed in 1995 (Zeller 2011). The AP report identified that terms like "sharpening the pencil" and "pencil engineering"—"the fudging of calculations and assumptions to yield answers that enable plants with deteriorating conditions to remain in compliance"—were widely used by nuclear engineers and former regulators to describe this process. The report itself identifies several areas of particular concern—brittle vessels, leaky valves, cracked tubing, and corroded piping—and provides several specific examples of problems and accidents. David Lochbaum, nuclear safety director at the Union of Concerned Scientists (which is not opposed to nuclear energy), has been consistently reporting on radioactive leaks because of broken equipment or inadequate worker training and on NRC negligence on safety.[30] In addition, much recent worry, after both the terrorist attacks on September 11, 2001, and the reactor meltdowns at Fukushima Daiichi, has turned to the storage of spent fuel at the reactor sites. Charles Perrow, writing for the *Bulletin of the Atomic Scientists,* suggests that some kinds of mishaps and accidents, even of the catastrophic variety, are the inevitable products of complex systems, yet most of the examples of negligence that are reported are of the predictable variety and could have been prevented with a better regulatory apparatus that did not yield so consistently to industry pressure (sometimes via state officials who are recipients of large campaign donations from the industry) (Perrow 2011). It may be, as Kaufman and Penciakova suggest, comparing the U.S. and Japanese nuclear regulatory environments, that the "regulatory laxity" of the NRC is largely a product of "lax enforcement" rather than "private sector deception," but even they identify the reliance of the NRC on industry funding and the influence wielded by revolving-door industry lobbyists and campaign contributions as problems (Kaufmann and Penciakova 2011).

It is not as though the government always turns a blind eye. The relaxed and often failed regulations of the NRC led the Subcommittee on General Oversight and Investigation in Congress to release a report in December 1987 titled "NRC Coziness with the Industry: Nuclear Regulatory Commission Fails to Maintain Arm's Length Relationship with the Nuclear Industry." The subcommittee found that the NRC had engaged in back-door meetings with nuclear utilities that granted those utilities exemptions from regulations, bowed to industry pressure over regulating drug and alcohol abuse problems at power plants, and more.[31] But the 2010 Union of Concerned Scientists's independent evaluation mentioned earlier, which found significant problems with the enforcement of safety rules, including cases where NRC inspectors knew about safety problems but did nothing to fix them, suggests that not much had changed in more than thirty years.[32] Many of these questions related to corporate influence on regulatory systems have been intensified post-Fukushima with what appear to be increasing tensions among commissioners and staff members at the NRC,[33] and recent attempts to impose relatively more expensive safety measures have faced pushback from both industry representatives and lawmakers (Lipton and Wald 2013).

The 2008 U.S.–Indian Nuclear Fuel Deal

The U.S.–Indian Nuclear Fuel Deal is a perfect example of what happens when a nuclear rebel state whose nuclear belligerence appears to be at odds with U.S. national security interests in nonproliferation also offers a massive and attractive investment destination for nuclear corporate interests searching for new markets. Beginning with the terrorist attacks on September 11, 2001, U.S.–Indian relations have undergone a dramatic transformation over the past decade. Despite its initial help in developing India's nuclear energy program (including building a nuclear reactor and providing nuclear fuel) under the Atoms for Peace program, the United States had long had a strained relationship with India because of disagreements over the latter's pursuit of nuclear weapons. Since around the time of India's first nuclear weapons test in 1974, the United States had put in place a moratorium on nuclear trade with India. When India next declared itself a NWS by conducting another round of tests in 1998, the United

States placed new economic sanctions on the country. Just three years later, however, and only ten days after the September 11, 2001, attacks, President George W. Bush lifted the sanctions that President Clinton had put in place. Soon after, the number of Indian companies on the Commerce Department's Entity List, which records companies on which the United States has placed import or export regulations, decreased from 159 to 2 (Hoey 2009). Additionally, the United States changed its licensing policy of denial for "nuclear- and missile-related technology" to a policy of case-by-case review (Hoey 2009). These changes were meant to reflect the "countries' new relationship and common strategic interests"—interests that included dealing with terrorist threats and containing the power of China.[34]

This new strategic relationship eventually led to the landmark 2008 U.S.–Indian Nuclear Fuel Deal. By March 2006, negotiations between the Bush administration and Indian prime minister Manmohan Singh led India to promise to place fourteen of its twenty-two nuclear power reactors under International Atomic Energy Association (IAEA) safeguards. In addition, India agreed to a moratorium on weapons testing. On October 1, 2008, the U.S. Congress officially approved the U.S.–Indian Civil Nuclear Cooperation Initiative, which allows the United States to engage in civilian nuclear commerce with India. Beyond what India had already agreed to, the deal stipulated that India would sign the Additional Protocol, which allows the IAEA to conduct even more rigorous inspections of civilian nuclear facilities; upgrade the security of its nuclear arsenal; negotiate a Fissile Material Cutoff Treaty in the future, which would ban the production of fissile material in India for weapons purposes; and support international nonproliferation efforts by preventing additional states from acquiring enrichment and reprocessing technologies.[35] This was accompanied by a Nuclear Suppliers Group (NSG) waiver that made it possible for India to engage in nuclear trade with other NWS.

The Nuclear Fuel Deal was successfully negotiated despite heavy objections by a variety of groups in both India and the United States.[36] Warnings by many arms control and disarmament advocates that a deal such as this was a major blow to the NPT's attempt to prohibit nuclear trading with a state not recognized as a NWS by the NPT went unheeded.[37] The NSG waiver was seen as an unprecedented exemption made by this suppliers' cartel to a state that had not signed either the NPT or the Comprehensive Test Ban Treaty (CTBT), with reportedly strong pressure used by the United States to secure the consent of objecting states.[38] In addition, critics suggested that there are several ways that these agreements on civilian nuclear commerce potentially impact India's nuclear weapons program. First, the deal allows India to purchase dual-use technology—technology that can be used for civilian purposes as well as military—from the United States, including items that could be used to help create nuclear bombs by enriching uranium or reprocessing plutonium. The agreement would also exempt from IAEA safeguards and inspections any facilities and stockpiles of nuclear fuel that India had produced before the agreement. Furthermore, because India's promise to place thermal and breeder reactors under IAEA safeguards only applied to civilian reactors, and India retained the right to determine and classify reactors as civilian, many have argued that the deal does not effectively regulate the military aspect of India's nuclear program at all.[39] Critics, such as Henry Sokolski of the Nonproliferation Education Center (who testified before the U.S. Congress on this) and Joseph Cirincione of the Carnegie Endowment for International Peace, warned that the U.S.–Indian Nuclear Fuel Deal and the NSG waiver allow India to free up its limited uranium resources, thus allowing uranium to be used for military purposes, that is, weapons production, without restricting the finite uranium for the civil nuclear industry. In contrast, Ashley Teller, from the Carnegie Center for International Peace, has argued that the deal would have no impact on India's nuclear weapons program, which can be sustained quite adequately with India's natural uranium reserves, but is instead really an effort to strengthen the country's civilian energy needs to satisfy rising electricity demand (Tellis 2006).[40]

Whether or not the deal can be considered a win for India's nuclear weapons program, the corporate interests in the United States, India, and other nuclear supplier countries are most certainly a beneficiary of it, as the deal allowed U.S. companies to sell nuclear fuel to India for civilian use and build nuclear reactors in the country, and the NSG waiver allowed other countries also to enter the Indian nuclear market. India's recalcitrance on nuclear nonproliferation had for some time stood in the way of opening up its large and growing energy market to the liberalizing forces that had first been unleashed in the early 1990s, and the Nuclear Fuel Deal finally made it possible and desirable again to import reactors and fuel, despite critics in India who bemoaned the loss of indigenous production and control over nuclear power.[41] It should be no surprise, then, that massive resources were expended by corporate lobby groups that had an enormous stake in this rapidly expanding energy market in an emerging economic power like India.[42] Indeed, the cinching of the fuel deal with such overwhelming support in the U.S. Congress was widely seen as evidence that the "India lobby" had finally established itself as a formidable force in Washington, D.C., much like the American Israel Public Affairs Committee, the pro-Israel lobby. Chennai-based journalist J. Sri Raman, writing for the *Bulletin of the Atomic Scientists,* reports that New Delhi paid two U.S.-based lobbying firms roughly $1.3 million to advocate in the U.S. Congress for the deal, and the Confederation of Indian Industry funded several trips to India for U.S. congressional delegations (Raman 2009; see also Raman 2012, appendix 2). The U.S.–Indian Business Council also hired a U.S. lobby firm, and spokespeople for the group gushed about the enormous economic possibilities for U.S. business interests in India (Kamdar 2007). Additionally, the U.S.–Indian Political Action Committee, the most influential Indian–American lobby, undertook a very substantial campaign to generate support for the U.S.–Indian nuclear deal in the U.S. Congress (Kirk 2008). Bringing together business interests, ethnic interests, and state interests, Temple describes the coordination of these various groups into the Coalition for Partnership with India, which hired in-house and outside lobby groups to convince U.S. congressional representatives of the enormous commercial benefits of the fuel deal for the U.S. economy. Executives from J. P. Morgan Chase, General Electric, Boeing, Bechtel, American International, Dow Chemical, and Lockheed Martin were all involved in these lobbying efforts (Temple 2009). Brahma Chellaney, writing for the Indian newspaper *The Hindu,* points to the influence of this global corporate nuclear lobby in pushing through the U.S.–Indian deal in India, as well (Chellaney 2011).[43]

That various business interests stood to gain from the opening up of an enormous Indian market in energy and weapons materials and technology via the Nuclear Fuel Deal and NSG waiver was quite clear. During the negotiations of the deal in 2008, the Manmohan Singh government had reportedly promised to buy reactors from U.S. companies like Westinghouse and General Electric that would cost $50 billion or more and generate a minimum of ten thousand megawatts of electricity (Ramana and Raju 2013). The deal was expected to draw business worth more than $100 billion and tens of thousands of jobs in both the United States and India and help revive the U.S. nuclear industry, whose domestic market had appeared to stagnate for about thirty years (Pant 2011, 46–47). Kamdar reports that major U.S. corporations were hoping that the nuclear deal would help secure military contracts as well as deals to build nuclear power plants, with Lockheed Martin pushing for a $4 billion to $9 billion contract for 120 fighter jets (Kamdar 2007). Raman reports that less than a year after the deal was finalized in the U.S. Congress, the Westinghouse Electric Company and the Mumbai-based Indian conglomerate Larsen and Toubro (L&T) signed a memorandum of understanding to "address the projected need in India for pressurized water nuclear reactors with modular construction technology" (Raman 2009). Four months later, U.S.-based GE Hitachi Nuclear Energy signed a similar memorandum with L&T for cooperation on boiling water reactors and advanced boiling water reactors. In July 2009, New Delhi set aside two sites in India on which U.S. companies could build nuclear reactors. During that same summer of 2009, the Indian government reportedly told the United States that it was willing to purchase $150 billion worth of nuclear reactors, equipment, and materials from U.S.-based companies (Raman 2009). For their role in helping secure the NSG waiver, Russia (specifically, the Russian state–controlled Rosatom) and France (specifically, the French firm Areva, which is the leader in the nuclear energy market) were awarded two nuclear reactor sites (Raman 2012, appendix 2).[44]

Although the deal initially appeared to be a major victory for business interests in the United States and India, legal issues hampered corporate plans between the two nations from coming to fruition. These legal issues all center on the current lack of nuclear liability protections under Indian law and the demand of U.S. firms for legislation that would exempt manufacturers and suppliers from liability payments and make operators solely liable for any mishaps.[45] In early 2010, legislation was introduced in the Indian parliament that would have protected "foreign equipment suppliers" from civil liability claims. The bill was quickly withdrawn by the Indian government because critics were unwilling to sign away the right of Indian citizens to go to court and receive compensation in the case of a nuclear accident, especially given the ill-handling of the 1984 Union Carbide industrial accident in Bhopal. This caused considerable frustration in the U.S. nuclear industry and among U.S. lawmakers, who saw state-protected France's Areva and Russia's Rosatom benefiting commercially from a deal largely brokered and made possible through U.S. efforts and resources (Hundley 2012). However, in August 25, 2010, India's parliament passed the Civil Liability for Nuclear Damage Bill. This legislation capped the amount of damages that could be paid by the operator (the Nuclear Power Corporation) of a nuclear plant at around $250 million and was seen as one of the last steps needed to solidify the 2008 U.S.–Indian Nuclear Fuel Deal. However, with pressure from concerned civil society groups, the Indian government allowed a small clause to be added that allows the operator—a public-sector company—to a "right of recourse" to claim some of the damages from the supplier, if an accident were found to be caused by reactor design. Unsurprisingly, Westinghouse and General Electric have been unwilling to sell reactors with the adoption of this unprecedented clause—despite the relatively small cap on liability damages that can be claimed for only a limited period—which led the Indian government to recently seek a legal opinion from the attorney general on whether the Nuclear Power Corporation could "choose not to exercise its right of recourse."[46] This naked attempt to surrender the rights of a public-sector company to the demands of a powerful private multinational company has generated another round of outrage among activists and concerned groups in India (Ramana and Raju 2013). As Ramana and Raju ask, "if Westinghouse genuinely believes that its reactors are so safe—in its public documents, it claims that a severe accident may occur only once in 3.5 million years—why is it so reluctant to accept responsibility for an accident?" Whether U.S. (and other) nuclear corporations are able to freely operate in India will largely depend on how this active contestation between powerful corporate interests, a state quite beholden to a neoliberal ideology, and various oppositional and democratic civil society groups plays out over time.

The State–Corporate Nexus in Japanese Nuclear Energy

A massive earthquake, followed by a tsunami, resulted in the loss of electricity to the Fukushima Daiichi nuclear power stations, which, coupled with the failure of backup systems, set in motion a massive crisis (partial core meltdowns at three reactors, hydrogen explosions damaging reactor buildings and leaking radioactive material, exposure of spent fuel rods) whose repercussions are still ongoing. Investigations conducted after the Fukushima accident have brought a great deal of renewed attention to the huge levels of collusion between the Japanese nuclear industry and the state, both in the marketing of nuclear power to a nuclear-wary nation and in compromising effective oversight of the nuclear industry and various regulatory mechanisms that should have been in place for early warning and prevention. On one hand, a huge ideological project undertaken by the state and the nuclear industry sought to make nuclear energy palatable to a country that, as the only victim of a nuclear bomb attack, has always been uneasy about nuclear power since the end of World War II. Fierce grassroots opposition to the setting up of nuclear power plants was reversed as rural towns all over Japan developed a stake in nuclear power. The state essentially was able to buy the support of these communities through generous subsidies, tax revenues, "anonymous" donations to local treasuries, big public works projects such as "sports parks," jobs, even compensation to individuals (Fackler and Onishi 2011).[47] This led to an enormous dependence on state and industry largess, especially as better-paying jobs in the nuclear industry replaced farming or fishing as modes of economic livelihood and poor, rural towns housing nuclear plants producing electricity largely for distant urban areas became much more vulnerable to safety hazards (Fackler and Onishi 2011). That the now-heavy reliance on nuclear energy has made Japan a breakout state—able to break into nuclear weapons at relatively short notice—despite the deep abhorrence to nuclear weapons among large segments of the Japanese population is evidence of the effectiveness of this corporate lobbying. It is in part the result of this deep and wide investment in nuclear power that has made it so difficult to either reform the nuclear industry and the regulatory apparatus despite political promises to do so during political campaigns or to decrease this dependence on nuclear power in the face of opposition to it.

The collusion between the state and the nuclear industry manifested itself through its impact on the regulatory apparatus established to ensure the safety of nuclear power plants. Regulation of the Japanese nuclear power industry began with the passage of the Atomic Energy Basic Law on December 19, 1955. The law was meant to outline a path for Japan's fledgling nuclear program that would productively grow the industry. As part of the law, Japan established the Atomic Energy Commission of Japan to act as the regulatory agency for the country's nuclear power program. The law also set up the Japanese Nuclear Safety Commission (NSC), which was meant to review the safety inspections that other agencies conducted. Although the process of regulations and review was vastly different from in the United States, Japan was still regulating the same categories of activities at the time, such as nuclear licensing, fuel allocation, and waste management. The primary difference between the U.S. and Japanese regulatory schemes was the lack of overlap between the commercial and military sectors because Japan did not have a weapons program. In 2001, the Nuclear and Industrial Safety Administration (NISA) was created and assumed much of the regulatory duties of Japan's Atomic Energy Commission. With the establishment of NISA, Japan had set up the nuclear regulatory framework that the country has in place today.

Although there has long been concern about Japan's regulatory apparatus, including questions raised by the IAEA in June 2007 about NISA and the NSC (Funabashi and Kitazawa 2012), recent events at Fukushima Daiichi have triggered a fairly extensive discussion about the ways that the long history of collusion between Japan's nuclear power industry, state regulators, and politicians has compromised nuclear safety. One of the primary criticisms had been the non-independence of Japan's primary nuclear regulatory organs, stemming from the fact that NISA fell under the purview of Japan's Ministry of Economy, Trade, and Industry (METI), that is, the industry that promotes the use of nuclear energy in the country.[48] In light of these criticisms, NISA was abolished in 2012 and replaced by the Nuclear Regulation Authority (patterned after the U.S. regulatory body—the NRC—discussed earlier), which is now housed under the Ministry of the Environment.[49] But investigations have also revealed how a revolving door among corporate executives[50] and state regulators— popularly termed the "nuclear power village"[51]—and close financial ties between politicians and industry elite meant that lapses in many safety regulations were routinely overlooked and that safety standards were lowered in the interest of keeping compromised nuclear reactors functioning (Onishi and Belson 2011).[52] It is also now clear that the Japanese government purposefully withheld damaging information about the unfolding disaster at Fukushima Daiichi to prevent costly evacuations and avoid casting the powerful nuclear industry in a negative light (Onishi and Fackler 2011).[53] The extent and effectiveness of the network of ties among state and industry interests is quite impressive. Pro-nuclear industry executives, politicians, regulators, government bureaucrats, scientists, and academics benefited from construction projects, lucrative jobs, and financial support, while critics denied promotions and support, ministry officials landed lucrative positions in the private nuclear industry, and industry officials served on government panels on devising safety regulations (Onishi and Belson 2011; Kaufmann and Penciakov 2011). Furthermore, lacking adequate technical expertise or an independent pool of experts from which to draw, NISA relied on industry experts to help draw up its regulations and procedures (Onishi and Belson 2011). This wide network of ties has meant that voices opposing nuclear power and the reach of the nuclear lobby—including through legal efforts to establish the dangers of nuclear reactors—were repeatedly silenced and defeated (Belson 2011).

Indeed, a massive public relations campaign by the nuclear establishment—the utility companies and the Ministry of Economy—marketed the "safety" of nuclear power using elaborate theme parks, advertisements, educational programs, and even government-mandated school textbooks (Onishi 2011). Organizations like the Japan Atomic Energy Relations Organization, funded partly by two ministries that oversee nuclear power and partly by plant operators, worked to produce what has been called the myth of the "absolute safety" of nuclear power—that is, a belief in the impossibility or extremely unlikely chance of a nuclear accident. This meant producing and disseminating information about nuclear power through, for instance, sending nuclear experts to speak at schools and colleges, but also by withholding undertaking public preparatory actions, such as earthquake drills, or publicly acknowledging nuclear risks that might cause "unnecessary anxiety and misunderstanding" (Onishi 2011; Funabashi and Kitazawa 2012, 14). After Chernobyl, nuclear plant operators created public relations buildings attached to the plants, aimed in particular at reassuring young parents of the safety of nuclear power, and school textbooks were revised to deemphasize the dangers of nuclear power (Onishi 2011). The safety myth helps explain "why in the only nation to have been attacked with atomic bombs, the Japanese acceptance of nuclear power was so strong that the accidents at Three Mile Island and Chernobyl barely registered. Even with the crisis at the Fukushima Daiichi nuclear power plant, the reaction against nuclear power has been, in some senses, much stronger in Europe and the United States than in Japan itself" (Onishi 2011).[54]

It should be clear from this section that there are complex and intersecting interests in the pursuit of nuclear power more broadly. The previous chapter discussed the many variables that scholars have argued influence the decision making that leads to the active pursuit of nuclear weapons. But the extent to which global corporate interests in nuclear energy affect corporate and state interests in nuclear weapons needs more attention. Some scholars have argued that in many cases, civilian nuclear assistance programs are motivated primarily by strategic concerns (Fuhrmann 2009a) and that legal transfer of peaceful nuclear technology significantly increases the risks of proliferation (Fuhrmann 2009b; Fuhrmann and Kreps 2010). Thus, it is suggested, focusing on supply-side factors, as opposed to the demand-side variables that now dominate the literature, is particularly important to understanding proliferation (Kroenig 2009). Whatever might be the balance between supply-side and demand-side variables in any actual decision to weaponize, attention to supply-side factors requires accounting for all the costs of investment in nuclear energy, despite what may appear to be their tangential connection to nuclear weapons proliferation. The animation of new fears of terrorist attacks on nuclear power plants and terrorist theft of nuclear materials for possible weapons production are evidence of some recognition of the potential weapons costs of nuclear energy (Allison 2004b; Hecker 2006; Nunn 2006). Indeed, securing nuclear materials is now widely recognized as one of the most urgent demands of the post–September 11, 2001, era. But given the sensitivity of nuclear materials and technology to such "national security" concerns, much of what happens in the nuclear energy industry (including the heavy role of corporations in cleanup and waste disposal efforts[55]) remains opaque to public scrutiny and accountability. In other words, the level of state secrecy and lack of transparency that attaches to nuclear weapons possession also ends up masking and protecting the nuclear energy industry. As I hope the three cases discussed in this section demonstrate, the pursuit of nuclear power has produced a highly compromised neoliberal state that can use "security" to inoculate itself from accountability.

The Real Costs of Unusable Weapons: Exploitation and Vulnerability

But the costs of nuclear weapons extend beyond the massive corporate interests invested in their production and sustenance. A Marxist analysis of commodity fetishism takes us, ultimately, to the labor and bodies affected by the production of commodities. This requires examining the working conditions in the nuclear power industry as well as following the production process to its origins by tracking the production of nuclear weapons from the mining of uranium through the several stages over which it is transformed into nuclear energy and weapons. Such a broad analysis would include examining the vast uranium mining and milling industry, the siting of nuclear power plants, and the various steps in nuclear weapons production, nuclear testing, and nuclear waste disposal.[56] Much of uranium mining occurs under exploitative conditions, the location of nuclear power plants carries a long history of land and resource appropriation, and nuclear testing has left many lasting traces on vulnerable populations. The storage and disposal of radioactive waste remains an unresolved issue involving many marginal communities around the world. Some of the (post)colonial relationships at play in many instances of uranium mine operations (especially in Africa), indigenous land appropriations for nuclear power plants, nuclear testing (such as in French testing in the Pacific and U.S. testing in the southwest), and nuclear waste disposal are being resuscitated as global nuclear power corporations with heavy clout set up shop among vulnerable communities around the world in the wake of rising demand for nuclear energy worldwide. This section makes an attempt at accounting for these sorts of costs of investment in nuclear power.

To support nuclear weapons development and the expansion of nuclear energy that has occurred over the past seventy years, countries have had to mine large amounts of uranium from the earth. After a decade of declining uranium production until 1993, world uranium production has been increasing. In 2011 alone, the world mined 53,493 tons of uranium, and in 2012, this increased to 58,394 tons.[57] The rising demand for uranium has created a worldwide market for uranium mining and production. Like many globalized markets, the largest market shares lie in the global North. Western countries, including France, Canada, Australia, and the United Kingdom, own 49 percent of the market of uranium mine production. Areva and Cameco, the largest French- and Canadian-owned mining corporations, respectively, control nearly 29 percent of the market, but the dramatic explosion of uranium mining that has occurred inside of Kazakhstan since 2004 has meant a steadily increasing share of mining by the state-owned KazAtomProm, whose share at 15 percent of the market has made it one of the leaders in the industry. In the last decade, uranium production in Kazakhstan has nearly quadrupled, making Kazakhstan the largest producer of uranium in the world, although Australia continues to have the largest known deposits. The expansion of uranium production in Kazakhstan has mirrored an expansion of worldwide production brought on by rising demand. This demand is being driven heavily by China's increasing reliance on nuclear power. Currently China is hoping to acquire roughly ten thousand tons of uranium oxide to meet its 2020 goals for nuclear power production (Hecht 2012a, 26). The expansion of the uranium market had also been driven by increased demand in Japan and France, both of which were looking for efficient and cleaner alternatives to coal, as well as by the more global "nuclear renaissance" that emerged from wider concerns about climate change. Rising demand had facilitated a dramatic rise in the spot price of uranium oxide over many years, but that price has declined since reaching an all-time high in 2007.

The history of uranium mining has extensive roots in the colonial pasts of Western nuclear states—imperial ties to uranium-rich parts of Africa and Australia helped Britain's nuclear program; the French have always depended heavily on the uranium reserves of their former African colonies; during apartheid, South Africa's uranium reserves helped keep in place its congenial relations with the West; the Soviet bomb program drew from mines in Uzbekistan and Kyrgyztan (as well as Eastern Europe); Australia, Canada, and the United States mined uranium on Aboriginal, First Nation, and Navajo lands, respectively; and India mined uranium on tribal lands (Hecht 2002; 2003; 2012a; 2012b; Yih et al. 1995).[58] These colonial ties are most evident in the relationship between Western corporations and African countries that possess vast reserves of uranium—Congo, Niger, South Africa, Gabon, Madagascar, and Namibia—documented carefully and brilliantly by Gabrielle Hecht's extensive archival and ethnographic work (Hecht 2012b). In Hecht's nuanced analysis, these colonial relations are "conjugated" through sociotechnical practices whose focus on modernization, development, and technology appears to mark a break or "rupture" from an overtly racist civilizing colonial mission, yet works in and through its categories of alterity and reproduces many of its material effects (Hecht 2002). During the Cold War, when demand for uranium production skyrocketed as countries tried to master nuclear power for weapons and civilian purposes, Africa was the most common source of uranium. At the time, anywhere from 20 to 50 percent of the Western world's uranium came from African countries. In Niger, for instance, the French Bureau de Recherches Geologiques et Minières first discovered uranium in the country in 1957, and the Commissarait a L'Energie Atomqiue (CEA)—now replaced by Areva—immediately started work extracting the precious resource from the country.[59] The colonial relationship between Western countries and African nations in uranium extraction was not restricted to the Cold War; the imbalanced power dynamic that was created allowed Western countries to establish a foothold in the uranium markets of African countries that remains to this day. The heavy economic, political, and military presence of France in its former African colonies in which it has mining interests is particularly noteworthy in this regard (Martin 1989; Hecht 2012b). Although Niger may have gained its independence from France in 1960, the CEA did not leave, and it continued to develop new uranium deposits as they were discovered (Hecht 2012a, 27). Today, Areva still controls the majority of Niger's uranium production. China has begun to establish a foothold in the region, however, and Chinese mining of the Azelik deposit in Niger's Agadez region has commenced (Hecht 2012a, 26).

Demonstrating the stakes involved in the technopolitical establishment of "nuclearity," Hecht points out that, at first, the West's attempt to monopolize the supply of uranium in an effort to limit its access to the Soviet Union in the early years of the Cold War made uranium the only ore subject to legislation that ensured secrecy in the conditions of its production, secrecy that fortified the ore's nuclearity. But when the discovery of multiple uranium sources made such secrecy impossible—leading to the emergence of a uranium market in which the ore had a market value—the mining industry actively resisted attempts to establish the nuclearity of uranium (Hecht 2006; 2012b). However, as Hecht points out, denuclearizing uranium and turning it into a "banal commodity" circulating in a "free market" "validated a political geography in which imperial powers could continue to dominate former colonies after independence" (Hecht 2012b, 35). At the same time, these shifting definitions of nuclear status— reflected also in the IAEA's safeguards lists[60]—affected not just the regulation of working conditions in those places but also workers' and communities' abilities to recognize and articulate the particular occupational hazards of uranium mining. The capacity of workers and workers' groups to seek and receive recognition and redress for the health hazards of uranium mining varied across different countries in Africa, depending on a variety of contextual historical, political, economic, and technological factors, but none achieved the kind of status that Chernobyl victims were able to craft to receive health care, welfare, and other resources (Hecht 2012b, 45).

In other words, although uranium mining has gained substantial profits for Western corporations, its health costs on the communities that possess minable uranium stockpiles has not always been easy to establish. The "radioactive colonialism" of Navajo lands and lives for the U.S. nuclear program has now been somewhat well documented and has received some public attention.[61] Little was admitted by the nuclear industry in the United States about the health effects of radiation exposure during the first few decades of nuclear production, and studies of these effects were conducted in great secrecy. But a standard for acceptable radiation exposure was established in 1971, and the Radiation Exposure Compensation Act—directed toward those who had suffered from the health effects associated with atmospheric nuclear testing and uranium mining—finally became law in 1990. But in parts of Africa, the causality from radon exposure to cancer has been much harder to document, given the focus of public health agencies on infectious diseases and malnutrition, the absence of national registries of cancer rates to provide baseline comparisons, and the general perception of the global health community that cancer is a "first world disease" that does not afflict parts of the world with lower longevity levels (Hecht 2012b, 40–43). Furthermore, the close ties between industry and regulators, that is, the kind of regulatory capture that the previous section documented in the case of the United States and Japan, can be even more severe in poorer countries in Africa, where independent sources of relevant expertise, as well as an adequate infrastructure of instruments and laboratories, may be absent, and the stakes for corrupt leaders reliant on uranium mining for driving an economy are even higher (Hecht 2012b, 320–28). It is in this sense that while radiation may not discriminate, "nuclearity" does discriminate along lines of class, race, and geography, leading to the differential valuation of human bodies involved in nuclear production (Hecht 2012b, 323–24). In effect, then, the value of the human bodies affected through the mundane production of nuclear power has differed quite dramatically at different times and places, and its slower, accumulating effects on the most vulnerable bodies are much harder to establish.[62]

It should not surprise us, then, as we are learning with the nuclear power industry in Japan, that much of the labor involved in the active day-to-day operations of power plants, which involves hazardous exposure to radiation, uses subcontracted, part-time temporary workers without adequate protections—termed "nuclear gypsies" by Kunio Horie (Chandler 2011). Hence, even when the nuclear effects are clear and visible—such as in the higher level of exposure resulting from major nuclear incidents such as the one at Fukushima Daiichi recently—it is the effects on the most vulnerable workers laboring at much more mundane levels that are the least visible. Large numbers of workers adversely affected by the economic downturn and from all across Japan have been traveling to Fukushima, despite the dangers, to work in the cleanup efforts. Most of these are un-skilled temporary migrant laborers contracted or subcontracted at very low wages, with no job security, benefits, or insurance for the effects of radiation exposure. But reporters point out that the Japanese nuclear in-dustry has always relied on such informal contract labor for most of its most demanding and dangerous jobs (Tabuchi 2011a; 2011c; McCurry 2011). Much like day laborers in the United States, workers exposed to the highest levels of toxicity within a short period are just rotated out, con-sidered largely "expendable" by the corporations running nuclear power plants (Dwyer 2012).[63] Drawing from the experience of Japanese work-ers and communities affected by the meltdowns in Fukushima, India is currently witnessing a massive public protest against the creation of the largest power plant ever proposed anywhere in the world in the Western coastal town of Jaitapur, a movement that began with protests against forc-ible land grabs by the government and that has now expanded to include nuclear safety issues (see Bajaj 2011; Dietrich 2011; Bidwai 2011). This land grab is occurring against the objections of local farmers and fishers fearing for their livelihoods and is made possible through the strong collusions between the nuclear industry and officials of the nuclear regulatory board. Similar examples of indigenous communities affected by the expansion of nuclear power are available elsewhere.

When fetishized nuclear weapons are so far removed from the process of production, and national security keeps the closed bidding of corpo-rate contracts in the industry so much under wraps, labor exploitation in the handling of materials and land appropriation for mining, testing, and setting up nuclear power plants can often occur without the protective apparatus of regulatory mechanisms. As the previous chapter argued, the fetishization of nuclear weapons conceals these collusions of corporate and state interests in nuclear power in the exploitation of vulnerable work-ers and communities. Moving beyond the fetishized nuclear weapons them-selves to reveal the conditions of their making lays bare the severe effects of nuclear nonuse.

Conclusion: The Political Economy of Waste

"If 'the hand mill gives you society with the feudal lord; the steam-mill, society with the industrial capitalist,' what are we given by those Satanic mills which are now at work, grinding out the means of human extermination?" was the question posed by Edward Thompson in 1982, echoing Marx in a world of nuclear weapons. Thompson suggested that we needed a new category of analysis—"exterminism"—to understand the internal logic and dynamic of a social system centered on the nuclear arms race that was driving the planet toward ultimate destruction. Although Thompson is quite clear that there would be nothing "accidental" in any future catastrophe, and fully acknowledges that there are human choices, class interests, and the always persistent profit motive that have contributed to this push toward such a bleak outcome, an analysis such as his yields a certain kind of technological determinism (Williams 1982). He provides an account of the inexorable thrust of an autonomous process in which nuclear weapons, which he recognizes are often fetishized as a "Thing," become "political agents" themselves, even as they "annihilate the very moment of 'politics,'" cumulatively militarizing all realms of life and society and leading us toward extermination (Thompson 1982, 3–8). But it is this very prospect of a future extermination that much of the theory and ideology of deterrence held at bay, seducing us into neglecting the more banal forms of exterminations already at play by keeping our focus so resolutely on the unusability of nuclear weapons. The preceding chapter suggested that the uselessness of nuclear weapons has only served to fetishize them as objects of deep desire, pursued by rich and poor countries alike, at least ostensibly for security and status. This chapter suggested how the pursuit of nuclear power has wrought its most damaging effects on the most vulnerable and marginal communities, in rich and poor countries alike.

If nuclear weapons are indeed unusable, then the massive resources invested in producing them—mining, processing, manufacturing, testing, storing, maintaining, and upgrading them—should, quite literally, be considered waste, and this chapter has drawn attention to the opportunity costs of investing in such useless and dangerous weapons. Poorer countries interested in joining the exclusive nuclear club find little improvement in the well-being of most of their populations through investment in nuclear weapons. India, Pakistan, and North Korea may be three of the select nine countries in the world to possess nuclear weapons, but the former two rank 136 and 146, respectively, on the United Nations Development Program's (UNDP) 2013 Human Development Index (HDI), and the latter's socioeconomic plight is a lot worse.[64] Iran is declining in its HDI ranking—currently at 76—even as it keeps alive a nuclear weapons program. One could suggest that the enormous amount of resources that could be productively *used* elsewhere to improve the well-being of large numbers of people is being spent on weapons that are, quite literally, *use-less*. In other words, one could conceptualize these sorts of expenditures as *waste*. Yet conceptualizing these weapons as essential in their very unusability has rendered them *necessary* for national security—in the nationalist imaginary, even if not in actuality. But any security and status enhancement that these weapons may provide hardly redounds to the well-being of the most vulnerable populations of any country in the nuclear club, populations who, needless to say, are already the ones most affected by the mundane costs of uranium production and nuclear testing and the least equipped to deal with any nuclear "accidents" that may occur.[65] These costs are enhanced when weapons costs are coupled with the additional necessary costs of nuclear energy, now considered vital for national development. And then there is, of course, the littering of the world with radioactive waste—waste in the most literal sense—dumped in peripheral communities inhabited by marginal populations who will bear its most vivid tolls for generations to come.

But these seemingly radically opposed ways of viewing the massive costs of nuclear power—as "waste" or as "necessary"—are twinned through the logic of fetishization that obscures the layers of exploitation that undergird its production as well as its function in propping up an unequal, capitalist world order managed through neoliberalism. In other words, nuclear consumption keeps in place a hierarchical nuclear order, within which postcolonial nuclear mimicry consigns poorer states to forever remain disadvantaged as they pour massive resources into wasteful nuclear projects that improve neither their global status nor the abject economic condition of most of their populations, while exposing large numbers of the most vulnerable peoples of the world to serious and long-term dangers. Nuclear weapons are exterminist not just in their use but also in their possession.

Decolonizing the Nuclear World

Can the Subaltern Speak?

MAINSTREAM INTERNATIONAL RELATIONS (IR) THEORY—
particularly in its neorealist and neoliberal incarnations—cannot
capture the "third world security predicament," argues Mohammed Ayoob.
This is what motivates Ayoob to create a version of realism that he calls
"subaltern realism," to capture the different dynamics of domestic variables and external pressures through which third world states express their
foreign policy behaviors. Ayoob is not interested in troubling the notion
of security or rejecting the state-centricity of traditional realism, but he
lambasts IR scholars for their ethnocentric generalizations from the experience of richer and more secure first world states, a neocolonial vantage
position from which they cannot hear how the subaltern speak their very
historically and geographically specific insecurities (Ayoob 1983–84; 1989;
1991; 1995; 1997; 1998; 2002). I find it hard not to be at least somewhat
sympathetic to Ayoob's attempts, against many criticisms over the course
of a long and distinguished career, to mark out a space of third world voice
within an overwhelmingly Eurocentric discipline. But can the third world
as subaltern really speak from this space?

In her widely influential piece titled "Can the Subaltern Speak?," postcolonial feminist theorist Gayatri Spivak raises this very question of the
"subaltern"—that most oppressed of figures, subordinated through structures of both imperialism and nationalism, and for whom many oppositional movements claim to speak (Spivak 2010a). Exemplified in some of
her other work by the severely exploited "tribal" Indian woman—made
abject through the multiple axes of gender, class, caste, and nation—Spivak
asks if and how the subaltern can speak in and through the existing discursive structures available to her (Spivak 1995; 2010a; 2010b). In the end, suggests Spivak, the subaltern cannot speak because her speech is inaudible
or unintelligible to those in power.

I want to take up this question of the space, medium, and audibility of subaltern speech in this concluding chapter by asking what we can learn from this study of the global nuclear order and its production of a certain kind of nuclear desire that may propel the so-called subaltern third world state to speak in the name of its security. Who speaks through nuclearization, and who is rendered inaudible? What can the many kinds of dreams of a nuclear-free world teach us about the differential effects of nuclear power pursuits on different spaces and bodies? How may we think about security if we really tried listening to the subaltern otherwise so illegible to IR theory? In the first part of this chapter, I recapitulate the argument of the book through this problematic of the subaltern, and then I follow that up in the second part with a critique of the subaltern state as Ayoob conceptualizes it. Pulling together the arguments of chapters 1 through 4, the next section largely summarizes my previous discussion of the production of the global nuclear order, the place and role of the desiring subaltern nuclear state within it, and the effects of nuclear pursuits on subaltern bodies and communities. The second section of the chapter interrogates the subaltern state as a vehicle for the subaltern voice. Discussing the profound impact of the "nuclear revolution" on the state-centered logic of security, I argue that the proliferation of nuclear weapons raises serious questions about the third world state's ability to deliver on the well-being of its most vulnerable members. Starting the following section with the well-meaning recent calls for "nuclear zero" as they have emerged from some of the most powerful corners of the global order, I finish this book by reiterating the importance of equality and justice as articulated in some of the most marginalized communities of the world as providing the most worthwhile paths to nuclear peace.

The Subaltern in the Global Nuclear Order

The Receding Goal of Nuclear Zero:
The Productive Failures of the Nuclear Nonproliferation Regime

Nuclear zero—a world without nuclear weapons—is the utopian dream of a new dystopia. The dystopia, captured in popular culture through tales of terrorists seeking the awesome, terrifying powers of the ultimate weapon, has reanimated fears of nuclear nonproliferation. What if al-Qaeda were to acquire a nuclear bomb? What if a rogue state, such as Iran, were willing to transfer nuclear materials, technology, or the bomb itself to Hezbollah?

What level of damage would an undeterrable nuclear terrorist be willing to inflict on a hapless world? It is in this context that concerns about the fraying of the Nuclear Non-Proliferation Treaty (NPT)—that also awesome linchpin of efforts to control the spread of nuclear weapons during the Cold War—have been revived. Quite remarkably, even ardent believers in the magic of nuclear deterrence at one time have now begun to preach universal nuclear disarmament. And so it came as a surprise to many in the nuclear peace movement when fierce cold warriors in the "gang of four"—George Shultz, William J. Perry, Henry Kissinger, and Sam Nunn—remade themselves as nuclear abolitionists, together mounting a public relations campaign to persuade current leaders and policy makers of the wisdom of moving to global nuclear zero.

That nuclear weapons are dangerous is a cliché. Their destructive power appears to escape the limits of epistemology. We already know something about the scale of destruction caused when atomic weapons were dropped on Hiroshima and Nagasaki, although estimates just of deaths still range between one hundred thousand and two hundred thousand. But it is not unusual to describe the scale of destruction that the currently existing stockpile of far more potent thermonuclear weapons could visit as "unthinkable" or "unimaginable." This destructive potential was recognized early. So it wasn't long after the development of the first atomic bombs that efforts began to control the spread of the technology, materials, and knowhow that could cause such immense harm. Out of these efforts emerged the massive, sprawling, complex, layered regime—the nuclear nonproliferation (NNP) regime—whose architecture I described in chapter 1.

The NPT—a near-universal treaty negotiated against many odds—has long had a special and central place within this regime. The NPT exists in close association with a number of other treaties, organizations, agencies, forums, and groups, working not in perfect harmony but in what may be considered an alignment of similar interests. In other words, the NPT is only one, albeit very prominent, node in this vast regime of agreements, associations, and interests that see their collective task as making the world safe from the horrific possible use of nuclear weapons. Instead of focusing solely on the NPT, chapter 1 took on the task of understanding the scope and reach of this larger regime; the massive constellation of actors, institutions, and interests that constitute it; the mechanisms that sustain it; and the criteria by which we may gauge its effectiveness.

To political realists in the field of IR, the fact that such a massive effort of state and nonstate cooperation across so many transnational borders could occur in the realm of security—that sacred ground of statist high politics—should be something of a puzzle. But for political liberals, well-intentioned believers in the possibility of trust and goodwill even under conditions of international anarchy, there is much cause for celebration in this. As the chapter described, the scale, scope, and reach of the NNP regime are truly staggering. The regime includes treaties, institutions, policies, organizations, think tanks, agencies, journals, and newsletters, which are engaged in tracking, monitoring, regulating, and raising public awareness and range from efforts to control and manage possible proliferation through officially sanctioned processes to advocacy efforts that document or suggest the harmful effects of nuclear weapons and nuclear weapons programs. These together form a complex network of scientific and public policy expertise, significant political interests, huge economic stakes, and massive investment of financial, bureaucratic, and voluntary resources, which, although polyvalent in emphases and commitments, are all engaged in the task of making peace in a nuclear world, at its minimum by helping prevent the harms of nuclear possession and use and at its most ambitious by ridding the world of nuclear weapons.

How should we gauge the effectiveness of the NNP regime? If liberal IR gives us a narrative of progressive regime building, then one measure of the success of this regime is to gauge the extent to which its good intentions are materialized. Although we are certainly nowhere near the peak of more than sixty-five thousand nuclear weapons at one time existent in the world, we are also nowhere close to nuclear zero, and there are no indications that we are progressing in that direction despite all the calls to get there.[1] We still have more than seventeen thousand warheads, about forty-three hundred of which are operational, and eighteen hundred of which are on high alert, and there is considerable capacity to deliver them across distances short and long. President Obama's June 2013 speech at Brandenburg calling on Russia to move beyond the limits of the New Strategic Arms Reduction Treaty and negotiate a mutual reduction in strategic nuclear warheads to a stockpile consisting of slightly more than one thousand may generate optimism but will in reality do little to alleviate the massive overkill capacity that nuclear weapons states possess and provides no reason to hope that the U.S. president is seriously willing to disarm, despite his allusions to universal nuclear disarmament every now and then. In that infamous triad of deterrence, arms control—

including nonproliferation—and disarmament, it may be safe to say that while there has been the occasional progress on arms control, too many states still continue to rely on or want to acquire the capacity for nuclear deterrence and that progress on universal disarmament can be considered an abysmal failure. Increasingly, progress on nonproliferation also appears precarious and will undoubtedly remain precarious as nuclear energy and weapons programs spread, increasing fears of horizontal, vertical, and diagonal proliferation and pushing the goal of disarmament, as always, to an indefinite future. Should we be surprised that the "gang of four" tempered their seemingly strong calls for universal disarmament to argue that the United States needed to maintain its deterrent capacity while nuclear weapons still existed?

None of this is to discount the genuinely good efforts and achievements that have emerged from the NNP regime. The fact there has been no wartime use of nuclear weapons since the conclusion of the Second World War; whatever role the imperfect NPT played in stemming the reach and speed of nuclear weapons spread; the various successfully negotiated regional nuclear weapons–free zones that may eventually help carve a pathway toward nuclear zero; the extensive data, information, and knowledge that we have of existing nuclear stockpiles and the environmental and health hazards posed by them thanks to the excellent empirical studies conducted by the *Bulletin of Atomic Scientists* and the International Physicians for the Prevention of Nuclear War are no small achievements. Needless to say, one could multiply these examples of the necessary and important work of tracking, demanding, regulating, and watching out for nuclear dangers that so many organizations and groups do on a regular and consistent basis, and occasionally against great odds. But even as we spend so much effort preventing the spread and use of nuclear weapons, the amount states spend on the pursuit of acquiring, maintaining, and modernizing nuclear weapons that ostensibly they do not intend to use (i.e., possess only for deterrent purposes), and at the expense of other kinds of public spending that could well be used for life-saving and life-enhancing purposes, also remains staggering. Indeed, if we are not sanguine about the possibility of achieving anywhere close to nuclear zero in the near future, as I am not, despite all that we have learned about nuclear dangers from the NNP regime, then how do we judge the effectiveness of a regime that multiplies and replicates itself through a variety of redundant efforts involving a massive commitment of resources?

For theorists of liberal IR, this kind of cooperation against all odds can only be explained through the good intentions of experts and policy makers who can push otherwise egoistic states toward more altruistic identities and interests. Suggesting that these liberal IR understandings of the NNP regime fall short of adequately grasping the complexity and functions of this regime, chapter 1 conducted a Foucauldian-inspired analysis of this regime in terms of its effects rather than its aims. In other words, the chapter asked what the NNP regime *does* that is more than the sum of the various liberal interests in simply ensuring the creation of a peaceful world, or how what may be considered the "failures" of the regime in creating nuclear peace are, indeed, *productive* in other ways. On one hand, I suggested that the NNP regime has been successful in extending the reach and power of the state in multiple ways, and this has only increased with the fears of nuclear terrorism. I return to this point later in this chapter. But relatedly, and more importantly, what the book has highlighted are the ways that the NNP regime has both kept in place and occluded a deeply hierarchical global order whose sustenance plays an instrumental role in the desire for, and proliferation of, nuclear weapons. In particular, I am interested in the ways that the various good efforts of the NNP have served to *depoliticize* the "problem of nuclear nonproliferation"—or how the complex mechanisms of tracking and the elaborate plans for restraining nuclear spread have deflected from the *politics* of the deep and enduring inequalities of a world of security-seeking states in alliance with a whole host of corporate interests. The rest of the book describes the structure and components of this global order and the production of nuclear desire as one product of this ordering.

A Colonial Nuclear Order

Chapter 2 interrogated the kind of global order both revealed and instantiated by the NPT. Although it is certainly not the only component in the NNP regime, the NPT may be considered its central and most important element. A near-universal treaty, it is considered by many to have been quite effective in preventing the horizontal spread of nuclear weapons. I am persuaded by the argument that many states not likely or able to develop nuclear weapons programs for all sorts of reasons signed on to the NPT because it provided them a bargaining and strategic tool that they would not otherwise have possessed. But I also think that it is difficult to dismiss the normative force the treaty has gathered and generated, in effect changing the strategic calculus for states considering nuclear weapons programs. In that sense, the NPT's role in preventing horizontal proliferation cannot be dismissed. Among some of its strongest supporters, its enshrinement of the principle of universal disarmament, weak though it may be, is also an important element of its force and provides at least some pressure on existing nuclear weapons states (NWS) to move toward global disarmament sometime in the future. However, over the last decade and a half, Indian, Pakistani, and North Korean nuclearization; the continuation of the Iranian nuclear program; the discovery of the vast transnational nuclear smuggling network run by A. Q. Khan; the Nuclear Fuel Deal with India; North Korea's continuing development of missile technology and nuclear testing; and the possibility of nuclear terrorism have all raised concerns about the unraveling of the NPT and its consequences for future proliferation. U.S. withdrawal from the Anti-Ballistic Missile Treaty, its active pursuit of missile defense, and its counterproliferation efforts have also generated concerns about the effects of great-power belligerence on nonproliferation efforts more generally. But although there is an occasional suggestion here or there about the dispensability of the NPT, most arms control and disarmament proponents very much argue for fortifying and strengthening the treaty, perhaps even creatively to account for a different configuration of power in the post–Cold War and post–September 11, 2001, world. I believe it is fair to say that there is generally little doubt about the excellent impulses of the NPT, its track record during the Cold War, and the need to preserve it, even if there is anxiety about its future. The purpose of chapter 2 was to interrogate some of the anxieties surrounding its unraveling and the calls to bolster it, but from a very specific vantage point—by examining what *kind of order* is kept in place by the NPT and its associated regime.

Continuing the inquiry from chapter 1, chapter 2 asked the question, What does the NPT *do* beyond its commitment to making the world safe from the terribly destructive power of nuclear weapons? Studying the NPT as a technology of ordering, I argued that the treaty and its institutional apparatus reflect and produce a hierarchical global order in which certain states are forever consigned to the "waiting room of history"— branded as pariahs if they choose to pursue the same nuclear weapons that the "nuclear five," whose possession of nuclear weapons is both recognized and legitimized by the treaty, consider so essential to their security. I made this argument by scrutinizing the debate surrounding William Walker's quite innovative argument that the NPT-centered regime institutional-izes a progressive global "nuclear order" embodying the Enlightenment values of reason and trust. In his important work, Walker celebrates the NPT as a universalist progressive global "Enlightenment project" that has helped avert nuclear catastrophe and can, if pursued sincerely and without hypocrisy, lead to a world without nuclear weapons. Not surpris-ingly, Walker's account of a liberal international order has been heavily critiqued by political realists for its rosy-eyed picture of the world and its unfounded and dangerous optimism. Piercing this idealism by pointing to the hard-nosed reality of the threats that exist out there, these critics find various "unenlightened others"—terrorists and terrorist-like rogue states—whose utter irrationality makes it necessary for those who can wield Enlightenment rationality to retain custody of nuclear weapons.

Chapter 2 undertook a critical postcolonial analysis of this debate, with particular focus on the common presuppositions of the non-Western world undergirding it. Rather than quarreling with Walker's characterization of the NPT as a progressive, utopian Enlightenment project, my interest was in interrogating the exclusionary logics through which *order* is conceptu-alized in conceptions of Enlightenment order more generally, revealing the limits of the geography of Enlightenment rationality. Much like the Enlightenment itself, the political order the NPT both represents and in-stantiates has always incorporated these deep prejudices about Europe's others. These are prejudices that have a long history in Enlightenment thought, and the many anxieties that attend the NPT's possible unravel-ing at least partially reflect a wider anxiety about the unraveling of that order and the resulting inability to manage an unruly (and dangerously armed) third world. Surely, I suggested, if the NPT was seen to provide some measure of stability despite the rapidly expanding and moderniz-ing arsenals of the superpowers during the Cold War—that is, the vertical proliferation the treaty does nothing to restrain—it could only be because of faith in not just the technical capability but also the willingness of the "nuclear five" to exercise effective restraint in the use of nuclear weapons that others simply wouldn't or couldn't. How could anyone, I asked, feel even relatively safe in a world with an NPT that makes so little demand on NWS to eliminate their massive arsenals of sophisticated and wide-ranging weapons, especially given the fact that one of those NWS is the only state in the world to have ever had the stomach to actually make wartime use of those weapons, and even as these NWS (none of which have evidenced clearly pacifist foreign policy behavior in the past) continue to update and expand their arsenals? Why is it that our most profound fears of nuclear danger come to be attached to the belligerent images of the endlessly lampooned late North Korean tyrant Kim Jong-il and the rhetorically provocative former Iranian president Mohammad Ahmedinejad but not to the armed-to-the-teeth and reckless, aggressive foreign policy behavior of a George W. Bush or even (the Nobel Peace Prize–winning, disarmament proponent) Barack Obama? Is that not in itself evidence of deeply and profoundly internalized prejudices about the global distribution of reason and trust?

It is important to note that Walker is certainly attentive to the inequality institutionalized within the NPT, and when he makes an impassioned plea to revive and reform a floundering treaty, he also pleads for NWS to make a sincere commitment to disarmament. But frankly, I find Walker's critics able to account for the *centrality of power* in international relations in a way that most liberal universalist accounts of international order, including Walker's, simply cannot. Walker's realist critics draw attention to this power in the creation and maintenance of international agreements and institutions, and although they make no apologies for the inequalities of a treaty that reflects the shape of an unequal world, their accounts recognize and take at least some stock of that inequality. For realists, the arrangement of the world into great powers and others is not incidental or just unfortunate but simply a fact, a given—it is the reality that must be contended with by all states and actors, and most of Walker's critics wear their prejudices about who can or cannot be trusted with nuclear weapons on their sleeves. It may also bear reminding here that it is arch neorealist Kenneth Waltz who called out the ethnocentrism of those who rely on nuclear deterrence for great-power security but deny its significance for third world states, including questioning the apocalyptic presentations of Iranian nuclearization (Waltz 2012).[2] For Waltz, nuclear weapons possession functions as a potential security equalizer in a world of unequal distribution of capabilities, but generally, inequality is not a *problem* for most realists—or a problem only insofar as it may affect great-power security, balance of power, and stability. Nor are realists particularly concerned about how that inequality is experienced or perceived by those who are on the short end of it. But at least inequality exists as a *structural fact*. It is this fact of inequality that liberal accounts of international relations gloss over too quickly and to which I have tried to draw attention in this book, albeit from a very different perspective than that of political realists. Where, then, as Mohammad Ayoob may be inclined to ask, does that leave the third world as subalterns of that unequal world?

How Can and Does the Subaltern Speak?

Chapter 2 ended with a discussion of the manner in which "nuclear apartheid" comes to be wielded by states pursuing nuclear weapons—India in 1998, charging discrimination by the nuclear club of five; Pakistan more recently, in its opposition to the 2008 U.S.–Indian nuclear fuel deal that allowed India to join the club of discriminators; North Korea and Iran every now and then as they flex their nuclear muscles against nuclear-armed big powers and their allies. It is thus that these countries claim to speak as the subaltern of the nuclear order, those excluded and marginalized by the powerful in a world divided into legitimate and illegitimate possessors of nuclear weapons. It is hard to deny that this is a powerful means for gaining recognition, even if it is to earn approbation and disapproval from many on the global stage. Indian nuclearization, especially since the nuclear fuel deal, has helped position India as an emerging global actor; Pakistan's possession of nuclear weapons, especially given the strategic position of the country in the war on terror, has made it an actor that simply cannot be ignored; Israel's powerful and difficult position in the Middle East has at least something to do with it being the sole possessor of nuclear weapons in the region; North Korea has long been able to extract all manner of concessions and deals on the threat of its nuclear weapons program, and there is every reason to think that this will continue under the regime of the new leader, Kim Jong-un; and Iran's nuclear program keeps it on the global radar as an actor that cannot be taken lightly. Perhaps one might argue that this is the kind of recognition that invites unwanted scrutiny and even imperils security, but for many, the message of the 2003 U.S. invasion of a nonnuclear Iraq was that the possession of nuclear weapons matters, especially for weak states with few other weapons to wield against superpower aggression. So can nuclearization enable the subaltern to speak and be heard? How effective is nuclearization as subaltern speech, and how may we judge its effectiveness? This is the question that is taken up by the following two chapters, beginning with a discussion of how nuclear desire is produced.

I started chapter 3 with a meditation on the contradictory powers of the atom as enshrined in the NPT. As a treaty that not just allows but encourages the exchange of knowledge, technology, and materials related to nuclear energy development, the purpose of the NPT is to prevent weapons proliferation, not nuclear proliferation. It is thus that the treaty establishes an ontological break between nuclear energy programs and nuclear weapons programs that is sometimes hard to determine in practice, recognizing the liberatory potential of the former and obvious dangers of the latter. But also implicit in this institutional recognition of the dangers posed by nuclear weapons is an assumption about the deep *desire* for nuclear weapons among states, a desire that appears to exist despite a strong normative constraint—even a *taboo*—against the use of these weapons. Nuclear energy, in this rendition, is a beneficent force, but that energy turned to weapons, even if the weapons are not likely to be used, is simply abhorrent. My interest was not in examining state motivations for acquiring nuclear weapons—national security, domestic bureaucratic or nationalist interests, normative status and prestige, all of which have been amply and well discussed. Even if states held off from actually acquiring nuclear weapons for reasons of cost or morality, or even security, I was curious about examining what makes nuclear weapons so terrifyingly desirable— for states that want to keep weapons far in excess of what is needed for deterrence, for states that want to acquire more and better kinds of them, for states that want to have the capacity to possess them even if they stop short of producing them, for states that take a moral absolutist stand against the possession of such weapons, and for all who want to abolish nuclear weapons altogether. What presuppositions are contained in the wide use of the terms *nuclear restraint* and *nuclear abstinence* to explain the decisions of non–nuclear weapons states? What kind of desire underlies the decision to acquire or *resist* acquiring nuclear weapons? In the absence of such a desire, one simply does not need the NPT, and its unraveling should not generate that much anxiety. The question that chapter 3 asked is how have supposedly tabooed and unusable nuclear weapons emerged as fetishized objects of state desire, especially in a postcolonial context. In other words, before examining how effective nuclear weapons are as a medium of subaltern speech, I think it is necessary to theorize the *allure* of nuclear weapons as a medium.

Chapter 3 theorized the allure underlying the potential demand for nuclear weapons through a conceptualization of nuclear weapons as "fetish commodities." In the chapter, I undertook an analysis of how commodities acquire social value, critically examining two different but connected logics of exchange through which nuclear weapons have emerged as particular kinds of fetish commodities—one logic simultaneously evacuating danger while endowing these objects with magical powers, and the other enhancing status through the acquisition of the object. As the "unimaginably" destructive power of nuclear weapons is wielded in the strategic logic of deterrence, it is their "unusability" that makes them so desirable, rendering them a seemingly perfect and costless instrument of ensuring absolute security. Or even when policy makers question the ability of nuclear weapons to provide the security they seek, the weapons can confront them as powerful in ways that make them seem irresistible (to acquire or to resist acquiring). At the same time, as a very particular class of fetish commodities—"luxury goods"—nuclear weapons become markers of status and rank, thus enhancing their exchange value even further. Here the NPT's demarcation of a world of nuclear haves and nuclear have-nots only raises the exchange value of nuclear weapons. In the highly regulated market of luxury goods, should we be surprised if nuclear weapons as fetish commodities that confer such awesome powers can, indeed, appear to provide an effective medium for subaltern speech?

But what kind of medium is it, and how well does it represent the interests of the subaltern? I take up this question in chapter 4, where I attempt to *politicize* the depoliticization that occurs when nuclear weapons as fetish objects serve as "solutions" to the problem of security and enmity, while concealing a remarkable set of institutions, interests, and practices that sustain this problem-solving exercise and that themselves profit from that exercise. Whereas chapter 3 attempted to politicize nuclear desire by showing how the fetishization of nuclear weapons does a certain kind of cultural work in producing nuclear desire, in chapter 4, I politicize nuclear fetishization by revealing how it sustains a political economy of nuclear weapons production that has enormous and global effects, whether or not nuclear weapons are used. These effects far exceed the geographical limits of the nuclear club of weapons possessors. It is with this in mind that I turn in this chapter from the demand side to the supply side of nuclear weapons, that is, to the material forces that make it possible to pursue and acquire these most desirable weapons and profit from that acquisition. In other words, chapter 4 examines the larger political economy through which nuclear weapons emerge as fetishized weapons and which often

gets short shrift in the prominence given to the institutional form of treaties like the NPT as mechanisms for preventing weapons proliferation.

I begin this discussion of political economy with a consideration of how
we understand "nuclear accidents." When not worried about nuclear use
by irresponsible others, much of our fear of nuclear weapons possession
and proliferation comes to reside in the real possibility of such accidents.
But this trope of nuclear accidents can sometimes be a distraction, I suggested, blinding us to the very predictable and sometimes quite mundane
dangers of nuclear weapons. When we look at the supply side of nuclear
weapons and begin accounting for the entire production cycle of nuclear
weapons from uranium mining to nuclear waste disposal, the dangers of
nuclear weapons possession and proliferation abound and reveal a whole
host of hierarchies and inequalities otherwise less visible. Chapter 4 revealed that the ontological distinction between nuclear energy programs
and nuclear weapons programs that the NPT makes is much harder to
sustain when one begins to account for these larger costs of nuclear weapons programs. After all, a treaty that forbids nuclear weapons proliferation
but encourages nuclear energy proliferation, in a world in which nuclear
power is a driver of development, a symbol of modernity, and a rectifier
of economic disparities as well as environmental challenges, must always
be susceptible to weakening, as it generates more and more potentially
weaponizable nuclear materials and undisposed waste worldwide. Thus
accounting for the production of nuclear weapons requires some level of
sensitivity to the costs of nuclear power more generally. Sketching out and
analyzing the resource and humans costs invested in the nuclear production process brings attention back to the continuities between nuclear
weapons and nuclear energy that the NPT's focus on fetishized weapons
tries to avoid.

The purpose of chapter 4 is to create a framework for analyzing the
costs of nuclear weapons, arguing that these costs are much larger than
simply the proportion of defense budgets spent on nuclear weapons programs and require a discussion of both nuclear weapons and energy pursuits. Neither the framework nor the analysis is exhaustive by any means;
the purpose instead is to provide some sense of the multifaceted and
complex kinds of costs already incurred in sustaining nuclear projects
globally. In addition to an examination of the global political economy of
nuclear weapons production, I chose to take a closer look at three very
different kinds of nuclear states—the United States, with its long and

well-established massive nuclear weapons program; India, a nonsignatory to the NPT, with its more recent active nuclear weapons program; and Japan, with its enormous investment in nuclear energy now imperiled by the Fukushima Daiichi disaster and yet remaining a state able to break out into nuclear weapons relatively quickly. In an attempt to create an expansive rubric of nuclear costs, the analysis relied on three related kinds of costs—first, examining the actual investments in nuclear weapons development, production, and maintenance, but more important, contrasting those with the opportunity costs of such investment; second, examining the extent to which the presence of global and national corporate interests in the nuclear industry compromises various regulatory mechanisms; finally, examining the working conditions in the nuclear power industry, including uranium mining, siting of nuclear power plants, nuclear weapons testing, and waste disposal efforts. What the analyses in these three categories reveal is that the pursuit of nuclear weapons, weapons that are meant to be unusable, comes at tremendous costs to the well-being of populations whose lives could have been improved if those public funds had been diverted toward other kinds of social spending; that the enormous corporate interests invested in the production of nuclear power creates a highly compromised neoliberal state heavily invested in delivering security, but with a weakened regulatory apparatus that has costly environmental and safety effects disproportionately borne by the most vulnerable peoples of the world; and that this production comes with significant labor exploitation and human vulnerability, often in places peripheral to the centers of nuclear power production.

One must conclude, then, that if nuclear weapons are a medium of subaltern speech, it is not a medium that really serves the subaltern of the world. All NWS developed their nuclear programs by displacing, testing on, and generally mistreating indigenous peoples within their territories or geographically distant colonized and poor peoples. For countries such as India, Pakistan, North Korea, and Iran, nuclear weapons have done little to alleviate the poverty of large numbers of the population and have only made their most vulnerable members without the means of adequate civil defense even more vulnerable. Indeed, nuclearization as subaltern speech is a ruse, the kind of colonial mimicry that only leaves the real subalterns of the world even more speechless. Any security and status enhancement that these weapons may provide hardly redounds to the well-being of the most deprived populations of any country that joins the nuclear club, populations who are already the ones most affected by the mundane costs of uranium production and nuclear testing and least equipped to deal with any nuclear "accidents" that may occur. In other words, nuclear production keeps in place a hierarchical nuclear order within which postcolonial nuclear mimicry—disguised as subaltern speech—consigns poorer states to forever remain disadvantaged as they pour massive resources into wasteful nuclear projects that improve neither their global status nor the abject economic conditions of most of their populations, while exposing large numbers of the most vulnerable peoples of the world to serious and long-term dangers. It is thus that the fetishization of nuclear weapons helps sustain a deeply unequal and violent world through the generation of unachievable ambitions for status and power, and "the neoliberal security state" fortifies itself and contributes toward the fortification of global hierarchies.

Thinking beyond the Subaltern State

Realists remind us that despite its attempt to transcend the state system, the NPT, like all international treaties, remains quite resolutely a state-centered treaty—created through hard bargaining among self-interested states, sustained through the voluntary acquiescence of states (after all, the treaty allows a state to withdraw only with a three-month notification), and ultimately ineffective in ensuring compliance because of the lack of an enforcement mechanism exceeding the will of individual states to undertake punitive measures. Despite whatever normative taboos treaties help institutionalize, that states make and break treaties does bear reminding. But what is more important, this book has argued, is the *kind* of state system any particular treaty and/or regime creates and helps reproduce. So far I have argued that this is a profoundly and fundamentally hierarchical state system, structured on inequalities between states and driven by powerful capitalist interests that both exceed and manage those states. The desire for nuclear weapons is deeply entrenched within those inequalities, and their elimination will need to take account of that.

In Mohammed Ayoob's writings, the state is the most important vehicle available to the third world for redressing international inequalities. *Subaltern state* is the term he uses to designate the weaker and powerless states within the economic and political hierarchies of international relations. In this final part of the book, I would like to examine a little more

carefully this focus on the subaltern state within Ayoob's writings, especially as it functions in a nuclear world. After briefly stating Ayoob's position on the role of the state within international relations, I look at the
challenge nuclear weapons pose to a state-centric logic of security and
how that challenge is evacuated by a nuclear state that produces docile
subjects willing to submit to the dictates of nuclear power. I then undertake a sympathetic critique of Ayoob's analysis of the important role the
subaltern state plays within a profoundly asymmetrical international system. I applaud Ayoob's understanding of the colonialist underpinnings
of any global order that attempts to transcend the state system without
remedying its underlying inequalities but argue that he stops short of interrogating the colonialist basis of the state system itself. I believe that his
arguments for inclusion rather than insurrection stop short of realizing the
potential of subaltern speech to overhaul the status quo. In the end, I suggest that if we are looking for the path to nuclear zero in a way that can create both peace and justice, we should look at all the ways that the subaltern
affected by nuclearization are already speaking, even though the vehicle of
the state makes us deaf to them.

From the "State in a Nuclear World" to the "Nuclear State"

Mohammed Ayoob's "subaltern realism" is resolutely state centered. Suspicious of attempts to expand and dilute the concept of security in the
critical security scholarship, Ayoob reiterates the importance of the political authority and legitimacy of the state as a provider of security in the
Hobbesian anarchy of international relations (Ayoob 1995; 1997; 2002).
What IR theorists miss, according to Ayoob, are the enormous internal
and quite different external challenges the postcolonial third world state
faces as a late entrant to an international context composed of more
mature and fuller-formed states (Ayoob 1983–84; 1989; 1995). But that
states—when fully formed and cohesive, and with sovereignty internally
and externally authorized and legitimated—can and should be the agents
of security is not in question for him. In a world where states are the primary security providers, third world states seeking the second-strike capabilities of nuclear weapons as a means to national security—as a Waltzian
framework on stability might suggest—appears to make sense. If nuclear
deterrence ensures great-power security, subaltern realism might suggest
that nuclearization is one avenue for also ensuring third world security.

Indeed, Ayoob has suggested that Iranian nuclearization makes strategic sense from the Iranian perspective and that the world needs to learn to live with a nuclear-capable Iran pursuing legitimate security concerns given its encirclement by nuclear weapons states (Ayoob 2011). However, nuclear weapons raise a larger question about the *capacity of the state* to deliver security, even in a realist world. Can nuclear technology affect the very *form of the state* as a viable security-providing unit? Where does that leave the subaltern state in the provision of security?

In his intellectual history of the effects of nuclear weapons development on American realist thought during the Cold War, Campbell Craig provides an account of the "politically eradicative" effects of nuclear weapons as conceptualized in the works of classical realists such as Reinhold Niebuhr and Hans Morgenthau, both of whom came to regard the continuation of international anarchy as unsustainable in the face of profound nuclear fear. Initially resistant to the possibility or desirability of a "world state," these early realists eventually came to a more acute understanding of the ways that security is so fundamentally reconfigured in the context of the explosive capacities of thermonuclear weapons and the range and speed of intercontinental ballistic missiles that states can no longer release society from insecurity in any viable fashion (Craig 2003).[3] Similarly, Daniel Deudney has argued that the *real state*—that is, the state as a mode of protection or security-providing unit as realists conceptualize it—has become functionally irrelevant in a nuclear world. Now the "third world security predicament," in Ayoob's analysis, arises precisely because such states have not formed themselves into effective "real states" of the sort to which Deudney refers—that is, apparatuses capable of ensuring "the provision of security through the maintenance of a monopoly of violence capability in a particular territory" (Deudney 1993, 24–25). They remain "weak states" or "quasi states" that, in terms of the classification Robert Jackson has popularized, have not transformed their juridical sovereignty into effective sovereignty (Ayoob 1983–84; 1995; 1997; 2002; Jackson 1990). Their primary security threats emerge from the severe domestic challenges encountered by these newer states aspiring to effectively monopolize legitimate violence within a territory beset by various sectarian divisions (Ayoob 1984; 1989). But, argues Deudney, nuclear states are simply *not* able to monopolize violence or ensure security; in the "planetary geopolitic" of a nuclear world, the possibility of annihilation makes the very question of territorial security moot. Many states forsake nuclear weapons, he suggests, precisely because they understand its perils for their own integrity *as states* (Deudney 1993; 1995). Thus, even if nuclear weapons have not made the state obsolete quite yet, they have severely curtailed its ability to function as a security-providing institution. How can subaltern realism withstand the challenge that nuclear weapons pose to the capacities of the "real state"? But before we get to that question, we must ask how existing "real states" have dealt with this challenge of nuclear weapons.

Even as the transformative effects of the "thermonuclear revolution" were recognized by some of the early realists, Bernard Brodie's articulation of deterrence appeared to make nuclear weapons "manageable," as I already discussed in an earlier chapter, providing a mechanism for states to contain a possibly radical threat to their own existence. Rather than dealing with its internal contradictions, "nuclear reason" ended up being reworked and reapplied through nuclear strategy as instruments of state security (Burke 2009). This, as we know, eventually yielded to the kind of nuclear optimism that we see in the work of Kenneth Waltz's neorealism.[4] Both Craig and Deudney rightly criticize Waltz's idealized state of perfect rationality, abstracted from the human fallibility that classical realists assumed (Craig 2003; Deudney 1993). But Deudney also differentiates between the overly optimistic "automatic deterrence statism" of Waltz and the "institutional deterrence statism" of those who argue that effective nuclear deterrence requires certain institutional and infrastructural prerequisites (Deudney 2007). While the former Waltzian view of the inherently stabilizing dynamics of deterrence has received a lot of critical attention, it is the latter form of managed deterrence that has come to be the dominant perspective among nuclear strategists and many IR theorists, albeit with some resistance. Deterrence, in this version, functions, but only insofar as states have found methods to restrain a hasty or accidental use of such weapons. Danger, then, becomes associated with rampant proliferation unaccompanied by adequate institutional support rather than with state possession of nuclear weapons per se. Both varieties of deterrence statism, thus, continue to take the state as given and help restore faith in its ability to guarantee security, even in a nuclear world. Presumably, even a third world state—especially an "effective" one in Ayoob's terms—that can demonstrate the establishment of the necessary institutional prerequisites can exercise nuclear deterrence.[5] Ayoob himself has suggested that the dangers of nuclear proliferation in the third world do not arise from the irrationality of particular leaders, but it is the "primitive" nature of the institutional infrastructures and procedures of immature states that is unable to restrain leader idiosyncrasies (Ayoob 1995, 154).

What is important here is that none of these approaches takes adequate stock of the potentially transformative effects of the profound existential dangers of nuclear weaponry on the very form of the state. Deterrence statism—in both forms—helps reproduce the logic of the state as the guarantor of security, appearing to tame the dangers posed by nuclear weapons. The premise underlying mutually assured destruction, after all, rested on making strategic use of the profound vulnerability revealed by nuclear weapons technology.[6] The fetishism of nuclear weapons discussed in chapter 3 only adds to the further domestication of these incredible dangers posed by nuclear weapons, making them objects of deep state desire. The threat to the state from potentially undeterrable nonstate actors, that is, terrorists, and the rise of nonstate networks of nuclear exchange, such as the A. Q. Khan network, have renewed calls to enhance statist measures of control and increase interstate cooperation and led to measures such as the Proliferation Security Measure and UNSC Resolution 1540, which attempt to bolster state power (Auerswald 2006–7; Curtis 2006; Van Evera 2006), as discussed in chapter 1.[7] Thus, despite these early attempts to think creatively about the impact of nuclear weapons on the forms, functions, and future of the state, the pursuit of state deterrence and state-led measures to control nonstate threats have served to reinforce the state's claims of its capacity to deliver security as well as enhance its global status via the pursuit of nuclear weapons. Despite its deep collusion with global capitalism and resulting compromised ability to ensure internal safety and security, as chapter 4 discussed, deterrence allows the nuclear state to speak as an effective provider of security.

One must, then, question *any* state that speaks in the name of security to pursue nuclear weapons, distracting us through its ideology of the dangers that vastly exceed its capacity to contain. If the claim to speak as the most effective provider of security bolsters the state's own power, this is further magnified with the possession of nuclear weapons. Scholars have examined how the imperatives of national security trump other human desires and needs in the production of a "national security state" that operates as the paternalistic protector of a docile citizenry (Campbell 1992; Weldes et al. 1999; Young 2003). The massive dangers associated with nuclear weapons do not just help reinforce the Weberian state's monopoly over the means of legitimate violence but also exacerbate the antidemocratic thrusts of the security state (Johansen 1992; Abraham 2009b). The catastrophic possibilities inherent in deploying "bomb power" provide a pretext to suspend constitutional rights and enhance executive powers, thus effectively normalizing a perpetual state of war (Wills 2010). The level of technical and strategic complexity of nuclear weapons programs appears to require some form of "nuclear guardianship" and alienates public participation, the secrecy and opacity surrounding nuclear programs keeping such guardians unaccountable and in effect immunizing the national security state from scrutiny (Dahl 1985; Abraham 1996; Taylor 2007; Taylor et al. 2007; Taylor and Hendry 2008; Chatterjee 1998). As I already alluded to in the previous chapter, many of these concerns about the authoritarian proclivities of the nuclear state have also been documented with respect to nuclear energy programs, especially as problems related to the disposal, storage, and dispersal of fissionable materials have been magnified with fears of nuclear terrorism. Despite the challenge nuclear weapons pose to the form of the state, the state has found in nuclear power ways to strengthen itself, even at the expense of imperiling the security of those it claims to protect. By wielding this most lethal power in the name of security, it asks citizens to consent to its unaccountable authority, deflecting from the dangers that nuclear pursuits pose to those the state can no longer protect. If subaltern realism looks to states for redemption from insecurity in a nuclear world, does it evacuate even more the radical possibilities of envisioning a new global politics toward which classical realists had begun to gesture?

The Subaltern State against a Nuclear World State

Recognizing the paradox that the "thermonuclear revolution" presents to the realist state's willingness to threaten and use force when necessary has possibly radical implications for the organization of international politics. Both Niebuhr and Morgenthau—albeit the former more tentatively than the latter—gestured toward the possibility of a world state, although neither thinker outlined the shape of it or indicated the path toward it (Craig 2003; Morgenthau 1964). Deudney laments the disappearance of these and other realist "nuclear one worldists" from the field of security studies—thinkers who at one time seriously contended with the radical implications of the nuclear revolution, some of whom even debated actively about the possibilities and contours of such a world state (Deudney 1995; 2007). Despite believing that the paralysis of the state as a war-

making body makes it ripe for abolition, Deudney himself is neither optimistic nor enthusiastic about the emergence of an "omni-state" that mo-
nopolizes nuclear capability, but he does see an alternative system slowly
replacing the state system as the organizing principle of international
relations. A form of global federal republican governance–"negarchical
Republicanism"—this would be a system built around constraining and
containing state violence through systems of institutionalized checks and
balances, where nuclear capability is effectively bound and paralyzed by
separating it from state control. Deudney sees the NNP regime as a weak
version of this kind of global governance structure but fleshes out the contours of a fuller version of a possible future "world nuclear government"
in his later work (Deudney 1993; 2007).[8] Without abolishing states altogether, this form of security union provides a mechanism for transcending
the limitations of states as sole authorizers of nuclear warring.

Ayoob, however, is very suspicious of any attempts to transcend a state-
centered world in which statehood provides at least some kind of vehicle
for the expression of third world aspirations and the protection of third
world interests. It is true that most of Ayoob's analysis is focused on making the case that possessing real and effective statehood by third world
states matters *in a world in which states are the primary players.* He berates
IR scholars for the disproportionate attention paid to nuclear weapons,
bipolarity, and Cold War nuclear deterrence and the almost complete neglect of the security concerns of the vast majority of the world. He reminds
these scholars that despite the moral questions raised by nuclear weapons,
security for great powers in the thermonuclear age—conceptualized as
"system security"—directly contributed to third world insecurity (Ayoob
1991, 257–58, 264–65, 272–73; 2002, 35–36). The hotness of the Cold War
for many people around the world in states that served as proxies for superpower rivalry might help make sense of the paranoia of a state like Iran,
an object of Cold War interventions and currently surrounded by the
presence of U.S. troops and weapons in its neighboring states. If states are
the only actors who can speak in this highly unequal world, then having a
"real state" appears vital, not just for domestic order and security, but also
to resist domination by great powers (Ayoob 1997).

But Ayoob is also fully aware that transcending the state system would
no more work in favor of third world interests than the current system has
and, in fact, advocates against "the supersession of the state by suprastate
or substate structures or entities for either moral or practical reasons"

(Ayoob 1997, 139–40). Although the bulk of his criticism of the neglect of third world security concerns is directed at political realists, he harbors deep suspicions of liberal globalist conceptions of world order, especially ones that ask third world states to join a global community on the basis of a shared mutuality. Calling out the ethnocentrism of a universalist liberal IR, Ayoob argues that neoliberal institutionalists operate with a false assumption of mutuality, interdependence, and absolute gains, ignoring the military and economic dependence of third world states on the first world (Ayoob 2002, 35–36, 38). He judges proposals for global governance designed in the West as a red herring, sharing the same "neocolonialist biases" that realism has suffered (Ayoob 1997, 140), and fears that any global order conceptualized on the basis of shared mutuality invites new forms of ("humanitarian") interventions in the name of a collective good.

In conceptualizing his version of one-worldism, Deudney acknowledges the fears of hierarchy and tyranny that calls for a world government evoke, and his federal–republican world nuclear government of checks and balances is an attempt to prevent such pitfalls (Deudney 2007, 262). In a wonderfully evocative metaphor, Deudney suggests that the "billiard balls" of realism are transformed into "eggs" in a nuclear world, thus recognizing their vulnerability to explode on contact. The negarchical republicanism of nuclear governance, then, is akin to enclosing these eggs in a carton, the restraints of the protective layers preventing any hasty or accidental explosions (Deudney 1993; 1995). But the metaphor of the carton brings to mind the image of equally sized eggs nesting within layers of equal restraints. One can miss here that some of these eggs are much larger than others, the shells on some thicker than others (as Ayoob would suggest), and the restraints on some stronger than on others. In other words, the protective layers of the metaphorical egg carton do not impose the same set of nuclear restraints nor distribute nuclear vulnerabilities equally. Ayoob himself sees great-power attempts to institutionalize international controls through the NPT to be a direct product of their own security interests because nuclear proliferation threatens system security in a way that previous forms of Cold War arms transfers, so common during the Cold War, did not (Ayoob 1991, 277–78; 1995, 105–6). Here Ayoob begins to hint at the transformative effects of nuclear weapons but elsewhere suggests that nuclear weapons are only a "second-order change," a continuation of the various revolutions in military affairs that may well have prevented superpower confrontation but has failed to end competition, war, and conflict in the wider world (Ayoob 2002, 33–34). What Ayoob understands, I believe, is that the statist resolution of the profound systemic dilemma posed by nuclear weapons has only secured the dominance of the great powers, allowing them to buy their security through a nonproliferation regime that keeps other states insecure. In other words, Ayoob's critique of the neocolonial domination of international relations helps him recognize that the shape of any future carton would reflect the shape of already existing inequalities between states. The hierarchy and tyranny that calls for a world government evoke among the powerful states of the world are already a reality for most of the poorer third world states. In that sense, it is worth pointing out that *the international anarchy that nuclear weapons appeared to make unsustainable was always structured through substantive inequality*, and treaties like the NPT only froze that inequality. For those living on the margins of nuclear pursuits, nuclear weapons posed no qualitative shift in their lived forms of daily insecurities. Yielding to any radical potential in the conception of a "world state" that the thermonuclear revolution suggested requires attending to this inequality. The question is, is the subaltern state the best vehicle for doing so?

Moving beyond the Subaltern State

How should third world states deal with the inequality that faces them in the world in which they emerged as the sovereign equals of other, more powerful states? Here Ayoob describes what he calls the "schizophrenia" of the third world in navigating the collective aspiration for global structural and redistributive changes, that is, "considerations of justice," and the individual imperative for self-preservation within a stable order, that is, "considerations of order" (Ayoob 1989, 70). Forums like the United Nations provide third world states with disproportionate levels of collective visibility and audibility to push for changes in global economic and political systems, yet they are pulled by the pursuit of self-help policies designed to ensure their own preservation as states within a state system in which they wield very little actual power (Ayoob 1989, 70). Given the highly insecure situation in which such states find themselves, this tension, argues Ayoob, is ultimately resolved in favor of narrow survivalist self-interests rather than abstract considerations of justice and the collective good (Ayoob 1989, 70). Ultimately and unfortunately, the structural imperatives of international relations to survive or perish make third world states "collaborators" who end up helping preserve an unequal and unjust international system within which they remain disadvantaged (Ayoob 1989, 70).[9]

Ayoob's delineation of the paradoxical position in which third world states find themselves within a hierarchical international order may be compelling, but his insistence on the state as the vehicle for third world security remains puzzling. Even though he fully understands how little any particular third world state can do to mitigate the wider structural conditions it faces in the world, there is no interrogation of the limits of the form of the state as a vehicle for structural change[10] and, furthermore, the implications of this failure on the third world state's capacity to actually provide security and well-being. The modern Westphalian state is, after all, one particular and contingent resolution of the question of political order, with its own complex history and economy (Ruggie 1986; Spruyt 1994; Walker 1993; Nandy 2003). This is a resolution that operates by deferring the problem of difference to the outside, fashioning and consolidating an internal uniformity by displacing fears and anxieties to an outside threat to be placated, obliterated, or assimilated (Inayatullah and Blaney 2004; Beier 2009). The defense of the state—in the name of security—is the primary mechanism for managing confrontation with others (internal and external). These state borders are only hardened when their actual porosity and the fact of shared vulnerability are so obvious, such as in a nuclear world. When third world states succumb to that logic, consolidating their internal hierarchies in the process of becoming effective "real" states, they submit to a "systemic stability" within which they will always remain marginal, perhaps even more so as newly threatening nuclear states.

Ayoob recognizes that state consolidation requires violence against recalcitrant groups and individuals and draws this lesson from the history of European state making (Ayoob 1995, 85). But European state formation, in his account, occurs autochthonously and then simply diffuses to the rest of the world. In this respect, Ayoob subscribes to what Grovogui has called "the Westphalian common-sense" of the discipline of IR (Grovogui 2002), which is part of what Blaut (1993) has called "the colonizer's model of the world." In contrast, postcolonial theorists have argued that similar to the other institutions of modernity, the internal consolidation of the European state system was coeval with colonial violence. Much as the development of capitalism was coincidental with and dependent on colonial conquest and trade, so the peace of Westphalia went hand in hand with the subjugation of the Americas, the rise of the transatlantic slave trade, the expansion of the British and Dutch East India Companies, and the violent expansion of European power more generally (Seth 2013a; Jones 2013). The subjugation and exploitation of colonized societies provided the resources that made effective state formation in the metropole possible, the consolidation of unitary state authority in Europe was based on lessons drawn from experiments with sovereignty in the colonies, and violent differentiation from colonial subjects helped suture and deflect from internal European differences and dissensions (Blaut 1993; Sen 2002; Inayatullah and Blaney 2004; Hansen and Stepputat 2005; Hindess 2005; Jones 2006a; Biswas and Nair 2010). For someone so attuned to the colonial continuities in the enduring inequalities of international relations theory and practice, and so insistent on restoring historicity and geographical specificity to the study of IR theory, it is curious that there is so little examination in Ayoob's writings of the colonialist history and underpinnings of the state system itself or a critique of the statist resolution of the question of order.

The dilemma, as Ayoob presents it, is both collective and historical—marginalization of third world states born into a post-Westphalian world forged in Europe, but the resolution he offers—more and enhanced statism—is both privatized and presentist. Individuated as states within a state system, third world states can only become better states, and he suggests that such states should draw historical lessons by looking back to an earlier stage of state making in Europe—the late medieval and early modern period, specifically (Ayoob 2002, 39, 42). Ayoob recognizes that the current ethnic and other communal divisions in the third world may have been caused by colonialism (Ayoob 1984, 1989), but the process of European state consolidation in his account is not co-constitutive with the pillage, plunder, and disordering of the colonies. The resolution of these sectarian divisions requires taking them as given, as *current* and *internal* problems without history, as problems that invite mimicry of the very form whose consolidation may have originated them. But if what appear as "deformed" or "incomplete" forms of postcolonial state-ness have been integral to the formation of the Westphalian state system, and their lack of cohesion and inability to secure a monopoly over the means of violence a result of the continuing culture and forms of (neo)colonial rule, then the "failure" of the third world to become "real" or "effective" states cannot be remedied simply by an emulation of the European state (Hansen and Stepputat 2005; Mbembe 2000; 2001). The birth of third world states into the unequal international system that Ayoob identifies is a result of the imperial process through which the Westphalian state system became global

(Hobson 2013). Both the problems—for instance, the challenges of aligning the nation(s) and state or the multiple and competing local relations of authority and loyalty not fully contained by the apparatus of the state—and their attempted resolution—for instance through spectacular displays of state power or the mimetic desire for modernity—are a product of that same process (Nandy 2003; Hansen and Stepputat 2005). Nuclearization may be one attempt to compensate for the lingering effects of this "derivative" character of the postcolonial state,[11] but it is not one that can rectify the global disparity of power and insecurity to which it is a response.

Thus, when Ayoob asks Eurocentric IR theorists to recognize the security problematic of the third world as the "growing pains of adolescence rather than the schizophrenia of the demented" (Ayoob 1989, 76–77), he replaces the narrative of third world madness with a narrative of childlike innocence, substituting one set of prejudices by another, and one, moreover, that appears, at least on the surface, less threatening to the West.[12] The assimilationist language of (nuclear) statism, even if it is to make a case for granting a standard of recognition to the third world against the presumption of its inherent savagery, as Ayoob aims to do, consigns the third world to a form of mimicry that both reproduces the conditions of its own subordination while dehistoricizing and depoliticizing those conditions (Ferguson 2006). The linear "catchup" narrative of Ayoob's subaltern realism only ends up reproducing a neocolonialist IR, despite his own strong critique of neocolonialism in IR. Discovering the statist language of the powerful, perhaps the subaltern state can speak, but does it speak for the subaltern?

From Inclusion to Insurrection: Listening to the Subaltern

It bears reminding here that Ayoob is well aware of the Gramscian concept of the subaltern as used in the work of postcolonial historians, but he quite self-consciously uses the term to designate states on the grounds that until we have progressed from an "international society" to a "world society," the only way to represent "the plight of the subaltern classes, groups, and individuals within Third World states" is via the state (Ayoob 2002, 46–47).[13] It is this very question of "representation"—in both senses of "speaking for" (*Vertretung*) in the form of political proxy and "re-presenting" (*Darstellung*) in the form of staging or signification—that Spivak takes up and critiques in her essay, pointing to the ways that both moves establish the authority of paternalistic heroes or agents of power, while the subaltern effectively stays mute (Spivak 2010a). The nuclear state may speak in the name of the subaltern, but does it represent the subaltern most affected by, and most vulnerable to, the nuclear pursuits discussed in chapter 4? Where else can we look for effective forms of challenge to the global nuclear order described in this book?

It is not unusual for books on nuclear politics to end with blueprints—detailed step-by-step proposals—to get us to the utopia of a nuclear-free world. Most of these look to the state to deliver us to that world, as do the bulk of efforts contained within the NNP that I described in chapter 1. But this book is much more about institutionalized forms of global inequality than how to pursue nuclear security or nuclear disarmament. Indeed, I have argued that if inequality or hierarchy were at the center of our analysis, we would see that nuclear weapons and energy programs are always already harmful to some and enormously beneficial to others. If we were to learn to think of the "costs" of nuclear weapons in the more expansive sense suggested in chapter 4, we would see that the costliness of nukes is more apparent in the peripheries of nuclear production than in the centers of nuclear decision making. So instead of looking to the pursuers of nuclear power, or for that matter, the consumers of more security and cheap electricity, perhaps we need to look to those exploited, displaced, tested on, and in general the most vulnerable to nuclear use and accidents for a path toward nuclear zero. Or instead of focusing one's energies on strengthening treaties such as the NPT or even bemoaning the end of the mass antinuclear peace movements in the West, perhaps we could turn our attention to facilitating and resuscitating the many grassroots anti-imperialist movements in many corners of the world (Vanaik 2009). What can we learn about "security" and the harms of nuclear possession and proliferation if we really tried listening to the subaltern?

Critical of what he sees as "fashionable" attempts at indiscriminate expansion of the concept of security to concerns of environmentalism, human rights, and emancipation, Ayoob argues for holding on to a more conventional definition of state security, especially for third world states that can ill-afford these luxuries that more stable and affluent societies can enjoy (Ayoob 1997, 125–28; 2002, 40). However, proposals for deepening or expanding the concept of security argue against subscribing to an abstract notion of security, making the case for restoring the experiential basis of security in people's everyday lived practices (Tuchman 1989;

Booth 1991; Tickner 1993; Jones 1999). Such accounts claim that global climate change, domestic violence, migration, corporate practices, and economic policies all affect people's actual experience of security, some even suggesting replacing state security with the more inclusive category of "human security." In that sense, calls to "re-vision," "re-map," "democ-ratize," "gender," "race," or "humanize" the concept of security appear to make the case for including the subaltern experience of insecurity. But subscribing to the logic of security in making the case for the subaltern voice is to surrender even more ground to the authority of the state, its vision of political order, and the institutional violence through which it maintains that order (Neocleous 2008). Rather than an ontologically pre-existing condition, the demarcation of areas of "insecurity" has, after all, always accompanied the provision of security (Weldes et al. 1999; Dillon 1996). As "the master narrative of the state," security is the technology through which the liberal, capitalist order is maintained and, ultimately, political practices neutralized and human lives administered (Neocleous 2008). In that sense, nuclear harms should simply be added to the long list of "shared human vulnerabilities" that could, in principle, enhance a global sensibility and global ethic, but securitizing such felt vulnerabilities is to extend the reach and power of the state, through the institutions of which we cannot hear the subaltern. Instead of speaking in the voice of the subaltern state to demand inclusion in an unequal world, perhaps we are better off looking to the subaltern made expendable in the production of a statist global order.

In her response to critics, Spivak clarifies that it is not that the subal-terns didn't speak but that "if there was no valid institutional background for resistance, it could not be recognized" (Spivak 2010b, 228). Resistance to uranium mining, nuclear testing, nuclear deployment, siting of nuclear power plants, storage of nuclear waste, by local communities directly af-fected by nuclear power, has existed for almost as long as the pursuit of nu-clear power by states. Members of the Navajo Nation in uranium mining areas in the United States, villagers resisting nuclear power in Kudankulam in southern India, fishers and farmers all over Japan currently, have been speaking their sorrows and their rage in all manners of protests—some or-ganized, some dispersed, some desperate. These do not all form one cohe-sive, singular opposition to nuclearization, and some are linked to the vast apparatus of the NNP regime in complex and contradictory ways. Neither are these groups entirely outside of the state, and the demands they make are often directed to the state. But it is not states—neither President Obama as the representative of the most prominent nuclear weapons state nor an Iranian leader speaking in the name of the subaltern state—that we should expect to convince us of the urgency of nuclear zero. In a world with far too many nuclear weapons and a growing consensus on nuclear energy as the solution to the limitations of fossil fuels, perhaps we may get to peace when we can find ways to hear the demands for justice that come from the subaltern, voices that we cannot hear when filtered through the institutional apparatus of the state.

The Nuclear Nonproliferation Regime

Treaties and Agreements

Antarctic Treaty (full treaty text): http://www.state.gov/www/
global/oes/oceans/antarctic_treaty_1959.html

Anti-Ballistic Missile Treaty (ABM) (full treaty text): http://
www.state.gov/t/avc/trty/101888.htm

Comprehensive Nuclear Test Ban Treaty (full treaty text): http://
www.state.gov/www/global/arms/treaties/ctb.html

Convention on the Physical Protection of Nuclear Material (full treaty
text): http://www.nti.org/e_research/official_docs/inventory/
pdfs/aptcppnm.pdf

Hague (International) Code of Conduct Against Ballistic Missile
Proliferation (HCOC) (full treaty text): http://www.armscontrol
.org/documents/icoc

Intermediate-Range Nuclear Forces Treaty (INF) (full treaty text):
http://www.state.gov/www/global/arms/treaties/inf2.html

International Convention for the Suppression of Acts of Nuclear
Terrorism (full text): http://www.un.org/en/sc/ctc/docs/
conventions/Conv13.pdf

Limited Test Ban Treaty (LTBT) or Partial Test Ban Treaty (PTBT)
(full treaty text): http://www.state.gov/www/global/arms/
treaties/ltbt1.html

Missile Technology Control Regime (MTCR) (including information
on regime guidelines): http://www.mtcr.info/english/

Mongolian Nuclear Weapons Free Zone (full document text): http://
cns.miis.edu/inventory/pdfs/aptmongolia.pdf

New Strategic Arms Reduction Treaty (START) (full treaty text and
protocol): http://www.state.gov/t/avc/newstart/index.htm

Nuclear Non-Proliferation Treaty (NPT) (full treaty text):

http://www.iaea.org/Publications/Magazines/Bulletin/
Bull104/10403501117.pdf

Outer Space Treaty (full treaty text): http://www.state.gov/www/
global/arms/treaties/space1.html

Peaceful Nuclear Explosions Treaty (PNE) (full treaty text): http://
www.state.gov/www/global/arms/treaties/pne1.html

Seabed Arms Control Treaty (full treaty text): http://www.state.gov/
www/global/arms/treaties/seabed1.html

Semipalatinsk/Central Asian Nuclear Weapons Free Zone (full treaty
text): http://cns.miis.edu/inventory/pdfs/aptcanwz.pdf

Strategic Arms Limitations Talks I (SALT I) (full treaty text and
subsequent protocols and publications): http://www.state.gov/
www/global/arms/treaties/abmpage.html

Strategic Arms Limitations Talks II (SALT II) (full treaty text):
http://www.state.gov/www/global/arms/treaties/inf2.html

Strategic Arms Reduction Treaty I (START I) (full treaty text and
protocols): http://www.state.gov/www/global/arms/starthtm/
start/toc.html

Strategic Arms Reduction Treaty II (START II) (full treaty text and
protocols): http://www.state.gov/www/global/arms/starthtm/
start2/st2intal.html

Strategic Offensive Reduction Treaty (SORT) (full treaty text):
http://www.fas.org/nuke/control/sort/sort.htm

Threshold Test Ban Treaty (TTBT) (full treaty text): http://
www.state.gov/www/global/arms/treaties/ttbt1.html

Treaty of Bangkok/Southeast Asia Nuclear Weapons Free Zone
(full treaty text): http://www.nti.org/e_research/official_docs/
inventory/pdfs/aptbang.pdf

Treaty of Pelindaba/African Nuclear Weapons Free Zone (full
treaty text): http://www.iaea.org/About/Policy/GC/GC40/
Documents/pelindab.html

Treaty of Rarotonga/South Pacific Nuclear Weapons Free Zone (full
treaty text): http://www.state.gov/www/global/arms/treaties/
spnfz.html#1

Treaty of Tlatelolco/Latin American and Caribbean Nuclear Weapons
Free Zone (full treaty text): http://www.nti.org/media/pdfs/
Treaty_of_Tlatelolco.pdf?_=1316643635

Wassenaar Arrangement on Export Controls for Conventional Arms and Dual-Use Goods and Technologies (Wassenaar Arrangement) (including export guidelines): http://www.wassenaar.org/

Organizations, Agencies, and Initiatives

Arms Control and Disarmament Agency (ACDA) Department: http://dosfan.lib.uic.edu/acda/abtacda.htm

Brazilian–Argentine Agency for Accounting and Control of Nuclear Materials (ABACC) (in English): http://www.abacc.org.br/?page_id=5&lang=en

Comprehensive Nuclear Test Ban Treaty Organization (CTBTO) (details on eventual responsibilities): http://cns.miis.edu/inventory/pdfs/ctbto_verif-regime.pdf

Comprehensive Nuclear Test Ban Treaty Organization (CTBTO): http://www.ctbto.org/

Container Security Initiative (CSI) (information at the Bureau of Customs and Border Protection): http://www.cbp.gov/border-security/ports-entry/cargo-security/csi/csi-brief

Defense Threat Reduction Agency (DTRA): http://www.dtra.mil/

Department of Homeland Security (overview of Secure Freights Initiative [SFI]): http://www.dhs.gov/secure-freight-initiative

Department of State Proliferation Security Initiative (PSI): http://www.state.gov/t/isn/c10390.htm

European Atomic Energy Community (EURATOM) establishment treaty: http://europa.eu/legislation_summaries/institutional_affairs/treaties/treaties_euratom_en.htm

European Atomic Energy Community (EURATOM): http://ec.europa.eu/energy/nuclear/euratom/euratom_en.htm

Information from the Department of Energy on the Global Threat Reduction Initiative: http://nnsa.energy.gov/aboutus/ourprograms/dnn/gtri

Information on Minatom/Rosatom: http://www.globalsecurity.org/wmd/world/russia/minatom.htm

Information on Nunn–Lugar Cooperative Threat Reduction (CTR): http://www.fas.org/nuke/control/ctr/index.html

International Atomic Energy Agency (IAEA) statute: http://www.iaea.org/About/about_statute.html

International Atomic Energy Agency (IAEA): http://www.iaea.org/

International Commission on Nuclear Non-Proliferation and Disarmament (ICNND): http://www.icnnd.org/Pages/default.aspx

International Framework for Nuclear Energy Commission (IFNEC): http://www.ifnec.org/

International Science and Technology Center (ISTC): http://www.istc.ru/istc/istc.nsf/fa_MainPageMultiLang?OpenForm&lang=Eng

Megaports Initiative: http://nnsa.energy.gov/aboutus/ourprograms/nonproliferation/programoffices/internationalmaterialprotectionandcooperation/-5

National Counterproliferation Center (NCPC): http://www.counterwmd.gov/

Nuclear Materials Management and Safeguard System (NMMSS): http://nnsa.energy.gov/aboutus/ourprograms/nuclearsecurity/nmmsshome

Nuclear Regulatory Commission (NRC): http://www.nrc.gov/

Nuclear Suppliers Group (NSG): http://www.nuclearsuppliersgroup.org/Leng/default.htm

Official Page of the Global Initiative to Combat Nuclear Terrorism (GICNT) through the State Department: http://www.state.gov/t/isn/c18406.htm

Text of the 1998 New Agenda Coalition declaration: http://www.ccnr.org/8_nation_declaration.html

U.S. official announcement of the first steps in the Next Steps in Strategic Partnership (NSSP): http://2001-2009.state.gov/r/pa/prs/ps/2004/36290.htm

STRATCOM Center for Combating Weapons of Mass Destruction (SCC WMD) Fact Sheet: http://www.stratcom.mil/factsheets/12/SCC_WMD/

Think Tanks and Nongovernmental Organizations

Acronym Institute: http://www.acronym.org.uk/index.htm

Alliance for Nuclear Accountability (ANA): http://www.ananuclear.org/Welcome/tabid/36/Default.aspx

Alsos Digital Library for Nuclear Issues: http://alsos.wlu.edu/

Arms Control Association: http://www.armscontrol.org/

Begin–Sadat Center for Strategic Studies (BESA): http://besacenter.org/

Belfer Center for Science and International Affairs: http://
belfercenter.ksg.harvard.edu/index.html

Brookings Institution Arms Control Initiative: http://www.brookings
.edu/projects/arms-control.aspx

Brookings Institution: http://www.brookings.edu/

Bulletin of Atomic Scientists: http://www.thebulletin.org/

Carnegie Endowment for International Peace: http://www
.carnegieendowment.org/

Carnegie Endowment's Nuclear Policy Program: http://
carnegieendowment.org/programs/npp/

Center for Arms Control and Non-Proliferation (CACNP) research
and policy pieces: http://www.armscontrolcenter.org/policy/

Center for Arms Control and Non-Proliferation (CACNP): http://
www.armscontrolcenter.org/

Center for International Security and Cooperation (CISAC): http://
cisac.stanford.edu/

Center for International Trade and Security (CITS) nuclear security
issues page: http://cisac.stanford.edu/research/2240/

Center for Policy Studies in Russia (PIR Center): http://
www.pircenter.org/en/

Center for Security Policy (CSP): http://www.centerforsecuritypolicy
.org/

Center for Strategic and International Studies (CSIS) publications
related to nuclear weapons: http://csis.org/taxonomy/term/3/
publication

CNS publications: http://cns.miis.edu/stories/index.htm

Congressional Research Service (CRS): http://opencrs.com/

Council for a Livable World: http://www.livableworld.org/

Council on Foreign Relations (CFR) (nuclear nonproliferation/
arms control): http://www.cfr.org/arms-control-disarmament-
and-nonproliferation/nuclear-nonproliferation/p21999

Delhi Policy Group (DPG) (nuclear policy and disarmament):
http://www.delhipolicygroup.com/programs/national-security/
nuclear-policy-and-disarmament.html

Eisenhower Institute: http://www.eisenhowerinstitute.org/

Federation of American Scientists (FAS) Nuclear Information
Project: http://www.fas.org/programs/ssp/nukes/index.html

Foreign Policy in Focus (FPIF): http://www.fpif.org/

George Soros Foundations: http://www.soros.org/

Hans Kristensen's Security Blog: http://blogs.fas.org/security/

Henry L. Stimson Center: http://www.stimson.org/

Heritage Foundation Arms Control and Non-Proliferation Program:
  http://www.heritage.org/Issues/Arms-Control-and-Non-
  Proliferation

Heritage Foundation: http://www.heritage.org/

IFPA publications: http://www.ifpa.org/publications/publications
  .htm

Institute for Foreign Policy Analysis (IFPA): http://www.ifpa.org/

Institute for Science and International Security (ISIS): http://
  isis-online.org/

Institute of Nuclear Materials Management (INMM): http://
  www.inmm.org/

Institute of Peace and Conflict Studies (IPCS) nuclear issues: http://
  www.ipcs.org/issues/nuclear/

Institute of Peace and Conflict Studies (IPCS): http://www.ipcs.org/

Institute on Global Conflict and Cooperation (IGCC): http://
  www-igcc.ucsd.edu/

International Commission on Nuclear Non-Proliferation and Disarmament (ICNND): http://www.icnnd.org/Pages/default.aspx

International Institute for Strategic Studies (IISS) nonproliferation
  and disarmament page: http://www.iiss.org/programmes/
  non-proliferation-and-disarmament/

International Institute for Strategic Studies (IISS): http://www.iiss
  .org/welcome/

International Network of Engineers and Scientists Against Proliferation (INESAP): http://www.inesap.org/

International Physicians for the Prevention of Nuclear War (IPPNW):
  http://www.ippnw.org/

Iran Watch: http://www.iranwatch.org/

James Martin Center for Nonproliferation Studies (CNS): http://
  cns.miis.edu/

Jamestown Foundation: http://www.jamestown.org/

Lowy Institute's Nuclear Policy Center: http://www.lowyinstitute
  .org/programs-and-projects/projects/nuclear-policy-centre

Managing the Atom: http://belfercenter.ksg.harvard.edu/project/3/
  managing_the_atom.html

Middle Powers Initiative (MPI): http://www.middlepowers.org/

National Institute for Public Policy (NIPP): http://www.nipp.org/index.html

Natural Resources Defense Council (NRDC) Nuclear Program: http://www.nrdc.org/nuclear/default.asp

Natural Resources Defense Council (NRDC): http://www.nrdc.org/

New America Foundation: http://www.newamerica.net/

Nonproliferation for Global Security (NPS Global): http://npsglobal.org/eng/

North Korea International Documentation Project: http://www.wilsoncenter.org/index.cfm?fuseaction=topics.home&topic_id=230972

Nuclear Age Peace Foundation: http://www.wagingpeace.org/

Nuclear Control Institute: http://www.nci.org/index.htm

Nuclear Security Project: http://www.nuclearsecurityproject.org/

Nuclear Threat Initiative (NTI): http://www.nti.org/index.php

Pacific Council: http://www.pacificcouncil.org/Page.aspx?pid=326

Parliamentarians for Nuclear Non-Proliferation and Disarmament (PNND): http://www.pnnd.org/

Partnership for Global Security (PGS): http://www.partnershipforglobalsecurity.org/

Policy Architects International (PAI): http://www.policyarchitects.org/

Program in Arms Control, Disarmament, and International Security (ACDIS): http://acdis.illinois.edu/

Program on Science and Global Security (SGS): http://www.princeton.edu/sgs/

Project on Government Oversight (POGO): http://www.pogo.org/

Project on Nuclear Issues (PONI) publications: http://csis.org/node/13398/publication

Pugwash Conferences on Science and World Affairs: http://www.pugwash.org/index.htm

Research and Development Corporation (RAND): http://www.rand.org/

Safeguarding the Atom Project: http://www.eisenhowerinstitute.org/programs/pastprograms.dot

South Asia Analysis Group nonproliferation page: http://www.southasiaanalysis.org/non-proliferation

South Asian Strategic Stability Institute (SASSI): http://www.sassu
.org.uk/

Stanley Foundation Nuclear Security Program: http://www
.stanleyfoundation.org/programs.cfm?id=2

Stanley Foundation: http://www.stanleyfoundation.org/

Stimson Nuclear Weapons Program: http://www.stimson.org/
topics/nuclear-weapons/

Stockholm International Peace Research Institute (SIPRI): http://
www.sipri.org/

U.S. Civilian and Research Development Foundation (CRDF):
http://www.crdf.org/

Union of Concerned Scientists: http://www.ucsusa.org/

Washington Institute for Near East Policy (WINEP) proliferation:
https://www.washingtoninstitute.org/policy-analysis/topic/
proliferation#categories=68

Washington Institute for Near East Policy (WINEP): http://
www.washingtoninstitute.org/

Wilson Center on International Security Studies: http://www
.wilsoncenter.org/index.cfm?fuseaction=topics.home&topic
_id=1416

Wisconsin Project on Nuclear Arms Control: http://www
.wisconsinproject.org/

Woodrow Wilson International Center for Scholars: http://
www.wilsoncenter.org/

World Security Institute: http://www.worldsecurityinstitute.org/

Notes

Introduction

1. http://www.youtube.com/watch?v=CCDcdnEjJHA.

2. Mueller's book was widely reviewed in both academic and nonacademic venues and received both favorable and quite critical commentaries. In this discussion, I am drawing from several reviews more generally: Collignon (2010), Craig (2011), DeGroot (2009), Freedman (2010), Gusterson (2011), Jervis (2009), Kurtz (2010), Olwell (2010), Schoenfeld (2009), Shariatmadari (2010), and Stigler (2011).

3. See Barkawi and Laffey (2006) for a critique of the Eurocentricity of security studies and Beier (2009) for an analysis of security studies (and international relations theory more broadly) as a form of advanced colonialism. Both direct their critiques at mainstream as well as critical approaches in the field.

4. As I described earlier, the last two, despite being nonsignatories of the NPT, are generally not represented as the "problem cases" these days.

1. Intentions and Effects

1. This would be five nuclear states (the United States, Russia, the United Kingdom, France, and China)—also the permanent members of the Security Council—who are recognized by the NPT as "nuclear weapons states" with no binding obligations to disarm.

2. The now widely circulated *Wall Street Journal* op-ed column by this "gang of four" first appeared in January 2007 (Shultz et al. 2007). See Taubman (2012) for a heroic narrative of the political evolution of this "gang of four" as well as for the contributions of theoretical physicist Sidney Drell, who has worked closely with this group. A video titled *Nuclear Tipping Point* that is largely based on conversations with this group was reportedly shown to President Obama in April 2010. Of the many emerging treatises elaborating a step-by-step approach to disarmament, see Cortright and Väyrynen (2009) for one inspired by the Schultz et al. piece. Another abolitionist project initiated by former government officials is the "Global Zero" movement, led by nuclear security expert Bruce Blair, that produced an also well-circulated *Countdown to Zero* video. See Taubman (2012) for an account of some of the tensions between these two campaigns.

3. There is a fairly energetic debate among South Asian strategic thinkers about the extent to which deterrence leads to nuclear stability in the Indian–Pakistani conflict (see, e.g., Ganguly and Kapur 2009; 2010). See O'Neil (2007) for an argument that the best approach to Northeast Asian nuclearization would emphasize deterrence and confidence-building measures over non- or counterproliferation. For arguments on the effectiveness of nuclear deterrence in Asia more broadly, see Alagappa (2008).

4. The terms *horizontal, vertical,* and now *diagonal* are used in the nuclear security literature to refer to the direction of proliferation. Horizontal proliferation refers to the acquisition of nuclear weapons by currently non–nuclear weapons states, vertical proliferation refers to the enhancement of the nuclear capabilities of existing nuclear weapons states, and diagonal proliferation refers to the spread of nuclear weapons to nonstate actors.

5. Of the three rogue states in the "axis of evil" identified by George W. Bush in his 2002 State of the Union address, Libya's nuclear weapons program was successfully dismantled, North Korea became a declared nuclear weapons state, and the weapons status of Iran's nuclear program continues to cause concern.

6. Graham Allison has become one of the most vocal proponents of the increased dangers of nuclear terrorism, which he assesses to be at 50 percent or higher likelihood over the next decade (Allison 2004a; 2004b; 2006). See also Cirincione (2007) for the dangers of nuclear terrorism. Mueller (2010) makes, in my view, a very strong case for why accounts such as Allison's exaggerate the intentions of, or capacities to, acquire nuclear weapons by terrorist groups such as al-Qaeda. It should be noted here that although most thinkers are concerned about the failures of deterrence in a world with terrorism, there are some who are arguing for a reformulated notion of "expanded deterrence" that might work in this world (Gallucci 2006).

7. See, e.g., the suggestions of the 1946 Acheson–Lilienthal Report on the International Control of Atomic Energy and the Baruch Plan submitted in 1946 by the United States to the United Nations International Atomic Commission.

8. Within IR literature, *high politics* generally refers to the high-stakes military–security issues faced by states in which states are least likely to cooperate, whereas *low politics* refers to issues not considered vital to the survival of the state.

9. Many scholars refer to this as the nonproliferation, arms control, and disarmament (NACD) establishment.

10. This special issue was published in 1983 as a volume edited by Stephen Krasner titled *International Regimes.* See also Young's (1986) review essay and Haggard and Simmons (1987) for continuing elaboration and questioning of the concept. Some of these lines of thinking on regimes can be traced to Karl Deutsch's (1957) study of "pluralistic security communities." See also Rittberger and Mayer (1995) and Hasenclever, Mayer, and Rittberger (1997).

11. See especially the essays by Arthur Stein (1982), Robert Keohane (1982), and Robert Jervis (1982). These draw from Robert Keohane and Joseph Nye's (2001) definition of regimes as "sets of governing arrangements" that include "networks of rules, norms, and procedures that regularize behavior and control its effects" (17), in a book first published in 1977.

12. See essays by Oran Young (1982) and Donald Puchala and Raymond Hopkins (1982). The English School tradition in IR, emerging from Hedley Bull's (1977) discussion of the importance of rules and institutions in the functioning of "international society," also traces its intellectual inspiration to Hugo Grotius.

13. This was also the analysis of Keohane and Nye (2001) in *Power and Interdependence,* who argued that when the stakes were sufficiently high, relations of "complex interdependence" that are amenable to regime formation would yield to a realist world where force predominates. Often this sort of analysis is conducted by contrasting the zero-sum, relative-power nature of security politics to the positive-sum, absolute-power nature of nonsecurity goods. Kenneth Oye's (1986) edited volume, *Cooperation under Anarchy,* popularized the extensive use of game-theoretic analysis for explaining the success or failure of cooperation.

14. Much of the work that does exist in this area is focused on regional security arrangements. See, e.g., the contributions to Adler and Barnett (1998).

15. Arthur Stein (1982, 309), in the same volume, makes a distinction between "dilemmas of common interests, in which actors have a common interest in insuring a particular outcome," and "dilemmas of common aversions," in which actors "have a common interest in avoiding a particular outcome." One might think that it would be easy to conceptualize the NNP regime as a solution to the latter kind of dilemma. Deudney (1993) suggests how accounting for the transformative role of nuclear technology on the form of the state may help realists explain the emergence of an NNP regime.

16. See also Volker Rittberger and Michael Zürn (1990) for an analysis of cumulative security cooperation between the United States and Soviet Union as one aspect of "regulated anarchy" in East–West relations.

17. This was the *International Organization* 46, no. 1 (1992) issue that was subsequently published in 1997 as a volume edited by Peter Haas (1997) titled *Knowledge, Power, and International Policy Coordination.*

18. In an earlier piece in *Daedalus* written in the aftermath of the dissolution of the Soviet Union, Adler (1991) sounds his optimism about the ability of a pluralistic security community emergent from various arms control agreements to prevent nuclear war, especially in Europe, but expresses concern about the ability of the existing NPT to restrain nuclear proliferation in a much more volatile third world.

19. The second essay in the volume by Jepperson, Wendt, and Katzenstein (1996) elaborates the conceptual apparatus for the volume.

20. For another important work on nonproliferation norms, using social

psychology, see Rublee (2008; 2009). I discuss Rublee's work in the following chapter.

21. A somewhat different version of this argument is made by William Walker (2007) about the NPT as an Enlightenment project establishing a progressive global order, an argument taken up through a different vein of critique of liberal IR in the following chapter.

22. See Joyner (2009) for an extensive account of the legal framework in and through which this regime functions. Joyner's book serves largely as a review piece on nonproliferation law, including the NPT as well as the chemical and biological conventional weapons conventions. Beyond explorations of standard treaties, Joyner also explores nonproliferation measures in the World Trade Organization and the use of the United Nations and the International Court of Justice as legal bodies to resolve nonproliferation disputes. He also explores the legality of measures taken in the wake of September 11, 2011, and the revelation of the A. Q. Khan network, including counterproliferation policy and preemptive warfare.

23. "Peaceful" here indicates not weapons related. There is nothing technologically distinctive about a nuclear explosion that makes it "peaceful"; rather, the characterization is based on the declaratory intent of the actor to not weaponize.

24. See the following Clinton administration release for a list of these conditions: http://www.fas.org/nuke/control/ctbt/text/ctbtsafeguards.htm.

25. The 2020 campaign was begun by Mayors for Peace, a grassroots organizing initiative to "eliminate the nuclear threat," which convened in Geneva in April 2008. As of 2010, 4,207 cities had signed on. http://www.2020visioncampaign.org/.

26. For more information (including full protocol text), see http://www.2020visioncampaign.org/filestorage/409/File/2/Hiroshima-NagasakiProtocol.pdf.

27. An IAEA document containing the Trigger List can be found at http://www.iaea.org/Publications/Documents/Infcircs/Others/inf209.shtml.

28. For the eight guidelines, see http://www.sipri.org/research/disarmament/nuclear/researchissues/strengthening_reduction/G8/partnership_documents/2. See also the press release from the summit: http://www.sipri.org/research/disarmament/nuclear/researchissues/strengthening_reduction/G8/partnership_documents/1.

29. The hierarchical structure of the NPT is discussed extensively in the next chapter, and its effects on nuclear materials proliferation are discussed in the chapter following that.

30. Index of Research Papers: http://www.icnnd.org/research/index.html.

31. Of course, many large and influential think tanks that are not primarily devoted to nuclear nonproliferation often have a fairly significant section dedicated to it. The Brookings Institution and the Heritage Foundation are both Washington, D.C.–based research organizations, the latter decidedly conservative in orientation, that focus on a range of issues, both domestic and international, and oc-

casionally release publications related to nuclear proliferation through their arms control programs. Among institutions focused on foreign policy, the highly prominent New York–based Council on Foreign Relations, which publishes the bimonthly journal *Foreign Affairs* and has a long list of notable members (including Barack Obama, Bill Clinton, and Henry Kissinger), publishes pretty extensively on proliferation. Partnered with the council is the Los Angeles–based Pacific Council on International Policy, which also occasionally publishes on nuclear issues. Washington, D.C.–based Foreign Policy in Focus publishes on nonproliferation and related issues with some frequency, despite not maintaining a dedicated section on nonproliferation, much like the more conservative Washington, D.C.–based Institute for Foreign Policy Analysis, which is aimed at helping senior policy makers, industry leaders, and public policy officials understand the global security environment. The New America Foundation, based in Washington, D.C., and Sacramento, California, publishes on the subject through its Nuclear Strategy and Nonproliferation Initiative, which is dedicated to empowering and aiding the Obama administration in its attempt to overhaul U.S. security policy, as does the more conservative Washington, D.C.–based Center for Strategic and International Studies through its Project on Nuclear Issues.

32. Also, there are still no treaties regulating tactical or short-range nuclear weapons.

33. Norris and Kristensen (2013). An op-ed in the *New York Times* in May 2010, by two professors of strategy, Gary Schaub Jr. from the Air War College and James Forsyth Jr. from the School of Advanced Air and Space Studies, suggests that of the 5,113 nuclear weapons the United States still has in its arsenal, 4,802 are simply excess, because 311 weapons (distributed within the triad) would be adequate to U.S. security. They reject the idea of a nuclear-free world as infeasible and argue the importance of deterrence but think that current levels are simply too "big, expensive and unnecessarily threatening to much of the world." Others have suggested that the land-based leg of the triad is quite dispensable for the purposes of deterrence, and still others that a small number of weapons limited to the most invulnerable leg of the triad—submarines—would be sufficient for deterrence. In any event, that the number and kinds of weapons that the United States possesses is far in excess of what it needs for deterrence is a relatively uncontroversial point to make.

34. Including specifically the ABM, from which the U.S. government withdrew shortly thereafter!

35. The doomsday clock is a metaphorical device used by the *Bulletin of the Atomic Scientists* to portend how close to nuclear destruction the world is positioned at any particular time.

36. Shultz et al. (2011). Taubman (2012) documents some of the disagreements and ambivalence among the members of the "gang of four," with Kissinger

in particular having misgivings about the project. I think it is safe to say that there really is no serious constituency for disarmament within the structure of the U.S. government, and it would be career suicide for most U.S. politicians even to bring that up as a real possibility (Price 2007). De Santana (2011) argues that the renewal of the pledge to disarm by the Obama administration and the gang of four becomes just another means to continue arms control and nonproliferation efforts that can secure the consent of other states without having to actually disarm.

37. http://cns.miis.edu/stories/100423_disarmament_proposals.htm. See Cortright and Väyrynen (2009) and Kelleher and Reppy (2011) for two more recent accounts that begin from the premise that global zero is possible and articulate road maps that suggest concrete institutional and other changes to get there.

38. http://www.armscontrol.org/system/files/ACA_2009–2010_ReportCard.pdf.

39. See Escobar (1994) for an excellent example of this.

40. Although his own study is quite localized and he is somewhat hesitant to make broad generalizations that might apply elsewhere, Ferguson (1994, 9) does note that the single project he examines might suggest what the "global development apparatus" may be all about.

41. Though certainly sympathetic to Marxism, Susan Strange was not a Marxist theorist of IR, yet her structuralist critique of regimes could be used to understand the NNP regime as simply a conduit for "real" material interests. I return to Strange's discussion of the conservative functions of liberal celebrations of regimes in the following chapter. There is an abundance of Marxist analysis of the armaments industry, but none that studies the NNP regime as an expression of capitalist interests. Most certainly, neo-Gramscian analyses of the institutions and discourses of the global political economy, so well done in many areas, could be used to explain the material interests undergirding the NNP regime, but none, to my knowledge, have been applied in that fashion.

42. Adler and Haas (1992, 370–71) mischaracterize "poststructural, postpositivist, and radical interpretive analyses," with their "exclusive focus on words and discourse" in which "the word is power and the only power is the word."

43. In his essay introducing the epistemic communities literature, Peter Haas (1992) recognizes the ways that the increasing bureaucratization and professionalization of public governance since the late nineteenth century have seen a rising reliance on "technical expertise" for the delineation and remedy of various public problems, yet he rejects a Foucauldian understanding of discourse as too determinist. In this, he appears to misread Foucault's conceptualization of discourse as devoid of internal disagreements or requiring a clear symmetry between knowledge and interests.

44. She describes the quandary faced by peace activists thus: "If we refuse to learn the language, we are virtually guaranteed that our voices will remain outside

the 'politically relevant' spectrum of opinion. Yet, if we do learn and speak it, we not only severely limit what we can say but we also invite the transformation, the militarization, of our own thinking" (Cohn 1987, 716). It is not that peace activists have not articulated other ways of speaking about nuclear weapons—such as, according to Gusterson (1998), through a form of deontological ethics targeted at "weapons of genocide" rather than the consequentialist ethics deployed by nuclear strategists—but being taken seriously within the NNP regime requires being able to talk and think in a certain way. See Gusterson (1998; 2004) for accounts of the ways that nuclear scientists come to understand the bomb and its place in the ordering of the world.

45. I have more to say on the nuclear state in the last two chapters of the book.

46. http://www.un.org/sc/1540/.

47. Given this, Mutimer (2011) suggests that denuclearization can only happen outside of the framework of arms control, for instance, through the articulation of national or regional security strategies that delegitimize nuclear weapons as weapons. But that still does not explain why states, qua states that are invested in a particular logic of security as governmentality (that reinforce their own power both within and outside their borders), would be inclined to do so in any serious fashion, especially for highly regulated and status-enhancing weapons.

2. Whose Nuclear Order?

1. Both North Korea and Iran, as well as Iraq and Libya at one time, developed their weapons programs covertly while they were parties to the NPT.

2. Many who consider the likelihood of massive proliferation to be fairly low find that the reasons for proliferation have little to do with the treaty itself. There has been a debate under way since the 2005 Review Conference among those who want to see the NPT salvaged through radical changes in U.S. policy (Hanson 2005; Carranza 2006), those who would like to see the NPT strengthened and supplemented through counterproliferation measures (Pilat 2007), those who would like to see it replaced with an altogether different regime that makes proliferation possible but limited (Wesley 2005), those who reject the usefulness of arms control treaties generally (Lyon 2005), those who think that the only way to deal with proliferation is on a case-by-case basis (Ayson 2005), and those who argue for a more inclusive and binding disarmament–prohibition convention to replace the NPT (Thakur 2000; Walker 2000; Sethi 2002; Johnson 2010). Also see the essays in Busch and Joyner (2009) for different approaches to dealing with nonproliferation, including possible futures for the NPT and the nonproliferation regime.

3. The full treaty text can be found at http://www.iaea.org/Publications/Magazines/Bulletin/Bull104/10403501117.pdf.

4. South Africa had an active nuclear weapons program from the 1950s to the 1980s and was reported to have produced six finished (and one incomplete) nuclear devices that it dismantled right before the end of apartheid in the early 1990s. It is the only country known to have actually dismantled its nuclear weapons program after successfully producing bombs. South Africa signed the NPT in 1991 and has emerged as one of the few powerful state voices in favor of universal disarmament on the global stage. The somewhat nascent Libyan nuclear weapons program—developed while Libya was formally a member of the NPT, and with assistance from the A. Q. Khan supply network—was successfully dismantled in 2006, after U.S. and British negotiations with the Qaddafi regime over the lifting of sanctions. Although the Iranian nuclear weapons program is much more advanced than Libya's was at the time of dismantlement, many recent commentators have used the Libyan case as an example of the effectiveness of sanctions in securing denuclearization, urging the international community not to ease sanctions on Iran.

5. Walker's more recent book is a somewhat more extensive discussion of the creation of an NPT-centered international order, continuing much of the discussion of these earlier pieces while underscoring the resilience of this order despite the stresses it endured during and after the Cold War, but with little discussion of this order as an Enlightenment order (Walker 2012). In the book, Walker continues to subscribe to the notion of the NPT-centered regime as a product of reasoned cooperation and conciliation toward a common purpose, but his tone, while still optimistic and forward looking, appears more pragmatic, muted, and cautionary here. My interest is in interrogating the underlying framework of liberal narratives of progress, and I think Walker's (2007) piece on Enlightenment values draws that out quite well (even though I have no way of ascertaining how strongly Walker continues to subscribe to the notion of the international nuclear order as an Enlightenment order). The larger point that I am trying to make in this chapter is about the conceptualization of "international order" in IR generally—in both realist and liberal accounts—and the debate between Walker and his critics about the Enlightenment values undergirding the international nuclear order is exemplary for that purpose.

6. Walker sees the echoes of the Reagan administration's disdain for arms control and its belief in invulnerability and unilateralism in the approaches that were gaining ascendancy in the later 1990s among Republican opponents of the Clinton administration. Much of this approach—which led to a move away from nonproliferation and toward counterproliferation—stemmed from a suspicion and distrust of irrational rogue states defined through a Huntingtonian "class of civilizations" framework (Walker 2000). In his Adelphi paper on this subject, Walker (2004, 52) sees the Bush administration's policies as making the journey from Francis Fukuyama's "assimilationism" through Samuel Huntington's "anx-

ious caution" about irredeemable civilizational differences on to Kagan's "imperial" and "brash incaution."

7. In his 2004 piece, Walker refers to the nuclear order as the "WMD order," recognizing the confusion of categories in the term *weapon of mass destruction* and suggesting that it is partly this lumping together of very disparate weapons systems—nuclear, chemical, and biological—that leads to some of the later difficulties with this order.

8. Here he suggests that dealing effectively with China and India as emerging global powers is going to be critical in the construction of that order, a point he develops more fully in Walker (2012).

9. Here he draws from Horkheimer and Adorno to refer to the paradox of Enlightenment rationality and mastery of technology.

10. Walker recognizes how important the extensive set of bilateral arms-control treaties negotiated between the United States and the Soviet Union, and of these the ABM Treaty in particular, was to this system of deterrence.

11. In his recent book, Walker modifies this somewhat to call it a combination of a "managed system of military engagement with nuclear technology (deterrence plus)" and a "managed system of military abstinence from, and civil engagement with, nuclear technology (non-proliferation plus)" with a set of norms, rules, institutions, and mutual obligations providing the "connecting instrumental and normative tissue." It is this latter normative tissue that Walker believes provides a certain degree of legitimacy to the existing nuclear order and keeps it from becoming an entirely self-serving and unjust apparatus of great power domination (Walker 2012; see the introduction to this volume). Toward the end of the book, Walker suggests a revision in the future management of an international nuclear order to account for India and China as major powers, so that this order would now be organized around two geographical hubs (Eurocentric and Asiacentric) of managed military engagement in addition to managed abstinence elsewhere (Walker 2012; see chapter 7 in this volume).

12. Hedley Bull's inspiration in Walker's thinking on international society is more fully elaborated in Walker (2012).

13. He points out that the treaty has no built-in sanctions regime, that it was of limited duration (and argues that its indefinite extension in 1995, which was accompanied by statements of strong political commitments from NWS, actually destroyed the productive ambiguity of the original treaty), and that its energy components allow dual-use technology, which works against the nonproliferation goals of the treaty.

14. China, France, and other nations did not sign until 1992; three nuclear powers have never signed the treaty; on negotiation, Western Europe had deep reservations, which were only resolved with firm commitments of U.S. extended deterrence and NATO nuclear sharing arrangements; a large number of states

party to the treaty did not have the financial and technical means to proliferate even if they had so desired, and the treaty offered them security guarantees that they would not otherwise have had; and many signed on cynically to exploit the access to nuclear technology that helped some of them build military programs in the future (Yost 2007).

15. Yost (2007) reminds readers that insistence on stronger language on disarmament at the time of negotiations was explicitly turned down and, if adopted, would have killed the treaty.

16. Nonaligned states and Sweden were the strongest proponents of disarmament, but there was disagreement among them as to how adamantly to pursue it, and many of these states were pushing for disarmament even as they were covertly pursuing their own nuclear weapons programs; the United States was most vested in nonproliferation, and the Soviet Union joined this effort only to prevent West Germany from possessing nuclear weapons; the United Kingdom was a reluctant participant, and France and China were opposed to the treaty; nonnuclear Western European states and Japan were quite skeptical about the treaty but wanted to ensure a security guarantee from the United States; and the "silent majority," which did not have the wherewithal to build programs of their own, supported any measure that reduced the number of nuclear weapons (Krause 2007).

17. Moreover, the ABM Treaty was hardly extensive, as it allowed each nation to explore short-range theater missile defense, something each nation pursued (Yost 2007).

18. For one of the clearest statements of this thesis, see Fairbanks and Shulsky (1987). However, not all realists come to the same conclusion about proliferation from this thesis. Both Lyon (2005) and O'Neil (2005b) make a realist argument for the ineffectiveness of arms control treaties out of sync with real-world strategic considerations, which effectively means that the NPT works best when it is needed least. But whereas Lyon, like many of Walker's critics, suggests that the problem with proliferation is not numbers (i.e., how many states have nuclear weapons) but identity (i.e., who has them), and hence that some states should simply be prohibited from acquiring nuclear weapons, O'Neil suggests that deterrence is the "least bad" of all available options and, with careful management and attention, could provide a stable international order.

19. Although Walker points his criticism quite strongly at the Bush administration, he does recognize the longer genealogy of many of the policies undertaken during that period (to the Reagan administration and then to the Republican-dominated Congress during the Clinton presidency).

20. As referred to in the previous chapter, this is the quite visible public campaign launched by George Shultz, Henry Kissinger (both former U.S. secretaries of state), William J. Perry (former U.S. secretary of defense), and Sam Nunn (former chairman of the U.S. Senate Foreign Relations Committee) to persuade cur-

rent leaders and policy makers to pursue nuclear disarmament. Walker applauds and discusses the impact of this campaign in his more recent work (Walker 2012).

21. It should be pointed out here that the internal logic of realism does not automatically lead to this form of ethnocentrism, as evidenced in the very controversial argument advanced famously by Kenneth Waltz in his "more may be better" piece—that is, that nuclear proliferation may well lead to stability, and to think otherwise may, indeed, be to fall prey to ethnocentrism (Waltz 1981). Beardsley and Asal's (2007) attempt to empirically prove Waltz's "nuclear optimism" also draws attention to the presence of such ethnocentric assumptions among "nuclear pessimists." There are others who argue that the "menace of nuclear proliferation" arises not so much from the irrationality of third world actors but from inadequate infrastructures of control (i.e., command, control, communications, and intelligence systems) in such places (Busch 2004).

22. And here it may be worthwhile to remember that the United States is the only state that has used a nuclear weapon in war.

23. This article by Mehta also appears as chapter 2 in his fuller exposition of the ways that nineteenth-century British liberal thought is shaped through its encounter with "the unfamiliar," an encounter whose background comprises the very real inequalities of power that form the British empire in India (Mehta 1999).

24. See here Susan Strange's (1982) trenchant critique of liberal regime analysis for focusing on the existing status quo and ignoring hidden agendas (such as regimes serving as instruments of new forms of nonterritorial imperialisms) as well as the complaints of the excluded or marginalized.

25. There is a long scholarly tradition of tracing some of the others excluded in liberalism—the propertyless or women—and Mehta alludes to these, but his primary focus is on colonial exclusions. For other discussions of how Enlightenment thought was more broadly shaped by perceptions of, knowledge about, and encounters with non-European others, see Hulme and Jordanova (1990), Rousseau and Porter (1990), and Eze (1997). For accounts of the cultural encounters (including the formative place of the European "discovery" of the Americas) that helped shape the foundations of mainstream IR as a discipline (in both its realist and liberal versions), see Jahn (2000) and Inayatullah and Blaney (2004), and for a broader account of the (multivalent) Eurocentricty of international theory, including in its critical offshoots, see Hobson (2012).

26. The exclusionary strategies that transform Locke's universalist impulses arise from largely tacit acceptance of certain conventional boundaries and social distinctions of his time and eventually make political inclusion contingent on an educated cultivation of the capacity to reason and exercise rational judgment, a very detailed and specific kind of educational practice thick with the inculcation of hierarchical and exclusionary credentials. Conversely, nineteenth-century British liberal thinkers such as James Mill and John Stuart Mill, thinkers for whom

India in particular played a very extensive role in their theoretical imaginations, "cultural difference" presents itself either as "inscrutability" or as a form of "civilizational infantilism"—both of which become the basis for political exclusion (Mehta 1990).

27. To be fair, Walker does recognize that the NPT serves great power interests and was a result of coercive diplomacy, but only in passing (Walker 2007, 437–38). Burke (2009), otherwise sympathetic to Walker's end goals of universal disarmament, is also critical of his general neglect of issues of power.

28. Of all of Walker's critics, Yost (2007) most understands the Enlightenment and counter-Enlightenment as complex phenomena with multiple meanings and forms. Here he attributes the "Reign of Terror" to be as much an Enlightenment project as the U.S. Constitution and the French Revolution (550) and the counter-Enlightenment as having both conservative and left-liberal forms, inspiring monarchism, nationalism, imperialism, and fascism (551). There is one fleeting moment when Walker suggests that the Bush administration's counter-Enlightenment may itself be based on an alternative Enlightenment ideal with roots in American political culture (Walker 2007, 432).

29. Walker reiterates this point in his more recent book, where he devotes a chapter to the question of disarmament. He identifies as a nuclear abolitionist but is not sanguine about the creation of a nuclear weapons–free world. However, he favors the pursuit of nuclear disarmament as a regulative ideal for what appear to be largely strategic or pragmatic purposes, that is, to help maintain the existing order of managed restraint (Walker 2012).

30. Indeed, in his book, Walker, invoking Amartya Sen, warns against any pursuit of justice that can imperil security, suggesting that complete nuclear disarmament may well turn out to be unjust if it produces insecurity (Walker 2012, 180).

31. Gray (1999a) argues that this will eventually coalesce into a "third nuclear age" organized around a single dominant axis of confrontation. It should be pointed out here that Gray (1999b) does express some reservations about the concept of the rogue state (13) and is critical of the ethnocentrism of some of the writings on proliferation, but he then goes on to warn against "uncritical relativism" (161–62) that might lead Western strategists to let their guard down. See Fred Iklé (2006) for a particularly alarmist narrative of how proliferation has increased the possibility of "annihilation from within," making the case for fortifying the U.S. state against forms of internal infiltration and threats. See Langewiesche (2007) for an apocalyptic narrative of the rise of what he calls the "nuclear poor." Gray, Payne, and Iklé have all made the case for an American strategy based on the premise that a nuclear war can be won. Lieber and Press (2006) argued that the United States had been pursuing and succeeding in achieving nuclear primacy, effectively eliminating the logic of MAD and bolstering its ability to use military might to achieve its foreign policy agenda, and urged (Lieber and Press

2009; 2011) the Obama administration to maintain a useable weapons capability necessary for the changed circumstances of a post–Cold War era.

32. The special place of Islam within this geography of fear may explain Roberts's (2007) dramatic claim about a potential "nuclear armed caliphate" that may confront the West in the future, an entirely unsubstantiated claim that has found plenty of currency within the right-wing Islamophobic discourse (such as in some of U.S. radio and in TV talk show host Glenn Beck's commentary) that has been circulating in the Western media.

33. See Caprioli and Trumbore (2005) for a critique of the rogue state concept and, in particular, assumptions about the foreign policy behavior of so-called rogue states, and see Litwak (2008) for a critique of a one-size-fits-all U.S. approach to the concept. Some have pointed out that if one looked at the foreign policy statements and postures of France and China at the time they acquired nuclear weapons, they could well have been considered rogue states as well (see Gavin 2009–10; Mueller 2010). See Muhula (2003) for a realist analysis that finds that security concerns explain the foreign policy behavior of rogue states like Iraq and North Korea (as well as South African reasons for disarmament) and Smith (2006) for an argument about how deterrence can be made to work even with rogue states. See Bleiker (2003) for a critique of the United States' treatment of North Korea as a rogue state.

34. Hedley Bull recognizes the fact of Western dominance over (and the revolt against it by) non-European peoples, yet Bull's writings, as well as the accounts of the English School more generally, are quite Eurocentric, offering a rather sanitized history of the "expansion" (a proxy for conquest and colonization) of an international society autochthonously generated in Europe, and one in whose constitution the third world plays the role of passive recipient or to which it simply reacts (Seth 2013a; Hobson 2012). Inayatullah and Blaney (2004) argue that the very formation of a society of states occurs through a deferral of the "problem of difference" faced by Europe in its encounters with others (both external and internal).

35. Wheeler (2009) makes his argument by drawing from the experience of Brazil and Argentina's eventual accession to the NPT, and the distrust to which he is referring is between those two countries, not in the larger colonial, hierarchical global order I am discussing here. However, I think Wheeler's thoughts on trust building can be seen in the context of his other work, which belongs within what is called the "solidarist" (distinguished from the "pluralist") wing of the English School tradition, arguing for the possibility and desirability of universal consensus on certain normative values (Wheeler 2000); both strands, in my view, are insufficiently attentive to questions of power and hierarchy. One can find discussions of the challenges and processes of building a genuine dialogue that acknowledge the traces of (colonial) history in some postcolonial scholarship (see, e.g.,

Todorov 1999; Nandy 1983; Inayatullah and Blaney 2004). As I will suggest, any dialogic moves toward nuclear disarmament will have to work through existing forms of "mistrust" by restoring global justice to the calls for global peace.

36. It should not be surprising that "trust" is the central issue that recurs in much of the public commentary on the possibilities of negotiations between Iran and the United States, although it is rarely historicized and conceptualized through the lens of colonial power. For a scholarly account that focuses on trust (while underplaying power) as a primary issue in U.S.–Iranian nuclear negotiations, see Beeman (2003; 2005).

37. It should be recalled that India had first tested a nuclear device in 1974 but claimed that it was a "peaceful nuclear explosion." Abraham (2009a) argues that the 1998 tests were a response to nonproliferation as a "discourse of control"—a way to settle the ambiguity that had surrounded India's national program—in a context in which the international community had never taken its peaceful intentions or its push for universal disarmament seriously.

38. The 2008 U.S.–Indian Nuclear Fuel Deal lifted years of sanctions on nuclear trade with India, providing legitimacy to India's nuclear weapons status, even though India remains outside of the NPT. I discuss the details of this agreement in chapter 4. It should also be noted that China has recently resumed nuclear energy cooperation with Pakistan, although this does not have the approval of the Nuclear Suppliers Group, as the deal with India does.

39. This is a "right" allowed by the NPT but considered a major loophole that enables states to develop an indigenous nuclear weapons program. I say more on this in the next chapter. There have been many proposals for creating an international nuclear fuel bank both in the past and more recently. See also Moshirsadeh (2007) for Iran's use of a discourse of justice, resistance, and independence to point to the hypocrisy of the NPT and claim equality.

40. See *CNN World* (2010). Israel occupies an odd position within the hierarchy of the NPT-centered order. It is a nuclear weapons–possessing state that is not party to the NPT, but its close military alliance with the United States has managed to protect it from the pariah or rogue label. From Iran's geopolitical perspective, in a context in which Israel frequently mentions its willingness to use military force to prevent Iranian nuclearization, Israel could certainly be depicted as an apartheid-practicing member of the nuclear club.

41. I trouble the idea of the so-called subaltern state seeking nuclearization in the name of the subaltern in the concluding chapter.

42. For an argument that vertical proliferation by existing NWS has an important effect on emergent proliferators' decisions to acquire nuclear weapons, see Sidel (2007).

43. He asks a few sentences later, "Yet, how much nuclear disarmament would have to occur before the critics are satisfied and doubts about the NWS' 'good

faith' removed?" (Rühle 2007, 515). Here he clearly conflates reductions with disarmament, not explaining why a certain level of nuclear reduction should be seen as compelling evidence of commitment to disarmament.

3. Unusable, Dangerous, and Desirable

1. It is generally understood in the proliferation literature that nuclear weapons development occurs in stages, with an active political decision to acquire weapons constituting the critical stage into proliferation. Stephen Meyer (1984) describes the multiple stage process that is widely discussed in the proliferation literature—from a latent capacity into an operational capacity, followed by actual operationalization. In practice, however, it appears to be quite difficult to determine when that happens. The latter applies also to states that explore a nuclear weapons option, only to decide to abandon it under duress, with appropriate external inducements and/or because of internal politics. There is a long list of these cases of "nuclear reversals" or "nuclear abstinence"—Iraq, Libya, South Africa, Argentina, Brazil, Taiwan, South Korea, Romania, Italy, Germany, Sweden, Egypt, and so on. This difficulty in determining the leap into weaponization is not just due to the heavy secrecy attending nuclear weapons programs and a lack of robust monitoring systems but also to internal contestation and government ambivalence about its own intentions with respect to nuclear power.

2. And one may argue by extension, terrorists, but the focus of the NPT is quite resolutely on proliferation to states. Efforts to prevent terrorists from acquiring nuclear weapons have inaugurated several new initiatives, most of which involve enhancing coordination among states to ensure maintaining state monopoly of the most extreme means of violence (see chapter 1).

3. Many recent commentators have worried aloud about the possible domino effect of Iranian nuclearization—starting with Middle Eastern states, such as Saudi Arabia and Turkey, and expanding to Asia and Africa.

4. Hymans (2006) suggests that the slow pace of proliferation is partly a result of state leaders' uncertainty about the security that will actually result from acquiring the bomb. Others, as seen later, make a similar point about acquisition of nuclear weapons increasing state vulnerability.

5. A term that comes from the title of an important 1993 edited volume by Zachary S. Davis and Benjamin Frankel. Many of the articles published in this volume are cited in this chapter from a 1993 special issue of the journal *Security Studies,* in which they were later reproduced.

6. For two reviews of literature on the causes of proliferation, see Ogilvie-White (1996) and Sagan (2011). This discussion has benefited greatly from both their discussions. A different variant of the question "why do states proliferate" is emphasized by T. V. Paul (2000) in the question that he poses in his book: "why

do nations forgo nuclear weapons?" Many studies on the causes of nuclear proliferation, as seen later, ask either one or both versions of these questions.

7. Supply-side factors that focus on the availability of fissile materials and the
technological capacity to produce a bomb have been widely critiqued for their
purported "technological determinism." I focus more on these in the following
chapter.

8. This article was republished in a slightly revised form in Sagan (2000).
A whole series of articles in the *Journal of Conflict Resolution* have attempted to
quantitatively evaluate different state motivations for proliferation (as well as
the consequences of proliferation). Despite the fact that Montgomery and Sagan
(2009, 322) find this resurgence in quantitative studies of proliferation dynamics
a "welcome advancement" (322), see their article for an extensive and excellent
critique of this literature that points out the measurement problems, the neglect
of unmeasurable but important variables, and the trivial findings that sometimes
result from these extensive analyses.

9. Stephen Meyer's (1984) book was an earlier attempt to divide the causes
of nuclear proliferation into what are now called supply-side and demand-side
variables. Meyer supplements the "technological imperative" (a necessary but not
sufficient condition), which produces a latent capability (supply side), with the
"motivational aspect," which includes national-level decision making or the exercise of an active choice (demand side) to move from latent to operational capability. These motives can vary from perceived military threats to nationalist rallying-
around-the-flag imperatives to the search for regional or global status.

10. For realist analyses of proliferation, see Zachary Davis's (1993) argument
that "classical realism" (more than both neorealism and liberalism) better explains
both proliferation and restraint; Richard Betts's (1993) realist explanation of
nuclear behavior as determined by the different positioning of different states—
driven by the twin motivations of fear–security and ambition–status—within anarchy; and Benjamin Frankel's (1993) structural realist account of the increased
proliferation possibilities in a multipolar world that more closely resembles an anarchic structure than the bipolar world of the Cold War, with its attendant superpower security guarantees. On the basis of an assessment of the different kinds
of likely motivations for Iranian nuclearization (and in the wider region), Bahgat
has consistently argued that security is the primary driver for proliferation in the
Middle East (see Bahgat 2004; 2005; 2006a; 2006b; 2007). See O'Neil (2007) for
a realist approach to proliferation in Northeast Asia, and see Alagappa (2008) for
Asia (including the Middle East) more broadly.

11. Another version of this domestic politics model was developed in Sagan's
(1994) now well-known response to Kenneth Waltz's "nuclear optimism," in
which he used organization theory to show how the internal dynamics of complex military organizations display strong tendencies toward the failure of "ratio-

nal deterrence," thus diminishing national security. Michael Reiss (1988) was one of the early scholars to emphasize that the "political motivations" of particular states to acquire or abstain from nuclear weapons mattered a great deal in the possibilities of proliferation, urging a case-by-case approach to understanding proliferation dynamics. A more recent case-by-case study of nuclear restraint can be found in Wirtz and Lavoy (2012).

12. This is the power of the "strategic enclave" of pro-bomb scientists and politicians that Itty Abraham's (1998) groundbreaking study of the Indian nuclear program reveals. Although this is the part of Abraham's study that seems to have received the most attention, it is his much more interesting analysis of postcolonial nuclear modernity on which I draw later in the chapter. See Vanaik (2004) for another discussion of the influence of the bomb lobby on India's 1998 decision to move from ambiguity to declared nuclear weapons status.

13. This, in her 2007 book, explains the lesser inclination to proliferate within outward-oriented East Asian states as compared to more inward-looking Middle Eastern states (Solingen 2007).

14. This recalls the argument of the previous chapter that the NPT-centered regime has established a particular kind of world order within which different states are positioned differently and the meaning of "responsibility" carries different connotations for differently positioned states.

15. For a shorter version of Hymans's essential argument, as applied to a different case study (North Korea), see Hymans (2008). Hymans's more recent book focuses on "domestic politics" factors to explain how internal state dynamics and political institutions that adversely affect the context of scientific professionalism and technical efficiency may thwart the motivation and will to nuclearize (Hymans 2012).

16. For a more concise articulation of a similar argument, see Rublee (2008). Rublee's argument echoes Tannenwald's (2007) discussion in some ways, although she is more interested in examining nuclear restraint exercised in the consideration to acquire weapons rather than nonuse of already acquired weapons.

17. Abraham (1998) can be read as an analysis of India's atomic pursuit as a form of colonial mimicry. One could also think of postwar British and French atomic pursuits as forms of postcolonial compensation for the loss of global power (Hecht 2006). For a more extensive discussion of the place of nuclear power in the imagination of post–World War II French national identity, see Hecht (1998). The emphasis on nuclear energy as a vehicle of modernity and progress was also a key aspect of nuclear relations within Soviet bloc countries, and indeed, both helped sustain the dependence of non-Russian territories and Eastern European satellite states on the Soviet Union, as well as allowing at least some Eastern European states to leverage the Soviet Union to develop their own nuclear expertise

(Schmid 2011). On a more complex notion of postcolonial mimicry as simultaneously imitative and subversive, see Bhabha (2004).

18. See, e.g., the argument that Charlotte Epstein (2008) makes about the modernity-producing functions of certain kinds of negative norms.

19. But Marx himself subscribes to a prejudiced view of primitive fetishisms, relying mostly on Africa for his analogies, where, according to Ferguson, that view of fetishism simply does not hold. Using Evans-Pritchard's classic study of Azande causal reasoning, Ferguson suggests that ethnography in much of Africa reveals that rather than endowing objects in the human world with mystified power, Africans search for human agency in all events, social and natural (Ferguson 2006, esp. chapter 3).

20. I will have more to say shortly on the way that Žižek understands ideological mystification as it works within commodity fetishism.

21. I will have more to say on the ways that this category of "accident" has functioned within nuclear doctrine and antinuclear politics in the following chapter. Burke (2009) points out that the debate between employing the strategy of deterrence versus relying on winnable nuclear strategies has been an ongoing feature of U.S. Cold War doctrine during and after the Cold War.

22. My intention is not to diminish the technical and resource challenges that poorer states face in building effective systems of control but rather to suggest that the presuppositions and prejudices about the limits of "Enlightenment rationality" that underlie some of the current fears of proliferation (as the previous chapter argued) also help define the borders of the community within which the effective communication that deterrence requires can function.

23. This, as far as I know, is the only piece Derrida has written on nuclear politics and is widely seen to have helped inaugurate a field of studies called "nuclear criticism" that set itself the task of applying literary theory to nuclear security. See chapter 1 of Solomon (1988) for a discussion of the political and professional contexts that led to the 1984 colloquium on "nuclear criticism" among literary theorists at Cornell University and formed the basis for the 1984 special issue of *Diacritics* on the subject, to which Derrida contributed the leading piece. Chapter 2 undertakes a sympathetic discussion of the Derrida piece, but the following chapter and the rest of the book attempt to restore a "nuclear referent" not entirely contained by textuality and that can open up the possibilities of productive communication and compromise between proponents and opponents of nuclear weapons without resulting in the endless aporias of literary discourse. I find Solomon's approach quite useful for my own thinking and am using this discussion of deterrence as semiotic precisely to draw attention to the materiality of the nuclear referent that deterrence attempts to transcend.

24. Unlike Baudrillard's acknowledgment of "real" nuclear use, Derrida's argument that nuclear war is a "fantasy" or "fiction" is based on the claim that, unlike other wars, a nuclear war has no precedent—is a "nonevent"—because the

atomic bombing of Japan was the end of a conventional war rather than a nuclear war (Derrida 1984). This too-easy dismissal of the nuclear events of World War II is, of course, problematic on its own terms (Norris 1994) but is also reliant on a certain kind of distinction between conventional and nuclear weapons and war that, I argue in the following section, itself contributes to the fetishization of nuclear weapons.

25. McCanles (1984, 13) suggests that Machiavelli may have been the first historical writer to be attentive to this power of deterrence, which lay not in actual use of weapons but in the threat of use, and where "the currency value of one's threats was not always proportional to the gold in one's vaults," thus making force subservient to discourse.

26. McCanles's goal is to reveal a series of paradoxes that result from deterrence as a semiotic regime and that make it continuously unstable, periodically undoing what is an unviable deterrence equilibrium and propelling it toward an accelerating arms race. Of all the pieces in the 1984 *Diacritics* special volume on nuclear criticism, I find McCanles's deployment of literary criticism in his analysis of deterrence as a semiotic regime to be the sharpest.

27. One should not be surprised here at how much of science fiction is devoted to imagining the unimaginable horrors of nuclear weapons.

28. Most studies have focused on language. For a study of nuclear iconography and the ways that nuclear images "de-materialize" their objects, see Taylor (2003).

29. Once again, please note my earlier comment about the mischaracterization of fetishism in African contexts as suggested by Ferguson (2006). Ward Wilson (2013) has also recently made use of de Santana's arguments to suggest why nuclear weapons can continue to serve as a currency of power despite being useless as weapons for most purposes.

30. There is a tendency to distinguish too bluntly between the early or young "idealist" Marx's focus on ideology (*The German Ideology* being the critical text here) and the later or more mature "materialist" Marx's focus on the commodity fetish in *Capital*. W. J. T. Mitchell (1986) makes a very compelling case for problematizing that distinction by viewing both ideology and fetishism as "varieties of idolatory." Raymond Williams (1982, 72–74) argues that deterrence as strategy was long ago surpassed during the Cold War arms race with the accumulation of increasing overkill capacity, as deterrence became an ideology whose purpose was deterrence of Communism.

31. This, of course, is a spin on Schelling's (1966; 1970) famous description of deterrence as the "rationality of irrationality." Indeed, several former nuclear warriors, such as Robert McNamara, who, like the Gang of Four, now reject nuclear weapons, have articulated cogent arguments precisely about this irrationality of allegedly rational deterrence (sometimes framed as the "madness of MAD"). See Robert Green, who served as the former commander of the British Royal Navy, and commander-in-chief of the U.S. Strategic Air Command General Lee Butler's

comments to the National Press Club in Washington, D.C., on December 4, 1996 (Green 2000). It is important to point out that Richard Nixon himself is said to have subscribed to the "madman theory"—that it would deter adversaries if they believed that he was a volatile, mad, irrational leader best not to provoke (Sagan 2003). There are also much more radical critiques of the alleged rationality undergirding the strategy of nuclear deterrence and the nuclear debate more generally. For instance, Zia Mian (1998) argues that having a nuclear debate itself is immoral, akin to a debate about the right to kill and eat children or to deliberately use famines as an instrument of population control, debates that no democratic society would consider having. See Bidwai and Vanaik (2000) and Hashimi and Lee (2004) for other discussions of the ethics of nuclear weapons and deterrence and the special issue of *Ethics* 95, no. 1 (1985), on "Ethics and Nuclear Deterrence," for a conversation among nuclear strategists and political philosophers.

32. But the rejection of a fetish object—especially when it is enunciated in the form of moral repudiation—may well consolidate its power, as I suggest a bit later. Like rejecting the power of money and wealth, a moral repudiation of the allure of nuclear weapons implicitly recognizes the presence of the fetish.

33. Ashis Nandy (1998) also calls nuclearism a "psychopathological syndrome," a kind of "genocidal mentality" that relies on psychic and moral numbing to contemplate and plan mass exterminations.

34. Appadurai himself does not discuss nuclear weapons as luxury goods but does, in one brief paragraph, allude to the strategic arms limitation talks as an example of a highly competitive realm of luxury trade, where the luxury in question is the nuclear restraint extracted from the trade (Appadurai 1986, 40).

35. The following chapter discusses the costs and opportunity costs of acquiring nuclear weapons.

36. It should be noted here that the land mine and chemical weapons taboos that were also initially taboos against use eventually became taboos against possession, felt acutely even by those who are recalcitrant in giving up their stockpiles. This may be another indication of the way that nuclear desire has been produced in a distinctive way through an articulation of its value through nonuse, which makes it harder to develop a taboo against possession. I owe this point to Marshall Beier.

37. Luckham (1984, 48–52) points to the ways that the armaments industry (with its cutting-edge and sophisticated armaments "packages") and associated military and technological culture (expertise, training, bureaucratic culture) both help reinforce the economic and cultural dependence of the third world on the West and bolster the dominance of third world ruling classes.

38. In Abraham's study, this technoaesthetic monumentalization of nuclear power compensated and substituted for the failures of the postcolonial state to deliver on "development" (via the science and technology of cheap nuclear energy). Sanadjian (2008) discusses the theatrical performances through which the

Iranian state helps turn enriched uranium into a fetishized commodity that depoliticizes and masks internal relations of authoritarian oppression.

39. There is plenty of evidence to suggest that the sharp distinction between conventional and nuclear weapons is somewhat suspect and that the category of WMD, which also includes biological and chemical weapons (whose potency is of an altogether different level), is also of dubious value. There is also contestation over the nuclear status of depleted uranium munitions or "dirty bombs" with significant radiological impact.

40. As Baudrillard (2001) says, reflecting on the ways that nuclear deterrence has made warfare hyperreal and empty, "if military power, at the cost of deescalating this marvelous practical madness to the second power, reestablishes the setting for warfare, a confined space that is in fact human, then weapons will regain their use-value and their exchange value: it will again be possible to *exchange warfare*" (194; emphasis original). Indeed, some argue that nuclear deterrence increases the possibility of conventional wars—called the *stability–instability paradox* in the literature on nuclear security.

41. It is this strange paradox that has led some scholars to ask whether we should think of nuclear weapons as weapons at all (Hallett and Summy 2003, 220–49). However, Hallett and Summy's concern is that using the term *weapons* connotes a possible use for nuclear weapons, which, given their inability to be discriminate or proportional to any legitimate war aid, are not considered to be effective as weapons of war by any serious defense planner. In making this argument, they are also drawing on, and reproducing, this absolute distinction between nuclear and other weapons, and in that sense, contributing toward the fetishism of nuclear weapons.

42. These same activists find themselves in the paradoxical position of demanding to "speak the unspeakable," to make nuclear weapons and their consequences "real" and "visible," while also enforcing "unspeakability" on those who might contemplate the actual use of nuclear weapons (Chaloupka 1992).

43. Luckham (1984) points out that even though the fetishism of the weapon, like other commodities, originates in capitalism and capitalist ideology, it functioned very much in the same way, although with important contextual valences, within the state socialism of the USSR, as well as in many non-Western cultures, thus making "armaments culture" both "capitalist *and* global" (43–52).

4. Costly Weapons

1. For two recent journalistic accounts that paint grim pictures with narratives of nuclear accidents, see Schlosser (2013) and Herzog (2012).

2. For an analysis of how the categories of "accidents" and "disasters" work to make poor, black, and brown bodies dispensable, see Agathengelou (2010).

3. I am not suggesting that those who document and study nuclear accidents

are referring to accidents only of this seemingly spectacular kind, but I am referring to how the trope of accident functions to connote a certain idea of the risks of nuclear possession. Although studies of nuclear accidents will often assess the possibilities of an accidental nuclear weapons detonation, the initiation of or escalation to a nuclear war, or a major catastrophe at a nuclear power plant, many also recognize the effects and risks of relatively low-level "accidents" in the production, handling, transportation, and day-to-day operations with respect to nuclear materials, weapons, and sites.

4. See Isao Hashimoto's simple but poignant video on the stream of nuclear explosions since the 1945 Trinity Tests, *Isao Hashimoto's Time Lapse of the 2053 Nuclear Explosions since 1945*, http://www.motherboard.tv/2010/7/13/isao-hashimoto-s -time-lapse-of-the-2053-nuclear-explosions-since-1945-video—2.

5. Henry Sokolski, executive director of the Nonproliferation Policy Education Center (http://www.npolicy.org/), has become one of the strongest public voices in the United States arguing that heavily state-subsidized nuclear energy programs, sold as the solution to global warming, have become prime movers of weapons proliferation. There is a debate on the question of how vulnerable to theft existing stockpiles of fissile material are, but there is no question that there is always the possibility of more weapons development from whatever materials do exist.

6. Japan is among a small handful of states without a nuclear weapons program but has had a commercial reprocessing plant that can produce plutonium for nuclear weapons and has civilian stocks of separated plutonium.

7. Hence Waltz, who makes the case for horizontal proliferation on grounds of security stability, is genuinely puzzled by vertical proliferation because, in his view, the logic of nuclear deterrence that can operate with a fairly limited force structure effectively eliminates any incentives for strategic arms racing (Waltz 1981). The "utility" of nuclear weapons held for nonuse cannot explain the massive resources expended in creating and maintaining large nuclear arsenals.

8. Kaldor does recognize that there are periods, such as was the case after World War II, when new industries were being established, when military spending can contribute to the accumulation process, but there is a point at which certain social relations (of security, of labor) become embedded in particular technomaterial infrastructures (of nuclear weapons production)—what she calls the *social* (rather than numerical) domination of dead over living labor—that contribute to diminishing rates of productivity (Kaldor 1982, 279).

9. During its first two years in office, the Obama administration increased funding for nuclear weapons and pledged to modernize the U.S. nuclear arsenal and production complex (Norris and Kristensen 2011). See Lieber and Press (2011) for a discussion about and defense of the contradictory policies of the Obama administration, which is pledging to reduce the size of the nuclear arsenal

even as it funds defense projects to modernize low-yield, higher-accuracy nuclear weapons that would be more "useable" in a conflict.

10. This eventually resulted in a book published by Brookings Institution titled *Atomic Audit: The Costs and Consequences of US Nuclear Weapons since 1940.* See http://www.brookings.edu/projects/archive/nucweapons/schwartz.aspx.

11. For instance, the construction of an expensive Chemistry and Metallurgy Research Replacement Nuclear Facility at Los Alamos was put on hold for at least five years. Additionally, a plan to increase the annual production of plutonium pits at Los Alamos from twenty to eighty was also being reassessed because it was predicted to cost nearly $6 billion (Kristensen and Norris 2012).

12. See http://energy.gov/sites/prod/files/FY13_SEWD_NNSABudget_USec _DAgostino_3–21–12.pdf for more specifics of the NNSA budget request.

13. See http://www.armscontrol.org/factsheets/USNuclearModernization for an extensive layout and breakdown of costs for various nuclear modernization projects. It should also be added here that although the United States has adopted a moratorium on conducting additional explosive nuclear testing, it has simultaneously invested significant resources into the technological infrastructure needed for laboratory-based simulated testing, which it considers vital to maintaining "safety" and "reliability" of its nuclear weapons. Thus, using the rubrics of "modification" and "enhancement," and suggesting no "new" production of nuclear weapons, the United States has been able to upgrade its warhead designs for post–Cold War missions (Taylor 2003, 11). For routine cost overruns in the Department of Energy's nuclear projects, including its warhead life-extension program, see this report by the Alliance for Nuclear Accountability: http://www .ananuclear.org/Portals/0/documents/high_risk_report.pdf.

14. http://cutnukes.globalzero.org/.

15. "World Nuclear Status," http://www.fas.org/programs/ssp/nukes/ nuclearweapons/nukestatus.html.

16. The early "Miliband–Poulantzas debate" on the degree of state autonomy in capitalist society dealt directly with the question of the role of the state but assumed that the state always acted to promote the legitimacy of capitalist society (Poulantzas 1960; Miliband 1970). For a classic piece that intervenes in this debate by analyzing the character of the overdeveloped postcolonial state, see Alavi (1972). This debate has been periodically renewed in different forms in the context of the internationalization of capital (Linklater 1990, esp. chapters 6 and 7). For example, in Wallerstein's world systems theory, the imperatives of market exchange at the international level curtail state autonomy so much so that nation-states are but superstructural appendages aiding in the reproduction of the modern global capitalist system (Wallerstein 1979; 1984), whereas other scholars stress how the state continues to play an important role in the internationalization and reproduction of capitalism (e.g., Murray 1971).

17. The literature on the military–industrial complex is enormous. For some of the more classical Marxist analyses of the military–industrial complex in the area of nuclear weapons, see Thompson (1982), Williams (1982), and Kaldor (1982). For a more recent investigative report of the emergence and influence of one of the leading U.S. nuclear weapons corporations, see Hartung (2012a).

18. This analysis draws heavily from Hartung (2012a).

19. These include the Congressional Shipbuilding Caucus and Submarine Caucus, which push for higher shipbuilding budgets, especially for ballistic missile submarines; the Congressional Long-Range Strike Caucus, which pushes not just for nuclear and conventional bombers but also for intercontinental ballistic missiles and cruise missiles; and a coalition of senators advocating for intercontinental ballistic missiles.

20. The three largest lobbying organizations that focus specifically on submarines are the Submarine Industrial Base Council, a group that claims to represent "more than 5,000 businesses across all 50 states that make up the nation's submarine industrial base" (http://www.submarinesuppliers.org/); the Naval Submarine League, self-described as "the professional organization for submarine advocates" (http://www.navalsubleague.com/); and the Naval League (http://www.navyleague.org/). The primary group that advocates on behalf of major air force weapons contractors is the Air Force Association (http://www.afa.org/).

21. Whether campaign contributions directly dictate policy is difficult to determine. On one hand, Hartung's report shows that there does appear to be a clear correlation between campaign contributions given and congressmen supporting pro-nuclear weapons-related legislation and projects. It is difficult to assess, however, whether the support for these projects is due to the campaign contributions given to congressional members or merely to the fact that projects that provide jobs to a specific district are generally supported by the member of Congress who represents that district. But sometimes efforts at influencing senators appear clearly unsuccessful, and Hartung provides the example of Senator Dianne Feinstein (Democrat-California), who has received more money from nuclear weapons corporations than any other member of the Senate, yet has been extremely critical of the NNSA (Hartung 2012a, 18).

22. See the website for the Center for Responsive Politics (http://www.opensecrets.org/) for more comprehensive information on corporate influence on U.S. politics, including considerable data on the nuclear industry and nuclear lobby groups.

23. For a comprehensive study of nuclear power subsidies in the United States, see Koplow (2010).

24. The nuclear energy industry's main trade association is the Nuclear Energy Institute (NEI) (http://www.nei.org/), which lobbies fairly heavily on the industry's behalf. The NEI has several registered federal lobbyists on its staff and also hires several outside lobbying firms and consultants. Individual nuclear en-

ergy companies, such as Entergy, Exelon, and Duke Energy, also conduct their own separate lobbying efforts, as do the utility companies that are not part of the NEI. The nuclear power industry also makes substantial campaign contributions, especially to members of select committees that make nuclear energy policy, and to members of districts where reactors are located or planned.

25. Usually, it is the engineers and technicians working for the NRC who often take up more lucrative positions in the nuclear energy industry or with lobby groups, but occasionally executives from the industry or officials from the Energy Department are appointed to the commission (see Zeller 2011).

26. See Charman (2010) and Stoett (2003) on the enormous efforts of the nuclear industry, post the nuclear incidents at Chernobyl and Three Mile Island, to rework its weathered image as unsafe and risky for the environment and proliferation into a more positive image of a "clean, carbon-free energy source" that solves the problem of climate change. The nuclear lobby in the United States spends millions of dollars to help secure the huge subsidies and loan guarantees that keep the nuclear energy industry competitive, and representatives of the NEI rushed to Congress immediately after the nuclear meltdown in Japan to reassure members that nuclear energy was safe.

27. A lot of this background is drawn from Buck (1983).

28. In both Japan (as we will see shortly) and India, the nuclear regulatory body has been located within the ministry in charge of promoting nuclear energy. Japan created a new regulatory body in 2012, which is housed under the Ministry of Environment.

29. http://www.ap.org/company/awards/part-i-aging-nukes.

30. See Lochbaum (2011) for a recent report that studies fourteen near-misses by the NRC during 2010, providing examples of both dangerous lapses and laudable catches. See the Nuclear Safety Project run by the Union of Concerned Scientists (http://www.ucsusa.org/) for discussions of nuclear hazards in the United States over the years.

31. http://research.greenpeaceusa.org/?a=view&d=6003.

32. http://www.ucsusa.org/assets/documents/nuclear_power/nrc-2010-full-report.pdf.

33. This eventually (in 2012) led to the resignation of Chairman Gregory B. Jaczko, who was supposedly pushing for tougher regulations.

34. See the "US–India Joint Statement on High Technology Commerce," related to trade in dual-use technology, released in November 2002: http://www.bis.doc.gov/news/2002/kijointstatementindia.htm.

35. See the report by Bajoria and Pan (2006) for details on the deal as well as some of the arguments made by proponents and critics. For step-by-step accounts of the deal making between and within India and the United States, see Mistry (2006) and Pant (2011) and several of the pieces in Chari (2009).

36. See Mistry (2006) for a discussion of the different domestic interests in

both the United States and India lobbying for and against this deal, although much of the focus in this article is on political groups rather than corporate interests. On the Indian opposition to the deal (primarily from leftist political parties, but initially also from the Hindu nationalist opposition party), much of which had to do with concerns about Indian sovereignty and U.S. power, see Chakravarti (2009). For a concise overview of arguments against the deal, see Milhollin (2006), and for a short summary of arguments in favor of the deal, see Mistry and Ganguly (2006). It should be noted that ElBaradei (2006), IAEA director general at the time, endorsed the deal as a "creative, outside-the-box" solution (although not without generating criticism).

37. See Abe (2009) and Fitzpatrick (2008b) for a discussion of some of the effects of the nuclear deal on the nonproliferation regime.

38. China has recently begun a new round of energy cooperation with Pakistan, with a commitment to build two new nuclear reactors in the port city of Karachi. This is a controversial deal that effectively provides a Chinese exception to nuclear-sanctioned Pakistan, but without NSG approval. Both countries have referred to the U.S. Nuclear Fuel Deal with India as a precedent for this cooperation.

39. See http://www.cfr.org/india/us-india-nuclear-deal/p9663 for a discussion of all these points.

40. It should be pointed out that Tellis served as senior adviser to the U.S. undersecretary of state for political affairs and was quite involved in negotiating the nuclear deal.

41. The negotiations of the U.S.–Indian nuclear deal was one instance in which differences of opinion within the Department of Atomic Energy were publicly aired (Raman 2012, appendix 2).

42. Reports indicate that India plans to build several nuclear power reactors over the next couple of decades, hoping to reach a target of forty thousand megawatts by 2020 and sixty-three thousand megawatts by 2032 and has identified four coastal cities (against serious resistance in those areas) to build gigantic, and some of the world's largest, nuclear parks or clusters (Reuters 2008; *Economic Times* 2010). As Raman (2012) points out, there has been a consistent and considerable gap between the achievements and projections of India's Department of Atomic Energy (DAE), and this is likely to continue in the future, even as the DAE uses these projections to secure state subsidies and bolster its own institutional power (Raman 2012).

43. *The Hindu* published a series of Wikileaks stories that eventually led to the (unproven) "cash for votes" scandal in which the ruling party was accused of bribing members of the opposition to buy their assent to the Nuclear Fuel Deal.

44. The latter of these two sites in Jaitapur, Maharashtra, has become the site of massive public protests, which I will discuss in the following section.

45. This kind of special protection is pretty standard in the nuclear industry,

in which many countries have adopted domestic laws that both indemnify the supplier from any financial liability and cap the liability of the operator (usually a public or private utility company) at a figure that is considerably smaller than the impact of a serious nuclear incident. These legislative concessions have largely been extracted by U.S. and Western European governments acting on behalf of corporate interests via a series of international liability conventions, effectively providing a subsidy to the nuclear power industry that is borne by potential victims and taxpayers. It is important to point out here that all three major nuclear accidents (Three Mile Island, Chernobyl, and Fukushima) were found to have been caused by some combination of design defects and operator error (Ramana and Raju 2013). It should also be noted that although the United States has been pressuring countries like India to ratify the Convention on Supplementary Compensation for Nuclear Damage, which sets the framework for these protections for the nuclear industry, a grandfather clause in the convention exempts the United States such that its own domestic law (the 1957 Price–Anderson Act) determines the liability of operators (currently capped at $12 billion) and also protects the rights of Americans to sue.

46. This was in the context of the Indian prime minister's very recent visit to Washington, D.C., that led to the signing of the first commercial agreement between Westinghouse and India.

47. See a similar story about France in Sayare (2012).

48. METI also promotes the nuclear energy sector overseas. The Japanese government and nuclear industry have been quite aggressive in lobbying for and helping secure nuclear reactor contracts in developing countries such as Vietnam, especially as demand within Japan has diminished in light of the Fukushima Daiichi incident.

49. The NRA recently issued a rare public scolding to the Tokyo Electric Company (TEPCO) about errors that led to the leakage of radioactive water into the Pacific Ocean (Fackler 2013).

50. From powerful power companies, such as TEPCO (the operator of the reactors at Fukushima Daiichi and Japan's largest utility company), and the industry's lobby group (the Federation of Electric and Power Companies).

51. The term used in Japan is nuclear *mura*, meaning "village" or "community" (Funabashi and Kitazawa 2012, 14). The term *amakudari*, or "descent from heaven," is used to describe the revolving-door practice in Japan in which government bureaucrats land lucrative positions in the industry they previously helped regulate; the lesser known practice of *amaagari*, or "ascent to heaven," is used to describe the dependence of regulatory agencies on expertise from retired or active engineers from the nuclear industry (Onishi and Belson 2011).

52. In addition, there was criticism that the first three contracts for decontamination and cleanup work at Fukushima Daiichi were awarded to three giant

construction companies, with no particular expertise in radiation cleanup, that were also heavily involved in the building of the nuclear industry (Tabuchi 2012). Public criticism of the government's decision to let TEPCO, the operator of the nuclear plant at Fukushima, handle the cleanup efforts finally led the government to take more control of the process in late 2013, although this still fell within the purview of the trade ministry. A major and risky effort to remove the spent fuel rods from the damaged reactor 4 building is currently under way. There have been demands and proposals for the Japanese government to yield cleanup responsibilities to international experts independent of TEPCO, who would be monitored by a civil society panel.

53. For a while, the financial health of TEPCO was really under question, and the two-decade-long push by a group of shareholders to end TEPCO's nuclear program seemed like it might receive more attention (Tabuchi 2011d). The Japanese government eventually passed a law to allow the provision of public funds to TEPCO to help cover the costs of compensation to victims of the Fukushima Daiichi disaster, helping keep the company afloat (Tabuchi 2011b).

54. Intensified public pressure post the Fukushima Daiichi accident had led the Japanese government to make a relatively weak commitment to go nuclear-free by 2040, but the recently elected prime minister, Shinzo Abe, who himself ran on a campaign pledge of moving Japan away from nuclear power, reversed that position within a week of assuming office and said that he would seek to build new nuclear reactors. This is no surprise given the generally pro-business orientation of Mr. Abe's party, which won on campaign promises of rejuvenating Japan's lagging economy, and the pressure from the largest business lobby, Keidenren, which has been urging the government to restart the majority of nuclear reactors that have been kept off-line in the wake of the antinuclear protests. Abe's mentor and former prime minister, Junichiro Koisume, who had once been an enthusiastic supporter of nuclear power, has very recently emerged as a strong public critic of it.

55. The Department of Energy in the United States receives the most number of no-bid contracts; most of these funds are directed at programs that clean up Cold War–era nuclear weapons sites and are awarded to large corporations.

56. This is the approach taken by the Nobel Peace Prize–winning organization International Physicians for the Prevention of Nuclear War, which has produced three volumes documenting the environmental and health effects at various nuclear sites around the world: *Radioactive Heaven and Earth* (Robbins, Makhijani, and Yih 1991) documents the effects of nuclear testing, *Plutonium: Deadly Gold of the Nuclear Age* (Hu, Makhijani, and Yih 1992) documents the hazards of plutonium production and nuclear waste storage, and *Nuclear Wastelands* (Makhijani, Hu, and Yih 1995) documents the effects of uranium mining and milling, plutonium reprocessing, and weapons assembly.

57. Many of the data here are from the World Nuclear Association (http://world-nuclear.org/), with supplementary information from the 2011 "Red Book" of the IAEA. For information on global stocks and distribution of highly enriched uranium and separated plutonium that is weapons usable, see appendix 7A in SIPRI (2011).

58. The uranium for the bomb dropped on Hiroshima came from Belgian Congo. The history of nuclear testing shows similar colonial patterns.

59. http://www.world-nuclear.org/info/inf110.html.

60. The 1997 Additional Protocols (although voluntarily adopted by states) made uranium mines and yellowcake plants subject to international inspections for the first time, although the ability and general desire of the IAEA to devote its scarce resources toward that, rather than toward the more visible nuclear power plants and weapons production facilities, is still fairly low.

61. This term is generally attributed to Ward Churchill and Winona LaDuke (Churchill and LaDuke 1992; Churchill 1993). A series of investigative articles by Judy Pasternak in 2006 in the *Los Angeles Times* about illnesses developed by specific members of the Navajo community continued to draw attention to this issue relatively recently. See Pasternak (2010), Brugge and Goble (2002), and Brugge, Benally, and Yazzie-Lewis (2006) for extensive documentation and discussion of the effects of uranium mining on Navajo Indians. Many of the debates on the differential distribution of (still lingering) dangers from uranium mining have been revived in the context of recent discussions on expanding mining in the United States, as demand from countries like China and Saudi Arabia expands and a program for diluting uranium from old Russian warheads for use in U.S. power plants expires. It should also be pointed out here that enormous corporate lobby groups have also pushed for uranium mining, especially in areas where there is local resistance (such as in recent efforts to lift a moratorium on uranium mining in the state of Virginia), but the focus of this section is much more specifically on exploitation and land appropriation. In general, the U.S. Environmental Protection Agency is responsible for dealing with the effects of uranium mining, while the processing and enrichment of ore in mills is the purview of the Department of Energy. For accounts of local communities in the United States affected by nuclear weapons production and testing, see Masco (2006), Harper (2007), and Titus (2001), and for nuclear waste disposal (particularly in the Yucca Mountain region), see Kuletz (1998). See Krupar (2013) for a sharp account of the ways that efforts to convert some of the highly contaminated decommissioned nuclear sites in the western United States into nature preserves obscure the costs of the ongoing hazards of exposure. For an account of a "networked U.S. empire" whose expansive geography incorporated a series of overseas island territories that effectively served as nuclear laboratories, see Oldenziel (2011). For an account of Australian uranium mining on Aboriginal lands as colonial practice, see Bannerjee (2000).

62. Any fuller accounting of nuclear costs in the production of nuclear power would have to account for not just uranium mining but also uranium milling, conversion, and separation; plutonium production and separation; fabrication of different weapons components; weapons assembly and dismantling; nuclear testing; weapons maintenance; and the handling, transportation, and operations of nuclear materials and processes, including the disposal and storage of waste. These include both radiation and other toxic hazards, and those affected are not just workers, including armed forces personnel, but also local communities living around nuclear production and testing sites, subjects of nuclear experiments, and future generations of the world, given the very long half-lives of nuclear materials. See Makhijani, Hu, and Yih (1995) for a fuller account of the different kinds and levels of occupational and health hazards encountered at these different stages.

63. For a report on the difficult conditions of work and life faced by all workers involved in cleanup efforts inside the plant, see McCurry (2013).

64. The HDI is a statistic designed to measure the socioeconomic well-being of a national population and is based on a composite of life expectancy, educational attainment, and income; it is used to rank countries based on what is considered a more holistic measure of economic development than what can be captured through figures that focus on economic growth: http://hdr.undp.org/en/reports/global/hdr2013/. There are no statistics available for North Korea in the UNDP report.

65. It is important to point out here, because this chapter started with the Waltz–Sagan debate, that Scott Sagan well recognizes that in the horizontal proliferation of nuclear weapons, it is the poorer, more recent entrants to the nuclear club who have to develop their weapons programs under the opaque conditions imposed by the nuclear taboo, and thus whose untested weapons programs are much less likely to have the necessary safety features designed and put in place by more mature nuclear states. The "accident proneness" of these states is at least partly a result of the global conditions imposed by the nuclear nonproliferation regime (Sagan 1994, 98–100).

Conclusion

1. Here I am clearly invoking a global "we," although much of my effort in the book, and in the rest of this chapter, is to scrutinize and critique the presumption of an alleged "international community" that is uniformly invested in nuclear arms control and disarmament.

2. It is important to point out that Waltz makes it clear in his response to Sagan that he is making this claim not on the basis of the universality of rationality but rather on the basis of "fear"—the fear of catastrophe that nuclear weapons can inflict (Sagan and Waltz 2003, 154). Although not written in direct response to

Waltz's piece on Iranian nuclearization, see Sagan (2006) for an argument against "deterrence optimism" that points to the loose infrastructure of control that Iran would possess rather than its inherent irrationality. This is similar to Sagan's position in his earlier debate with Waltz.

3. In a conceptualization of the impact of nuclear technology on the nation (rather than just the state as an apparatus of security), Masco suggests that the permeability of national borders to long-range missiles and the immediacy of destruction also confounds the sense of national time and space. In addition, the long-term toxicity of nuclear materials (calculated in thousands of years) disrupts any reasonable conception of nation-time (Masco 2006, chapter 1).

4. Of course, there is a sense in which Waltz also conceptualizes nuclear weapons as transformative in that they provide "absolute security," or such a unique restraining influence on state behavior that they engender systemic stability. Waltz came to this conclusion about the systemic effects of nuclear weapons later in his writings. In this respect, Mearsheimer, who at one time also argued for the stabilizing effects of limited, well-managed proliferation, no longer thinks that they have subdued the potential for systemic conflict and instability (Roth 2007; Wheeler 2009).

5. This is a key question in debates on how well deterrence actually functions or can be made to function in the geopolitical rivalry in South Asia (Ganguly and Kapur 2009; 2010; Basrur 2006; Rajagopalan 2008; Khan 2011).

6. The irony here, of course, is that this involves risking the very survival of the subjects of state security to make them secure. Agreements like the Anti-Ballistic Missile Treaty and doctrines emphasizing countervalue (targeting of cities and civilian population centers rather than weapons systems) were similarly premised on recognition of the profound vulnerability posed by nuclear weapons and made strategic use of the exposure to such vulnerability.

7. Arguing that even proliferation optimists such as Waltz and Mearsheimer are unable to account for nuclear terrorism, Ariel Roth (2007) concludes that if states can no longer perform their existential task of providing security, perhaps one needs a new paradigm for organizing social units. In contrast, and representing the much more common view on the question of nuclear terrorism, Walker (2012) suggests that the increasing challenges posed by what he calls "irregular social interaction" require a strengthening of the "regular" domain of interstate and intrastate order.

8. The fuller version that Deudney (2007) outlines would include some form of collective international control as conceptualized in the eventually discarded 1946 Baruch Plan, a form of "recessed deterrence" in which universal disarmament is accompanied by the ability to effectively rearm if needed, as proposed by Jonathan Schell, and some form of "concurrent authority," in which any nuclear

use must be authorized by multiple agents, as proposed by Leonard Beaton (see Deudney 2007, chapter 9).

9. Yet, suggests Ayoob, the desire for independence from great power management of the global order persists and manifests itself primarily in "questions of status," which is precisely how Ayoob sees the opposition of India, Pakistan, Israel, and, at the time, Argentina, Brazil, and South Africa to the NPT (Ayoob 1989, 72–74; 1991, 276–78). In fact, says Ayoob (1989, 77), status is experienced as security for many of these states with active memories of colonial domination, who see their own survival at stake in their ability to write the terms of the international system.

10. I don't pursue the collective organizing possibilities available to the third world via the vehicle of the state. This, for instance, was the basis for the 1955 Bandung conference that gave rise to the Non-Aligned Movement (NAM), the G-77, third worldism as an organizing principle, and demands for a New International Economic Order. As Pasha (2013) points out, despite the eventual fractures and the failures to live up to the promise of effecting structural change, that decolonial "impulse" of Bandung lives on as an aspiration that animates many projects for global justice. See Potter and Mukhatzhanova (2013) for an evaluation of the historical influence and future potential of NAM for tackling issues related to nuclear disarmament and nonproliferation.

11. Here I am drawing from and reformulating Partha Chatterjee's (1993a) discussion of nationalism as a "derivative discourse."

12. Ashis Nandy (1983) suggests that of the two primary figures of alterity in resistance to the British Empire in India, it is Gandhi's more childlike and feminized mode that was ultimately more threatening to the colonizing powers than the masculinist, angrier version that mimicked the terms of the colonial binary of civilized–savage in the process of reversing it. However, the model of imitative childishness that Ayoob offers is quite different from the unruly childishness of Nandy's account.

13. The Subaltern Studies group emerged out of the work of a set of Indian historians who set themselves the task of writing a history of subordinated groups whose voices had been absent in the archives from which both colonial and nationalist historiographers drew their material. For an elaboration of the methodological approach and the concept of the subaltern as used in this project, see the preface and first chapter of Guha and Spivak (1988).

Bibliography

Abe, Nobuyasu. 2009. "Rebuilding the Nuclear Disarmament and Non-Proliferation Regime in the Post-US-India Deal World." *Asia Pacific Review* 16, no. 1: 56–72.

Abraham, Itty. 1996. "Science and Power in the Postcolonial State." *Alternatives* 21: 321–39.

———. 1998. *The Making of the Indian Atomic Bomb: Science, Secrecy, and the Postcolonial State.* New Delhi: Orient Longman.

———. 2009a. "Contra-Proliferation: Interpreting the Meanings of India's Nuclear Tests in 1974 and 1998." In *Inside Nuclear South Asia,* edited by Scott D. Sagan, 106–133. New Delhi: Orient Blackswan.

———. 2009b. *South Asian Cultures of the Bomb: Atomic Publics and the State in India and Pakistan.* New Delhi: Orient Blackswan.

Adler, Emanuel. 1991. "Arms Control, Disarmament, and National Security: A Thirty Year Retrospective and a New Set of Anticipations." *Daedalus* 120, no. 1: 1–20.

———. 1992. "The Emergence of Cooperation: National Epistemic Communities and the International Evolution of the Idea of Nuclear Arms Control." *International Organization* 46, no. 1: 101–45.

Adler, Emanuel, and Michael Barnett. 1998. *Security Communities.* Cambridge: Cambridge University Press.

———. 1998. "Security Communities in Theoretical Perspective." In *Security Communities,* edited by Emanuel Adler and Michael Barnett, 3–28. Cambridge: Cambridge University Press.

Adler, Emanuel, and Peter M. Haas. 1992. "Conclusion: Epistemic Communities, World Order, and the Creation of a Reflective Research Program." *International Organization* 46, no. 1: 367–90.

Agathangelou, Anna M. 2010. "Necro-(neo) Colonizations and Economics of Blackness: Of Slaughters, 'Accidents,' 'Disasters' and Captive Flesh," in *International Relations and States of Exception: Margins, Peripheries, and Excluded Bodies,* edited by Shampa Biswas and Sheila Nair, 186–209. London: Routledge.

Agathangelou, Anna M., and L. H. M. Ling. 2009. *Transforming World Politics: From Empire to Multiple Worlds.* London: Routledge.

Ahmed, Aijaz. 1992. *In Theory: Classes, Nations, Literatures.* New York: Verso.

Alagappa, Muthiah, ed. 2008. *The Long Shadow: Nuclear Weapons and Security in 21st Century Asia.* Stanford, Calif.: Stanford University Press.

Alavi, Hamza. 1972. "The State in Post-Colonial Societies: Pakistan and Bangladesh," *New Left Review* 74: 59–81.

Allison, Graham. 2004a. "How to Stop Nuclear Terror." *Foreign Affairs* 83, no. 1: 64–74.

——. 2004b. *Nuclear Terrorism: The Ultimate Preventable Catastrophe.* New York: Times Books.

——. 2006. "The Will to Prevent: Global Challenges of Nuclear Proliferation." *Harvard International Review* 28, no. 3: 50–55.

Anderson, Benedict. 1991. *Imagined Communities: Reflections on the Origin and Spread of Nationalism.* London: Verso.

Anghie, Antony. 2006. "Decolonizing the Concept of 'Good Governance.'" In *Decolonizing International Relations,* edited by Branwen G. Jones, 109–30. Lanham, Md.: Rowman and Littlefield.

Appadurai, Arjun. 1986. *The Social Life of Things: Commodities in Cultural Perspective.* New York: Cambridge University Press.

Auerswald, David P. 2006–7. "Deterring Nonstate WMD Attacks." *Political Science Quarterly* 121, no. 4: 543–68.

Ayoob, Mohammed. 1983–84. "Security in the Third World: The World About to Turn?" *International Affairs* 60, no. 1: 41–51.

——. 1989. "The Third World in the System of States: Acute Schizophrenia or Growing Pains?" *International Studies Quarterly* 33, no. 1: 67–79.

——. 1991. "The Security Problematic of the Third World." *World Politics* 43, no. 1: 257–83.

——. 1995. *The Third World Security Predicament: State Making, Regional Conflict, and the International System.* Boulder, Colo.: Lynne Rienner.

——. 1997. "Defining Security: A Subaltern Perspective." In *Critical Security Studies: Concepts and Cases,* edited by Keith Krause and Michael Williams, 121–46. Minneapolis: University of Minnesota Press.

——. 1998. "Subaltern Realism: International Relations Theory Meets the Third World." In *International Relations Theory and the Third World,* edited by Stephanie G. Neumann, 31–54. Basingtoke, U.K.: Macmillan.

——. 2002. "Inequality and Theorizing in International Relations: The Case for Subaltern Realism." *International Studies Review* 4, no. 3: 27–48.

——. 2011. "Can the World Live with a Near-Nuclear Iran?" http://www.cnn.com/2011/12/14/opinion/ayoob-iran-nulcear.

Ayson, Robert. 2005. "Selective Non-proliferation or Universal Regimes?" *Australian Journal of International Affairs* 59, no. 4: 431–37.

Bahgat, Gawdat. 2004. "Weapons of Mass Destruction in West Asia." *Korean Journal of Defense Analysis* 16: 131–52.

———. 2005. "Nuclear Proliferation in the Middle East: Iran and Israel." *Contemporary Security Policy* 26, no. 1: 25–43.

———. 2006a. "Nuclear Proliferation: The Islamic Republic of Iran." *Iranian Studies* 39, no. 3: 307–27.

———. 2006b. "Nuclear Proliferation: The Case of Saudi Arabia." *Middle East Journal* 60, no. 3: 421–43.

———. 2007. *Proliferation of Nuclear Weapons in the Middle East.* Gainesville: University Press of Florida.

Bailey, Kathleen C., ed. 1994. *Weapons of Mass Destruction: Costs versus Benefits.* New Delhi: Manohar.

Bajaj, Vikas. 2011. "Resistance to Jaitapur Nuclear Plant Grows in India." *New York Times,* April 13.

Bajoria, Jayshree, and Esther Pan. 2006. "The US–India Nuclear Deal," Council on Foreign Relations Publication 9663. http://www.cfr.org/india/us-india-nuclear-deal/p9663.

Bannerjee, Subhabrata Bobby. 2000. "Whose Land Is It Anyway? National Interest, Indigenous Stakeholders, and Colonial Discourses: The Case of the Jabiluka Uranium Mine." *Organization and Environment* 13, no. 1: 3–38.

Barkawi, Tarak, and Mark Laffey. 2006. "The Postcolonial Moment in Security Studies." *Review of International Studies* 32: 329–52.

Basrur, Rajesh M. 2006. *Minimum Deterrence and India's Nuclear Security.* Stanford, Calif.: Stanford University Press.

Baudrillard, Jean. 1987. "Forget Baudrillard: An Interview with Sylvere Lotringer." In *Forget Foucault,* 65–135. New York: Semiotext(e).

———. 1994. *Simulacra and Simulation.* Ann Arbor: University of Michigan Press.

———. 2001. "Fatal Strategies." In *Jean Baudrillard: Selected Writings,* edited by Mark Poster, 188–209. Stanford, Calif.: Stanford University Press.

Beardsley, Kyle, and Victor Asal. 2007. "Proliferation and International Crisis Behavior." *Journal of Peace Research* 44, no. 2: 139–55.

Beeman, William O. 2003. "Iran and the United States: Postmodern Culture Conflict in Action." *Anthropological Quarterly* 76, no. 4: 671–91.

———. 2005. *The "Great Satan" vs. the "Mad Mullahs": How the United States and Iran Demonize Each Other.* Chicago: University of Chicago Press.

Beier, Marshall. 2009. *International Relations in Uncommon Places: Indigeneity, Cosmology, and the Limits of International Theory.* New York: Palgrave Macmillan.

Belson, Ken. 2011. "Two Voices Are Heard after Years of Futility." *New York Times,* August 19.

Betts, Richard K. 1993. "Paranoids, Pygmies, Pariahs, and Nonproliferation Revisited." *Security Studies* 2: 100–24.

Bhabha, Homi. 2004. *The Location of Culture.* New York: Routledge.

Bidwai, Praful. 2011. "The Truth behind India's Nuclear Renaissance." *The Guardian,* February 8.

Bidwai, Praful, and Achin Vanaik. 2000. *New Nukes: India, Pakistan, and Global Nuclear Disarmament.* New York: Olive Branch Press.

Biswas, Shampa. 2001. "'Nuclear Apartheid': Race as a Postcolonial Resource?" *Alternatives* 26, no. 4: 485–522.

Biswas, Shampa, and Sheila Nair. 2010. "Introduction: International Relations and 'States of Exception.'" In *International Relations and States of Exception: Margins, Peripheries, and Excluded Bodies,* edited by Shampa Biswas and Sheila Nair, 1–30. London: Routledge.

Bjork, Rebecca S. 1995. "Public Policy Argumentation and Colonialist Ideology in the Post–Cold War Era." In *Warranting Assent: Case Studies in Argument Evaluation,* edited by Edward Schiappa, 211–38. Albany: State University of New York Press.

Blainey, Geoffrey. 1973. "Paradise Is a Bazaar." In *The Causes of War,* edited by Geoffrey Blainey, 18–32. New York: Free Press.

Blair, Bruce G., and Matthew A. Brown. 2011. "World Spending on Nuclear Weapons Surpasses $1 Trillion per Decade." http://www.globalzero.org/files/gz_nuclear_weapons_cost_study.pdf.

Blaut, J. M. 1993. *The Colonizer's Model of the World: Geographical Diffusionism and Eurocentric History.* New York: Guilford Press.

Bleiker, Roland. 2003. "A Rogue Is a Rogue Is a Rogue: US Foreign Policy and the Korean Nuclear Crisis." *International Affairs (Royal Institute of International Affairs)* 79, no. 4: 719–37.

Boese, Wade. 2005. "U.S.–Indian Nuclear Prospects Murky." *Arms Control Today,* October.

Booth, Ken. 1991. "Security and Emancipation." *Review of International Studies* 17, no. 4: 313–26.

———, ed. 2005. *Critical Security Studies and World Politics.* Boulder, Colo.: Lynne Rienner.

Bracken, Paul. 1999. *Fire in the East: The Rise of Asian Nuclear Power and the Second Nuclear Age.* New York: HarperCollins.

———. 2012. *The Second Nuclear Age: Strategy, Danger, and the New Power Politics.* New York: Times Books.

Broad, William J. 2011. "Iran Unveils Missile Silos as It Begins War Games." *New York Times,* June 27.

Brodie, Bernard. 1965. *Strategy in the Missile Age.* Princeton, N.J.: Princeton University Press.

Brugge, Doug, Timothy Benally, and Esther Yazzie-Lewis, eds. 2006. *The Navajo People and Uranium Mining.* Albuquerque: University of New Mexico Press.

Brugge, Doug, and Rob Goble. 2002. "The History of Uranium Mining and the Navajo People." *American Journal of Public Health* 92, no. 9: 1410–19.

Buck, Alice L. 1983. *A History of the Atomic Energy Commission*. Washington, D.C.: U.S. Department of Energy.

Bull, Hedley. 1977. *The Anarchical Society*. London: Macmillan.

Burke, Anthony. 2009. "Nuclear Reason: At the Limits of Strategy." *International Relations* 23, no. 4: 506–29.

Busch, Nathan. 2002. "Risks of Nuclear Terror: Vulnerabilities to Theft and Sabotage at Nuclear Weapons Facilities." *Contemporary Security Policy* 23, no. 3: 19–60.

———. 2004. *No End in Sight: The Continuing Menace of Nuclear Proliferation*. Lexington: University of Kentucky Press.

Busch, Nathan E., and Daniel H. Joyner. 2009. *Combating Weapons of Mass Destruction: The Future of International Nonproliferation Policy*. Athens: University of Georgia Press.

Byrne, John, and Steven M. Hoffman. 1996. *Governing the Atom: The Politics of Risk*. New Brunswick, N.J.: Transactions.

Campbell, David. 1992. *Writing Security: United States Foreign Policy and the Politics of Identity*. Minneapolis: University of Minnesota Press.

———. 1993. *Politics without Principle: Sovereignty, Ethics, and the Narratives of the Gulf War*. Denver, Colo.: Lynne Rienner.

Caprioli, Mary, and Peter Trumbore. 2005. "Rhetoric versus Reality: Rogue States in Interstate Conflict." *Journal of Conflict Resolution* 49, no. 5: 770–91.

Carr, E. H. 1940. *The Twenty Year Crisis, 1919–1939: An Introduction to the Study of International Relations*. London: Macmillan.

Carranza, Mario E. 2006. "Can the NPT Survive? The Theory and Practice of US Nuclear Non-Proliferation Policy after September 11." *Contemporary Security Policy* 27, no. 3: 489–525.

———. 2007. "From Non-Proliferation to Post-Proliferation: Explaining the US–India Nuclear Deal." *Contemporary Security Policy* 28, no. 3: 464–93.

Carter, Ashton B. 2006. "America's New Strategic Partner?" *Foreign Affairs* 85, no. 4: 33–44.

Chakrabarty, Dipesh. 2000. *Provincializing Europe: Postcolonial Thought and Historical Difference*. Princeton, N.J.: Princeton University Press.

Chakravarti, Rekha. 2009. "Internal Roadblocks to the Indo–US Nuclear Deal." In *Indo–US Nuclear Deal: Seeking Synergy in Bilateralism,* edited by P. R. Chari, 60–75. New York: Routledge.

Chaloupka, William. 1992. *Knowing Nukes: The Politics and Culture of the Atom*. Minneapolis: University of Minnesota Press.

Chandler, Michael Alison. 2011. "In Japan, New Attention for Longtime Antinuclear Activist." *Washington Post,* April 10.

Chari, P. R., ed. 2009. *Indo–US Nuclear Deal: Seeking Synergy in Bilateralism.* New York: Routledge.

Charman, Karen. 2010. "Half-Truths, Errors, and Omissions Propel Current 'Nuclear Revival.'" *Capitalism Nature Socialism* 31: 20–28.

Chatterjee, Partha. 1993a. *Nationalist Thought and the Colonial World: A Derivative Discourse.* Minneapolis: University of Minnesota Press.

———. 1993b. *The Nation and Its Fragments: Colonial and Postcolonial Histories.* Princeton, N.J.: Princeton University Press.

———. 1998. "How We Loved the Bomb and Later Rued It." *Economic and Political Weekly,* June 13.

Chellaney, Brahma. 2011. "Corrupt Means Taint the Nuclear Deal." *The Hindu,* March 23.

Chilton, Paul. 1982. "Nukespeak: Nuclear Language, Culture, and Propaganda." In *Nukespeak: The Media and the Bomb,* edited by Crispin Aubrey, 94–112. London: Comedia.

Chowdhry, Geeta, and Sheila Nair, ed. 2002. *Power, Postcolonialism, and International Relations: Reading Race, Gender, and Class.* New York: Routledge.

Churchill, Ward. 1993. *Struggle for the Lank: Indigenous Resistance to Genocide Ecocide and Expropriation in Contemporary North America.* Monroe, Maine: Common Courage Press.

Churchill, Ward, and Winona LaDuke. 1992. "Native North America: The Political Economy of Radioactive Colonialism." In *The State of Native America: Genocide, Colonization, and Resistance,* edited by M. Annette Jaimes, 241–66. Boston: South End Press.

Cirincione, Joseph. 2005. "Lessons Lost." *Bulletin of the Atomic Scientists* 61, no. 42: 43–53.

———. 2007. *Bomb Scare: The History and Future of Nuclear Weapons.* New York: Columbia University Press.

CNN World. 2010. "Iran Calls Fuel Bank 'Nuclear Apartheid.'" *CNN World,* December 4.

Cohn, Carol. 1987. "Sex and Death in the Rational World of Defense Intellectuals." *Signs: Journal of Women in Culture and Society* 12, no. 4: 687–718.

———. 1993. "War, Wimps, and Women: Talking Gender and Thinking War." In *Gendering War Talk,* edited by Miriam Cooke and Angela Woolacott, 227–46. Princeton, N.J.: Princeton University Press.

Collignon, Fabienne. 2010. "Review of John Mueller 'Atomic Obsession: Nuclear Alarmism from Hiroshima to Al-Qaeda.'" *Journal of American Studies* 44: 1–2.

Corera, Gordon. 2006. *Shopping for Bombs: Nuclear Proliferation, Global Insecurity, and the Rise and Fall of the A. Q. Khan Network.* New York: Oxford University Press.

Cortright, David, and Raimo Väyrynen. 2009. *Towards Nuclear Zero.* Adelphi Papers 49, no. 410.

Cox, Robert. 1986. "Social Forces, States, and World Orders: Beyond International Relations Theory." In *Neorealism and Its Critics,* edited by Robert Keohane, 204–54. New York: Columbia University Press.

Craig, Campbell. 2003. *Glimmer of a New Leviathan: Total War in the Realism of Neibuhr, Morgenthau, and Waltz.* New York: Columbia University Press.

———. 2011. "Review of Atomic Obsession: Nuclear Alarmism from Hiroshima to al-Qaeda." *Critical Studies on Terror* 4, no. 1: 115–24.

Curtis, Charles B. 2006. "Curbing the Demand for Mass Destruction." *Annals of the American Academy of Political and Social Science* 607: 27–32.

Dahl, Robert A. 1985. *Controlling Nuclear Weapons.* Syracuse, N.Y.: Syracuse University Press.

Daley, Tad. 2010. *Apocalypse Never: Forging the Path to a Nuclear Weapon-Free World.* New Brunswick, N.J.: Rutgers University Press.

Darby, Phillip. 1998. *The Fiction of Imperialism: Reading between International Relations and Postcolonialism.* London: Cassell.

———, ed. 2006. *Postcolonizing the International: Working to Change the Way We Are.* Honolulu: University of Hawai'i Press.

Davis, Zachary S. 1993. "The Realist Nuclear Regime." *Security Studies* 2: 79–99.

Davis, Zachary S., and Benjamin Frankel, ed. 1993. *The Proliferation Puzzle: Why Nuclear Weapons Spread and What Results.* London: Frank Cass.

DeGroot, Gerard. 2009. "Dismissing Doomsday." *Arms Control Today* 39, no. 9: 49–52.

Derrida, Jacques. 1984. "No Apocalypse, Not Now (Full Speed Ahead, Seven Missiles, Seven Missives)." *Diacritics* 14, no. 2: 20–31.

de Santana, Anne Harrington. 2009. "Nuclear Weapons as the Currency of Power: Deconstructing the Fetishism of Force." *Nonproliferation Review* 16, no. 3: 325–45.

———. 2011. "The Strategy of Non-proliferation: Maintaining the Credibility of an Incredible Pledge to Disarm." *Millennium: Journal of International Studies* 40, no. 1: 3–19.

Deudney, Daniel. 1993. "Dividing Realism: Structural Realism versus Security Materialism on Nuclear Security and Proliferation." In *The Proliferation Puzzle: Why Nuclear Weapons Spread and What Results,* edited by Zachary S. Davis and Benjamin Frankel, 7–36. London: Frank Cass.

———. 1995. "Nuclear Weapons and the Waning of the Real-State." *Daedalus* 124, no. 2: 209–31.

———. 2007. *Bounding Power: Republican Security Theory from the Polis to the Global Village.* Princeton, N.J.: Princeton University Press.

Deutsch, Karl, Sidney Burrell, Robert Kann, Maurice Lee Jr., Martin Lichterman, Raymond Lindren, Francis Loewenheim, and Richard Van Wagenen. 1957. *Political Community and the North Atlantic Area.* Princeton, N.J.: Princeton University Press.

Dietrich, Gabriele. 2011. "From Tarapur to Jaitapur." *Economic and Political Weekly,* June 4, 25–29.

Dillon, Michael. 1996. *The Politics of Security: Towards a Political Philosophy of Continental Thought.* New York: Routledge.

Dirlik, Arif. 1997. "The Postcolonial Aura: Third World Criticism in the Age of Global Capitalism." In *Dangerous Liaisons: Gender, Nation, and Postcolonial Perspectives,* edited by Anne McClintock, Aamir Mufti, and Ella Shohat, 501–28. Minneapolis: University of Minnesota Press.

Dwyer, Jim. 2012. "From Japan, Bearing Witness in Debate Over Indian Point." *New York Times,* March 6.

Economic Times. 2010. "India Eyeing 63,000 MW Nuclear Power Capacity by 2032: NPCIL." October 11.

ElBaradei, Mohamed. 2006. "Rethinking Nuclear Safeguards." *Washington Post,* June 14.

Epstein, Charlotte. 2008. *The Power of Words: Birth of An Anti-Whaling Discourse.* Cambridge, Mass.: MIT Press.

Escobar, Arturo. 1994. *Encountering Development: The Making and Unmaking of the Third World.* Princeton, N.J.: Princeton University Press.

Eze, Emmanuel Chukwudi, ed. 1997. *Race and the Enlightenment: A Reader.* Cambridge, Mass.: Blackwell.

Fackler, Martin. 2013. "Watchdog Scolds Operator of Fukushima Plant." *New York Times,* October 4.

Fackler, Martin, and Normitsu Onishi. 2011. "In Japan, a Culture That Promotes Nuclear Dependency." *New York Times,* May 30.

Fairbanks, Charles H., Jr., and Abram N. Shulsky. 1987. "From 'Arms Control' to Arms Reductions: The Historical Experience." *Washington Quarterly* 10, no. 3: 59–73.

Ferguson, James. 1994. *The Anti-Politics Machine: "Development," Dopoliticization, and Bureaucratic Power in Lesotho.* Minneapolis: University of Minnesota Press.

———. 2006. *Global Shadows: African in the Neoliberal World Order.* Durham, N.C.: Duke University Press.

Fitzpatrick, Mark. 2008a. "Will Nuclear Energy Plans in the Middle East Become Nuclear Weapons Strategies?" *International Relations* 22, no. 3: 381–85.

———. 2008b. "US–India Nuclear Cooperation Accord: Implications for the Non-proliferation Regime." *Asia-Pacific Review* 15, no. 1: 76–85.

Foucault, Michel. 1995. *Discipline and Punish: The Birth of the Prison.* New York: Vintage Books.

Frankel, Benjamin. 1993. "The Brooding Shadow: Systemic Incentives and Nuclear Weapons Proliferation." *Security Studies* 2: 37–78.

Freedman, Lawrence D. 2010. "Review of Atomic Obsession: Nuclear Alarmism from Hiroshima to Al-Qaeda." *Foreign Affairs* 89, no. 2: 158–59.

Fuhrmann, Matthew. 2009a. "Taking a Walk on the Supply Side: The Determinants of Civilian Nuclear Cooperation." *Journal of Conflict Resolution* 53, no. 2: 181–208.

———. 2009b. "Spreading Temptation: Proliferation and Peaceful Nuclear Cooperation Agreements." *International Security* 34, no. 1: 7–41.

Fuhrmann, Matthew, and Sarah Kreps. 2010. "Targeting Nuclear Programs in War and Peace: A Quantitative Empirical Analysis, 1941–2000." *Journal of Conflict Resolution* 54, no. 3: 1–29.

Funabashi, Yoichi, and Kay Kitazawa. 2012. "Fukushima in Review: A Complex Disaster, a Disastrous Response." *Bulletin of the Atomic Scientists* 68, no. 9: 9–21.

Gaddis, John Lewis. 1987. *The Long Peace: Inquiries into the History of the Cold War.* New York: Oxford University Press.

Gallucci, Robert L. 2006. "Averting Nuclear Catastrophe: Contemplating Extreme Responses to U.S. Vulnerability." *Annals of the American Academy of Political and Social Science* 607 (September): 51–58.

Gandhi, Leela. 1998. *Postcolonial Theory: A Critical Introduction.* New York: Columbia University Press.

Ganguly, Sumit, and S. Paul Kapur, eds. 2009. *Nuclear Proliferation in South Asia: Crisis Behavior and the Bomb.* New York: Routledge.

———. 2010. *India, Pakistan, and the Bomb: Debating Nuclear Stability in South Asia.* New York: Columbia University Press.

Gavin, Francis J. 2009–10. "Same As It Ever Was: Nuclear Alarmism, Proliferation, and the Cold War." *International Security* 34, no. 3: 7–37.

Gray, Collin. 1999a. *The Second Nuclear Age.* Boulder, Colo.: Lynne Rienner.

———. 1999b. *Modern Strategy.* New York: Oxford University Press.

Green, Robert. 2000. *The Naked Nuclear Emperor: Debunking Nuclear Deterrence, a Primer for Safer Security Strategies.* Christchurch, New Zealand: Disarmament and Security Centre.

Gregory, Shaun. 1990. *The Hidden Cost of Deterrence: Nuclear Weapons Accidents.* London: Brassey's.

Grovogui, Siba N'Zatioula. 1996. *Sovereigns, Quasi-Sovereigns, and Africans: Race and Self-Determination in International Law.* Minneapolis: University of Minnesota Press.

———. 2002. "Regimes of Sovereignty: International Morality and the African Condition." *European Journal of International Relations* 8, no. 3: 315–38.

———. 2006. *Beyond Eurocentrism and Anarchy: Memories of International Order and Institutions.* New York: Palgrave Macmillan.

Guha, Ranajit, and Gayatri Chakravorty Spivak, eds. 1988. *Selected Subaltern Studies.* New York: Oxford University Press.

Gusterson, Hugh. 1998. *Nuclear Rites: A Weapons Laboratory at the End of the Cold War*. Berkeley: University of California Press.

———. 1999. "Nuclear Weapons and the Other in the Western Imagination." *Cultural Anthropology* 14, no. 1: 111–43.

———. 2004. *People of the Bomb: Portraits of America's Nuclear Complex*. Minneapolis: University of Minnesota Press.

———. 2011. "Atomic Escapism?" *American Scientist* 99: 72–73.

Haas, Ernst B. 1982. "Words Can Hurt You; or, Who Said What to Whom About Regimes." *International Organization* 36, no. 2: 207–43.

Haas, Peter M. 1989. "Do Regimes Matter? Epistemic Communities and Mediterranean Pollution Control." *International Organization* 43, no. 3: 377–403.

———. 1992. "Introduction: Epistemic Communities and International Policy Coordination." *International Organization* 46, no. 1: 1–35.

———. 1997. *Knowledge, Power, and International Policy Coordination*. Columbia: University of South Carolina Press.

Haggard, Stephan, and Beth Simmons. 1987. "Theories of International Regimes." *International Organization* 41, no. 3: 491–517.

Hallett, Brian, and Ralph Summy. 2003. "Detooling the Language of the Master's House: The Case of Those 'Nuclear Things.'" *Peace and Change* 28, no. 1: 220–49.

Hansen, T. B., and F. Stepputat, eds. 2005. Introduction to *States of Imagination: Ethnographic Explorations of the Postcolonial State*. Durham, N.C.: Duke University Press.

Hanson, Marianne. 2005. "The Future of the NPT." *Australian Journal of International Affairs* 59, no. 3: 301–16.

Hardin, Russell, and John J. Mearsheimer. 1985. Introduction to the special issue "Symposium on Ethics and Nuclear Deterrence." *Ethics* 95, no. 3: 411–23.

Harper, Janice. 2007. "Secrets Revealed, Revelations Concealed: A Secret City Confronts Its Environmental Legacy of Weapon Production." *Anthropological Quarterly* 80: 39–64.

Hartung, William D., with Christine Anderson. 2012a. "Bombs versus Budgets: Inside the Nuclear Weapons Lobby." http://www.ciponline.org/images/uploads/publications/Hartung_IPR_0612_NuclearLobbyReport_Final.pdf.

———. 2012b. *Prophets of War: Lockheed Martin and the Making of the Military–Industrial Complex*. New York: Nation Books.

Hasenclever, Andreas, Peter Mayer, and Volker Rittberger. 1997. *Theories of International Regimes*. Cambridge: Cambridge University Press.

Hashimi, Sohail H., and Steven P. Lee, eds. 2004. *Ethics and Weapons of Mass Destruction: Religious and Secular Perspectives*. New York: Cambridge University Press.

Hassner, Pierre. 2007. "Who Killed Nuclear Enlightenment?" *International Affairs* 44, no. 3: 455–67.

Hecht, Gabrielle. 1998. *The Radiance of France: Nuclear Power and National Identity after World War II.* Cambridge, Mass.: MIT Press.

———. 2002. "Rupture-Talk in the Nuclear Age: Conjugating Colonial Power in Africa." *Social Studies of Science* 32, nos. 5–6: 691–727.

———. 2003. "Globalization Meets Frankenstein? Reflections on Terrorism, Nuclearity, and Global Technopolitical Discourse." *History and Technology* 19, no. 1: 1–8.

———. 2006. "Nuclear Ontologies." *Constellations* 13, no. 3: 320–31.

———. 2012a. "An Elemental Force: Uranium Production in Africa, and What It Means to Be Nuclear." *Bulletin of Atomic Scientists* 68, no. 22: 22–33.

———. 2012b. *Being Nuclear: Africans in the Global Uranium Trade.* Cambridge, Mass.: MIT Press.

Herzog, Rudolph. 2012. *A Short History of Nuclear Folly.* Brooklyn, N.Y.: Melville House.

Hindess, B. 2005. "Citizenship and Empire." In *Sovereign Bodies: Citizens, Migrants, and States in the Postcolonial World,* edited by T. B. Hansen and F. Stepputat, 241–56. Princeton, N.J.: Princeton University Press.

Hobson, John M. 2012. *The Eurocentric Conception of World Politics: Western International Theory, 1760–2010.* Cambridge: Cambridge University Press.

———. 2013. "The Other Side of the Westphalian Frontier." In *Postcolonial Theory and International Relations: A Critical Introduction,* edited by Sanjay Seth, 32–48. New York: Routledge.

Hoey, Matthew. 2009. "India's Quest for Dual-Use Technology." *Bulletin of the Atomic Scientists* 65: 43–59.

Hook, Glenn D. 1984. "The Nuclearization of Language: Nuclear Allergy as Political Metaphor." *Journal of Peace Research* 12, no. 3: 259–75.

Hu, Howard, Arjun Makhijani, and Katherine Yih. 1992. *Plutonium: Deadly Gold of the Nuclear Age.* Cambridge, Mass.: International Physicians Press.

Hulme, Peter, and Ludmilla Jordanova, eds. 1990. *The Enlightenment and Its Shadows.* London: Routledge.

Hundley, T. 2012. "Countdown to Zero Dollars." *Foreign Policy,* August 9, 1–4.

Hymans, Jacques E. C. 2006. *The Psychology of Nuclear Proliferation: Identity, Emotions, and Foreign Policy.* New York: Cambridge University Press.

———. 2008. "Assessing North Korean Nuclear Intentions and Capacities: A New Approach." *Journal of East Asian Studies* 8, no. 2: 259–92.

———. 2012. *Achieving Nuclear Ambitions: Scientists, Politicians, and Proliferation.* Cambridge: Cambridge University Press.

Iklé, Fred Charles. 2006. *Annihilation from Within: The Threat to Nations.* New York: Columbia University Press.

Inayatullah, Naeem, and David L. Blaney. 2004. *International Relations and the Problem of Difference*. New York: Routledge.

Jackson, Robert H. 1990. *Quasi-States: Sovereignty, International Relations, and the Third World*. New York: Cambridge University Press.

Jahn, Beate. 2000. *The Cultural Construction of International Relations: The Invention of the State of Nature*. Hampshire, U.K.: Palgrave.

Jepperson, Ronald L., Alexander Wendt, and Peter J. Katzenstein. 1996. "Norms, Identity, and Culture in National Security." In *The Culture of National Security: Norms and Identity in World Politics*, edited by Peter J. Katzenstein, 33–78. New York: Columbia University Press.

Jervis, Robert. 1976. *Perception and Misperception in International Politics*. Princeton, N.J.: Princeton University Press.

———. 1982. "Security Regimes." *International Organization* 36, no. 2: 357–78.

———. 2009. "Or: How I Learned to Stop Worrying." *The National Interest*, November/December, 73–84.

Jo, Dong-Joon, and Erik Gartzke. 2007. "Determinants of Nuclear Weapons Proliferation." *Journal of Conflict Resolution* 51, no. 1: 167–94.

Johansen, Robert C. 1992. "Military Policies and the State System as Impediments to Democracy." *Political Studies* 40: 99–115.

Johnson, Rebecca. 2010. "Rethinking the NPT's Role in Security: 2010 and Beyond." *International Affairs* 86, no. 2: 429–45.

Jones, Branwen Gruffydd. 2006a. "Introduction: International Relations, Eurocentrism, and Imperialism." In *Decolonizing International Relations*, edited by Branwen Gruffydd Jones, 1–22. Lanham, Md.: Rowman and Littlefield.

———, ed. 2006b. *Decolonizing International Relations*. Lanham, Md.: Rowman and Littlefield.

———. 2013. "Slavery, Finance, and International Political Economy: Postcolonial Relations." In *Postcolonial Theory and International Relations: A Critical Introduction*, edited by Sanjay Seth, 49–69. New York: Routledge.

Jones, Richard Wyn. 1999. *Security, Strategy, and Critical Theory*. Boulder, Colo.: Lynne Rienner.

Joyner, Daniel H. 2009. *International Law and the Proliferation of Weapons of Mass Destruction*. New York: Oxford University Press.

Kaldor, Mary. 1982. "Warfare and Capitalism." In *Exterminism and the Cold War*, 261–87. London: Verso.

Kamdar, Mira. 2007. "Forget the Israel Lobby: The Hill's Next Big Player Is Made in India." *Washington Post*, September 30.

Katzenstein, Peter. 1996. *The Culture of National Security: Norms and Identity in World Politics*. New York: Columbia University Press.

Kauffman, Charles. 1989. "Names and Weapons." *Communication Monographs* 56: 273–85.

Kaufmann, Daniel, and Veronika Penciakova. 2011. "Preventing Nuclear Meltdown: Assessing Regulatory Failure in Japan and the United States." Brookings Opinion. http://www.ap.org/company/awards/part-i-aging-nukes.

Kazmi, Zahir. 2010. "Neo-Nuclear Apartheid." *Dawn,* December 31.

Kelleher, Catherine McArdle, and Judith Reppy, eds. 2011. *Getting to Zero: The Path to Nuclear Disarmament.* Stanford, Calif.: Stanford University Press.

Keohane, Robert O. 1982. "The Demand for International Regimes." *International Organization* 36, no. 2: 1325–55.

Keohane, Robert O., and Joseph S. Nye. 2001. *Power and Independence.* 3rd ed. New York: Longman.

Khan, Saira. 2002. *Nuclear Proliferation Dynamics in Protracted Conflict Regions: A Comparative Study of South Asia and the Middle East.* Aldershot, U.K.: Ashgate.

Khan, Zulfqar, ed. 2011. *Nuclear Pakistan: Strategic Dimensions.* Karachi: Oxford University Press.

Kirk, Jason A. 2008. "Indian-Americans and the US–India Nuclear Agreement: Consolidation of an Ethnic Lobby?" *Foreign Policy Analysis* 4: 275–300.

Klein, Naomi. 2007. *The Shock Doctrine: The Rise of Disaster Capitalism.* New York: Metropolitan Books.

Koplow, Doug. 2010. "Nuclear Power: Still Not Viable without Subsidies." *Union of Concerned Scientists,* February.

Krasner, Stephen D. 1982a. "Regimes and the Limits of Realism: Regimes as Autonomous Variables." *International Organization* 36, no. 2: 497–510.

———. 1982b. "Structural Causes and Regime Consequences: Regimes as Intervening Variables." *International Organization* 36, no. 2: 185–205.

———, ed. 1983. *International Regimes.* Ithaca, N.Y.: Cornell University Press.

Krause, Joachim. 2007. "Enlightenment and Nuclear Order." *International Affairs* 83, no. 3: 483–90.

Krause, Keith. 2011. "Leashing the Dogs of War: Arms Control from Sovereignty to Governmentality." *Contemporary Security Policy* 32, no. 1: 20–39.

Krause, Keith, and Michael Williams, eds. 1997. *Critical Security Studies: Concepts and Cases.* Minneapolis: University of Minnesota Press.

Krishna, Sankaran. 2001. "Race, Amnesia, and the Education of International Relations." *Alternatives* 26, no. 4: 401–24.

———. 2009a. *Globalization and Postcolonialism: Hegemony and Resistance in the Twenty-first Century.* Plymouth, U.K.: Rowman and Littlefield.

———. 2009b. "The Social Life of a Bomb: India and the Ontology of an 'Overpopulated' Society." In *South Asian Cultures of the Bomb: Atomic Publics and the State in India and Pakistan,* edited by Abraham Itty, 68–88. New Delhi: Orient Blackswan.

Kristensen, Hans M., and Robert S. Norris. 2012. "US Nuclear Forces, 2012." *Bulletin of the Atomic Scientists* 68, no. 3: 84–91.

Kroenig, Matthew. 2009. "Importing the Bomb: Sensitive Nuclear Assistance and Nuclear Proliferation." *Journal of Conflict Resolution* 53, no. 2: 161–80.

Krupar, Shiloh. 2013. *Hot Spotter's Report: Military Fables of Toxic Waste*. Minneapolis: University of Minnesota Press.

Kuletz, Valerie L. 1998. *The Tainted Desert: Environmental Ruin in the American West*. New York: Routledge.

Kurtz, Lester R. 2010. "Review of Atomic Obsession: Nuclear Alarmism from Hiroshima to Al-Qaeda." *Times Higher Education*, July, 57.

Langewiesche, William. 2007. *The Atomic Bazaar: The Rise of the Nuclear Poor*. New York: Farrar, Straus, and Giroux.

Larsen, Neil. 2000. "DerbiNation: Postcolonialism, Poststructuralism, and the Problem of Ideology." In *The Pre-Occupation of Postcolonial Studies*, edited by Fawzia Afzal-Khan and Kalpana Seshadri-Crooks, 140–56. Durham, N.C.: Duke University Press.

Lavoy, Peter R. 1993. "Nuclear Myths and the Causes of Nuclear Proliferation." *Security Studies* 2: 192–212.

Lazarus, Neil. 2001. "The Fetish of 'the West' in Postcolonial Theory." In *Marxism, Modernity, and Postcolonial Studies*, edited by Crystal Bartolovich and Neil Lazarus, 43–64. Cambridge: Cambridge University Press.

Lieber, Keir A., and Daryl G. Press. 2006. "The Rise of U.S. Nuclear Primacy." *Foreign Affairs* 85, no. 2: 42–54.

———. 2009. "The Nukes We Need: Preserving the American Deterrent." *Foreign Affairs* 88, no. 6: 39–51.

———. 2011. "Obama's Nuclear Upgrade." *Foreign Affairs*, July 6, http://www .foreignaffairs.com/articles/67973/keir-a-lieber-and-daryl-g-press/ obamas-nuclear-upgrade.

Lifton, Robert J., and Richard Falk. 1982. *Indefensible Weapons: The Political and Psychological Case Against Nuclearism*. New York: Basic Books.

Linklater, Andrew. 1990. *Beyond Realism and Marxism: Critical Theory and International Relations*. New York: St. Martin's Press.

Lipschutz, Ronnie D. 1995. "On Security." In *On Security*, edited by Ronnie D. Lipschutz , 1–23. New York: Columbia University Press.

Lipton, Eric, and Matthew L. Wald. 2013. "Post-Fukushima, Arguments for Nuclear Safety Bog Down." *New York Times*, February 26.

Litwak, Robert S. 2008. "Regime Change 2.0." *Wilson Quarterly* 32, no. 4: 22–27.

Lochbaum, David. 2011. "Nuclear Power Plant Safety in 2010: A Brighter Spotlight Needed." http://www.ucsusa.org/assets/documents/nuclear_power/ nrc-2010 full-report.pdf.

Luckham, Robin. 1984. "Of Arms and Culture." *Current Research on Peace and Violence* 7, no. 1: 1–64.

Lyon, Rod. 2005. "Nuclear Weapons, International Security, and the NPT." *Australian Journal of International Affairs* 59, no. 4: 425–30.

Makhijani, Arjun, Howard Hu, and Katherine Yih, eds. 1995. *Nuclear Wastelands: A Global Guide to Nuclear Weapons Production and Its Health and Environmental Effects.* Cambridge, Mass.: MIT Press.

Makhijani, Arjun, and Scott Saleska. 1995. "The Production of Nuclear Weapons and Environmental Hazards." In *Nuclear Wastelands: A Global Guide to Nuclear Weapons Production and Its Health and Environmental Effects.* Cambridge, Mass.: MIT Press.

Malik, Mohan J. 1998. "India Goes Nuclear: Rationale, Benefits, Costs, and Implications." *Contemporary South Asia* 20, no. 2: 191–215.

Martin, Guy. 1989. "Uranium: A Case Study in Franco-African Relations." *Australian Outlook* 43, no. 3: 89–101.

Marx, Karl. 1977. *Capital.* Vol. 1. New York: Vintage Books.

———. 1978. "On the Jewish Question." In *The Marx–Engels Reader,* 2nd ed., edited by Robert C. Tucker, 26–52. New York: W. W. Norton.

Masco, Joseph. 2006. *The Nuclear Borderlands: The Manhattan Project in Post–Cold War New Mexico.* Princeton, N.J.: Princeton University Press.

Mathai, Manu V. 2013. *Nuclear Power, Economic Development Discourse, and the Environment: The Case of India.* London: Routledge.

Mbembe, Achille. 2000. "At the Edge of the World: Boundaries, Territoriality, and Sovereignty in Africa." *Public Culture* 12, no. 1: 259–84.

———. 2001. *On the Postcolony.* Berkeley: University of California Press.

McCanles, Michael. 1984. "Machiavelli and the Paradoxes of Deterrence." *Diacritics* 14, no. 2: 11–19.

McCurry, Justin. 2011. "Fukushima Cleanup Recruits 'Nuclear Gypsies' from Across Japan." *The Guardian,* July 13.

———. 2013. "Plummeting Morale at Fukushima Daiichi as Nuclear Cleanup Takes Its Toll." *The Guardian,* October 15.

Mehta, Uday. 1990. "Liberal Strategies of Exclusion." *Politics and Society* 18, no. 4: 427–54.

———. 1999. *Liberalism and Empire: A Study in Nineteenth-Century British Liberal Thought.* Chicago: University of Chicago Press.

Meyer, Stephen M. 1984. *The Dynamics of Nuclear Proliferation.* Chicago: University of Chicago Press.

Mian, Zia. 1998. "Why Pakistan Should Renounce the Nuclear Option." in *The Nuclear Debate: Ironies and Immoralities,* edited by Zia Mian and Ashis Nandy, 23–56. Colombo, Sri Lanka: Regional Center for Strategic Studies.

Milhollin, Gary. 2006. "The U.S.–India Nuclear Pact: Bad for Security." *Current History,* November, 371–74.

Miliband, Ralph. 1970. "The Capitalist State: Reply to Nicos Poulantzas." *New Left Review* 59: 53–60.

Mistry, Dinshaw. 2006. "Diplomacy, Domestic Politics, and the U.S.–India Nuclear Agreement." *Asian Survey* 46, no. 5: 675–98.

Mistry, Dinshaw, and Sumit Ganguly. 2006. "The U.S.–India Nuclear Pact: A Good Deal." *Current History,* November, 375–78.

Mitchell, Timothy. 2000. "The Stage of Modernity." In *Questions of Modernity,* edited by Timothy Mitchell, 1–34. Minneapolis: University of Minnesota Press.

Mitchell, W. J. T. 1986. *Iconology: Image, Text, Ideology.* Chicago: University of Chicago Press.

———. 2005. *What Do Pictures Want? The Lives and Loves of Images.* Chicago: University of Chicago Press.

Montgomery, Alexander H., and Scott D. Sagan. 2009. "The Perils of Predicting Proliferation." *Journal of Conflict Resolution* 53, no. 2: 302–28.

Morgenthau, Hans. 1964. "The Four Paradoxes of Nuclear Strategy." *American Political Science Review* 58, no. 1: 23–35.

Moshirzadeh, Homeira. 2007. "Discursive Foundations of Iran's Nuclear Policy." *Security Dialogue* 38, no. 4: 521–43.

Mueller, John. 1989. *Retreat from Doomsday: The Obsolescence of Major War.* New York: Basic Books.

———. 2010. *Atomic Obsession: Nuclear Alarmism from Hiroshima to Al-Qaeda.* New York: Oxford University Press.

Muhula, Raymond. 2003. "Rogue Nations, States of Concern, and Axes of Evil: Examining the Politics of Disarmament in a Changing Geopolitical Context." *Mediterranean Quarterly* 14, no. 4: 76–95.

Muppidi, Himadeep. 2012. *The Colonial Signs of International Relations.* New York: Columbia University Press.

Murray, Robin. 1971. "The Internationalization of Capital and the Nation-State." *New Left Review* 67: 84–109.

Mutimer, David. 2000. *The Weapons State: Proliferation and the Framing of Security.* Boulder, Colo.: Lynne Rienner.

———. 2011. "From Arms Control to Denuclearization: Governmentality and the Abolitionist Desire." *Contemporary Security Policy* 32, no. 1: 57–75.

Nandy, Ashis. 1983. *The Intimate Enemy: Loss and Recovery of Self under Colonialism.* Delhi: Oxford University Press.

———. 1998. "The Epidemic of Nuclearism." In *The Nuclear Debate: Ironies and Immoralities,* edited by Zia Mian and Ashis Nandy, 1–4. Colombo, Sri Lanka: Regional Center for Strategic Studies.

———. 2003. *The Romance of the State: And the Fate of Dissent in the Tropics.* New Delhi: Oxford University Press.

Neocleous, Mark. 2007. "Security, Commodity, Fetishism." *Critique: Journal of Socialist Theory* 35, no. 3: 339–55.

———. 2008. *Critique of Security.* Montreal: McGill–Queen's University Press.

Norris, Christopher. 1994. "'Nuclear Criticism' Ten Years On." *Prose Studies* 17: 130–39.

Norris, Robert S., and Hans M. Kristensen. 2011. "US Nuclear Forces, 2011." *Bulletin of the Atomic Scientists* 67: 66–76.

———. 2013. "Global Nuclear Weapons Inventories, 1945–2013." *Bulletin of the Atomic Scientists* 69, no. 5: 75–81.

Nunn, Sam. 2006. "The Race between Cooperation and Catastrophe: Reducing the Global Nuclear Threat." *Annals of the American Academy of Political and Social Science* 607: 43–50.

Nye, Joseph S., Jr. 1987. "Nuclear Learning and U.S.–Soviet Security Regime." *International Organization* 41, no. 3: 371–402.

Ogilvie-White, Tanya. 1996. "Is There a Theory of Nuclear Proliferation? An Analysis of the Contemporary Debate." *The Nonproliferation Review* 4, no. 1: 43–60.

Ogultarhan, Adem. 2010. "Iran's Nuclear Program: The US Misses Opportunities? An Examination of US Policies in the Middle East and Implications of Those Policies on the US Global Position." *Alternatives: Turkish Journal of International Relations* 9, no. 1: 112–47.

Oldenziel, Ruth. 2011. "Islands: The United States as a Networked Empire," in *Entangled Geographies: Empire and Technopolitics in the Global Cold War,* edited by Gabrielle Hecht, 13–42. Cambridge, Mass.: MIT Press.

Olwell, Russell. 2010. "Two Views of Cassandra: Lawrence Badash *A Nuclear Winter's Tale* John Mueller, *Atomic Obsession.*" *Technology and Culture* 51, no. 4: 1002–5.

O'Neil, Andrew. 2007. *Nuclear Proliferation in Northeast Asia: The Quest for Security.* New York: Palgrave Macmillan.

———. 2005a. "Learning to Live with Uncertainty: The Strategic Implications of North Korea's Nuclear Weapons Capability." *Contemporary Security Policy* 26, no. 2: 317–34.

———. 2005b. "Nuclear Proliferation and Global Security: Laying the Groundwork for a New Policy Agenda." *Comparative Strategy* 24, no. 4: 343–59.

Onishi, Normitsu, and Martin Fackler. 2011. "Japan Held Nuclear Data, Leaving Evacuees in Peril." *New York Times,* August 8.

Onishi, Normitsu. 2011. "'Safety Myth' Left Japan Ripe for Nuclear Crisis." *New York Times,* June 24.

Onishi, Normitsu, and Ken Belson. 2011. "In Japan's Nuclear Nexus, Safety Is Left Out." *New York Times,* April 26.

Oye, Kenneth A., ed. 1986. *Cooperation under Anarchy.* Princeton, N.J.: Princeton University Press.

Pant, Harsh V. 2011. *The US–India Nuclear Pact: Policy, Process, and Great Power Politics.* New Delhi: Oxford University Press.

Parry, Benita. 2004. "The Institutionalization of Postcolonial Studies." In *The Cambridge Companion to Postcolonial Literary Studies,* edited by Neil Lazarus, 66–82. Cambridge: Cambridge University Press.

Pasha, Mustapha Kamal. 2013. "The 'Bandung Impulse' and International Relations." In *Postcolonial Theory and International Relations: A Critical Introduction*, edited by Sanjay Seth, 144–65. New York: Routledge.

Pasternak, Judy. 2010. *Yellow Dirt: An American Story of a Poisoned Land and a People Betrayed*. New York: Free Press.

Paul, T. V. 2000. *Power versus Prudence: Why Nations Forgo Nuclear Weapons*. Montreal: McGill-Queen's University Press.

———. 2009. *The Tradition of Non-Use of Nuclear Weapons*. Stanford, Calif.: Stanford University Press.

Payne, Keith B. 1996. *Deterrence in the Second Nuclear Age*. Lexington: University Press of Kentucky.

Perkovich, George. 1998. "Nuclear Proliferation." *Foreign Policy*, no. 112, 12–23.

———. 1999. *India's Nuclear Bomb: The Impact on Global Proliferation*. Berkeley: University of California Press.

Perkovich, George, and James M. Acton. 2008. *Abolishing Nuclear Weapons. Adelphi Papers* 396. New York: Oxford University Press for the International Institute for Strategic Studies.

Perrow, Charles. 2011. "Fukushima and the Inevitability of Accidents." *Bulletin of the Atomic Scientists* 67, no. 6: 44–52.

Pilat, Joseph F. 2007. "The End of the NPT Regime?" *International Affairs* 83, no. 3: 469–82.

Potter, William C., and Gaukhar Mukhatzhanova, eds. 2010a. *Forecasting Nuclear Proliferation in the 21st Century: The Role of Theory*. Vol. 1. Stanford, Calif.: Stanford University Press.

———, eds. 2010b. *Forecasting Nuclear Proliferation in the 21st Century: The Role of Theory*. Vol. 1. Stanford, Calif.: Stanford University Press.

———. 2013. *Nuclear Politics and the Non-Aligned Movement: Principles vs Pragmatism. Adelphi Papers* 427. London: Routledge Press for the International Institute for Strategic Studies.

Poulantzas, Nicos. 1960. "The Problem of the Capitalist State." *New Left Review* 58: 67–78.

Price, Richard. 2007. "Nuclear Weapons Don't Kill People, Rogues Do." *International Politics* 44, no. 2: 232–49.

Puchala, Donald J., and Raymond F. Hopkins. 1982. "International Regimes: Lessons from Inductive Analysis." *International Organization* 36, no. 2: 245–75.

Rajagopalan, Rajesh. 2008. "India: The Logic of Assured Retaliation." In *The Long Shadow: Nuclear Weapons and Security in 21st Century Asia*, edited by Muthiah Alagappa, 188–214. Stanford, Calif.: Stanford University Press.

Raman, J. Sri. 2009. "The US–India Nuclear Deal—One Year Later." *Bulletin of the Atomic Scientists*, October 1. http://www.thebulletin.org/web-edition/features/the-us-india-nuclear-deal-one-year-later.

Raman, M. V. 2012. *The Power of Promise: Examining Nuclear Energy in India.* New Delhi: Penguin.

Ramana, M. V., and Suvrat Raju. 2013. "The Impasse Over Liability Clause in Indo–US Nuclear Deal." *New York Times,* October 15.

Reddy, Rammanohar C. 2003. "Nuclear Weapons versus Schools for Children: An Estimate of the Cost of the Indian Nuclear Weapons Programme." In *Prisoners of the Nuclear Dream,* edited by M. V. Ramana and C. Rammanohar Reddy, 360–408. New Delhi: Orient Longman.

Reiss, Mitchell. 1988. *Without the Bomb: The Politics of Nuclear Nonproliferation.* New York: Columbia University Press.

———. 2004. *The Nuclear Tipping Point.* Washington, D.C.: Brookings Institution Press.

Reuters. 2008. "Westinghouse, Areva Eye India Nuclear Plants-Paper." August 18.

Rhodes, Richard. 1986. *The Making of the Atomic Bomb.* New York: Simon and Schuster.

Rittberger, Volker, and Peter Mayer, eds. 1995. *Regime Theory and International Relations.* Oxford: Oxford University Press.

Rittberger, Volker, and Michael Zürn. 1990. "Towards Regulated Anarchy in East–West Relations: Causes and Consequences of East–West Regimes." In *International Regimes in East–West Politics,* edited by Volker Rittberger, 9–63. London: Pinter.

Robbins, Anthony, Arjun Makhijani, and Katherine Yih. 1991. *Radioactive Heaven and Earth: Report of the International Physicians for the Prevention of Nuclear War International Commission to Investigate the Health and Environmental Effects of Nuclear Weapons Production and the Institute for Energy and Environmental Research.* London: Apex Press.

Roberts, Brad. 2007. "'All the King's Men'? Refashioning Global Nuclear Order." *International Affairs* 83, no. 3: 549–74.

Rosow, Stephen J. 1989. "Deterrence, State Legitimation, and Liberal Democracy." *Polity* 21, no. 3: 563–86.

Roth, Ariel Ilan. 2007. "Nuclear Weapons in Neo-Realist Theory." *International Studies Review* 9, no. 3: 369–84.

Rousseau, G. S., and Roy Porter, eds. 1990. *Exoticism in the Enlightenment.* Manchester, U.K.: Manchester University Press.

Rublee, Maria Rost. 2008. "Taking Stock of the Nuclear Nonproliferation Regime: Using Social Psychology to Understand Regime Effectiveness." *International Studies Review* 10, no. 3: 420–50.

———. 2009. *Nonproliferation Norms: Why States Choose Nuclear Restraint.* Athens: University of Georgia Press.

Ruggie, John. 1986. "Continuity and Transformation in the World Polity: Toward a Neorealist Synthesis." In *Neorealism and Its Critics,* edited by Robert Keohane, 131–57. New York: Columbia University Press.

Rühle, Michael. 2007. "Enlightenment in the Second Nuclear Age." *International Affairs* 83, no. 3: 511–22.

Sagan, Scott D. 1994. "The Perils of Proliferation: Organization Theory, Deterrence Theory, and the Spread of Nuclear Weapons." *International Security* 18, no. 4: 66–107.

———. 1996–97. "Why Do States Build Nuclear Weapons? Three Models in Search of a Bomb." *International Security* 21, no. 3: 54–86.

———. 2000. "Rethinking the Causes of Nuclear Proliferation: Three Models in Search of a Bomb." In *The Coming Crisis: Nuclear Proliferation, U.S. Interests, and World Order,* edited by Victor A. Utgoff, 17–50. Cambridge, Mass.: MIT Press.

———. 2003. "The Madman Nuclear Alert: Secrecy, Signaling, and Safety in October 1969." *International Security* 27, no. 4: 150–83.

———. 2006. "How to Keep the Bomb from Iran." *Foreign Affairs* 85, no. 5: 45–59.

———. 2011. "The Causes of Nuclear Weapons Proliferation." *Reviews in Advance,* February 18, 225–46. http://www.annualreviews.org.

Sagan, Scott D., and Kenneth N. Waltz. 2003. *The Spread of Nuclear Weapons: A Debate Renewed.* New York: W. W. Norton.

Said, Edward. 1979. *Orientalism.* New York: Vintage Books.

Sajed, Alina. 2013. *Postcolonial Encounters in International Relations: The Politics of Transgression in the Maghreb.* Milton Park, U.K.: Routledge.

Samet, Jonathan M., Daniel M. Kutvirt, Richard Waxweiler, and Charles R. Key. 1984. "Uranium Mining and Lung Cancer in Navajo Men." *New England Journal of Medicine* 310: 1481–84.

Sanadjian, Manuchehr. 2008. "Nuclear Fetishism, the Fear of the 'Islamic' Bomb, and National Identity in Iran." *Social Identities* 14, no. 1: 77–100.

Sanger, David E., and Eric Schmitt. 2001. "Pakistani Nuclear Arms Pose Challenge to U.S. Policy." *New York Times,* January 31.

Sang-Hun, Choe, and Steven Lee Myers. 2011. "Seoul Sets Terms for Resuming Talks with North Korea." *New York Times,* July 29.

Sayare, Scott. 2012. "Wishing Upon an Atom in a Tiny French Village." *New York Times,* February 2.

Schaub, Gary, Jr., and James Forsyth Jr. 2010. "An Arsenal We Can All Live With." *New York Times,* May 23.

Schell, Jonathan. 1998. *The Gift of Time: The Case for Abolishing Nuclear Weapons Now.* New York: Metropolitan Books.

———. 2000. *The Fate of the Earth and the Abolition.* Stanford, Calif.: Stanford University Press.

Schelling, Thomas C. 1966. *Arms and Influence.* New Haven, Conn.: Yale University Press.

———. 1970. *The Strategy of Conflict.* Cambridge, Mass.: Harvard University Press.

Schiappa, Edward. 1989. "The Rhetoric of Nukespeak." *Communication Monographs* 56: 253–71.

Schlosser, Eric. 2013. *Nuclear Weapons, the Damascus Accident, and the Illusion of Safety.* New York: Penguin Press.

Schmid, Sonja D. 2011. "Nuclear Colonization? Soviet Technopolitics in the Second World." In *Entangled Geographies: Empire and Technopolitics in the Global Cold War,* edited by Gabrielle Hecht, 125–54. Cambridge, Mass.: MIT Press.

Schoenfeld, Gabriel. 2009. "Why Worry? If Iran and North Korea Want the Bomb So Badly, We Should 'Let Them Have It.'" *Wall Street Journal,* October 29.

Schulte, Paul. 2007. "Universal Vision or Bounded Rationality?" *International Affairs* 83, no. 3: 501–10.

Schwartz, Stephen I., and Deepti Choubey. 2009. "Nuclear Security Spending: Assessing Costs, Examining Priorities." Carnegie Endowment for International Peace. http://carnegieendowment.org/files/nuclear_security_spending_high.pdf.

Sen, Sudipta. 2002. *Distant Sovereignty.* New York: Routledge.

Seth, Sanjay. 2013a. "Postcolonial Theory and the Critique of International Relations." In *Postcolonial Theory and International Relations: A Critical Introduction,* edited by Sanjay Seth, 15–31. New York: Routledge.

———, ed. 2013b. *Postcolonial Theory and International Relations: A Critical Introduction.* New York: Routledge.

Sethi, Manpreet. 2002. "Steps to Devalue/Delegitimize Nuclear Weapons." *International Studies* 39, no. 1: 65–78.

Shariatmadari, David. 2010. "Sanctions and Dr. Strangelove." *The Guardian,* July 22.

Shultz, George P., William J. Perry, Henry A. Kissinger, and Sam Nunn. 2007. "A World Free of Nuclear Weapons." *Wall Street Journal,* January 4.

———. 2011. "Deterrence in the Age of Nuclear Proliferation." *Wall Street Journal,* March 7.

Sidel, Victor W. 2007. "Vertical Nuclear Proliferation." *Medicine, Conflict, and Survival* 33, no. 4: 249–58.

Singer, Peter. 2007. *Corporate Warriors: The Rise of the Privatized Military Industry.* Ithaca, N.Y.: Cornell University Press.

Singh, Jaswant. 1998. "Against Nuclear Apartheid." *Foreign Affairs* 77, no. 5: 41–52.

Singh, Sonali, and Christopher R. Way. 2004. "The Correlates of Nuclear Proliferation: A Quantitative Test." *Journal of Conflict Resolution* 48, no. 6: 859–85.

SIPRI. 2011. *Armaments, Disarmament, and International Security: SIPRI Yearbook 2011.* Oxford: Oxford University Press.

Smith, Derek Delbert. 2006. *Deterring America: Rogue States and the Proliferation of Weapons of Mass Destruction.* Cambridge: Cambridge University Press.

Sokolski, Henry D. 2007. "Towards an NPT-Restrained World That Makes Economic Sense." *International Affairs* 83, no. 3: 531–48.

Solingen, Etel. 1994a. *The Domestic Sources of Nuclear Postures: Influencing Fence Sitters in the Post–Cold War Era*. IGCC Policy Paper 8. Irvine: University of California.

———. 1994b. "The Political Economy of Nuclear Restraint." *International Security* 19, no. 2: 126–69.

———. 2007. *Nuclear Logics: Contrasting Paths in East Asia and the Middle East*. Princeton, N.J.: Princeton University Press.

———, ed. 2012. *Sanctions, Statecraft, and Nuclear Proliferation*. Cambridge: Cambridge University Press.

Solomon, Fisher J. 1988. *Discourse and Reference in the Nuclear Age*. Norman: University of Oklahoma Press.

Spivak, Gayatri Chakravorty, trans. 1995. *Imaginary Maps: Three Stories by Mahasweta Devi*. New York: Routledge.

———. 2010a. "Can the Subaltern Speak?" In *Can the Subaltern Speak? Reflections on the History of an Idea*, edited by Rosalind C. Morris, 22–78. New York: Columbia University Press.

———. 2010b. "In Response." In *Can the Subaltern Speak? Reflections on the History of an Idea*, edited by Rosalind C. Morris, 227–36. New York: Columbia University Press.

Spruyt, Hendrick. 1994. *The Sovereign State and Its Competitors: An Analysis of Systems Change*. Princeton, N.J.: Princeton University Press.

Stein, Arthur A. 1982. "Coordination and Collaboration: Regimes in an Anarchic World." *International Organization* 36, no. 2: 299–324.

Stigler, Andrew L. 2011. "Review of Mueller, John. *Atomic Obsession: Nuclear Alarmism from Hiroshima to Al Qaeda*." *Naval War College Review* 64, no. 4: 149–50.

Stoett, Peter J. 2003. "Toward Renewed Legitimacy? Nuclear Power, Global Warming, and Security." *Global Environmental Politics* 3: 99–116.

Strange, Susan. 1982. "Cave! Hic Dragones: A Critique of Regime Analysis." *International Organization* 36, no. 2: 479–96.

Tabuchi, Hiroko. 2011a. "Economy Sends Japanese to Fukushima for Jobs." *New York Times*, June 8.

———. 2011b. "Japan Passes Law Supporting Stricken Nuclear Plant's Operator." *New York Times*, August 3.

———. 2011c. "Japanese Workers Braved Radiation for a Temp Job." *New York Times*, April 9.

———. 2011d. "Tepco Quells Push by Shareholders to End Nuclear Program." *New York Times*, June 28.

———. 2012. "A Confused Nuclear Cleanup." *New York Times*, February 10.

Tannenwald, Nina. 1999. "The Nuclear Taboo: The United States and the Normative Basis of Nuclear Non-Use." *International Organization* 53, no. 3: 433–68.

———. 2005. "Stigmatizing the Bomb: Origins of the Nuclear Taboo." *International Security* 29, no. 4: 5–49.

———. 2007. *The Nuclear Taboo: The United States and the Non-Use of Nuclear Weapons since 1945*. New York: Cambridge University Press.

Taubman, Philip. 2012. *The Partnership: Five Cold Warriors and Their Quest to Ban the Bomb*. New York: HarperCollins.

Taylor, Bryan C. 2003. "'Our Bruised Arms Hung Up as Monuments': Nuclear Iconography in Post–Cold War Culture." *Critical Studies in Media Communication* 20, no. 1: 1–34.

———. 2007. "'The Means to Match Their Hatred': Nuclear Weapons, Rhetorical Democracy, and Presidential Discourse." *Presidential Studies Quarterly* 37, no. 4: 667–92.

Taylor, Bryan C., and Judith Hendry. 2008. "Insisting on Persisting: The Nuclear Rhetoric of Stockpile Stewardship." *Rhetoric and Public Affairs* 11, no. 2: 303–34.

Taylor, Bryan C., William J. Kinsella, Stephen P. Depoe, and Maribeth S. Metzler, eds. 2007. *Nuclear Legacies: Communication, Controversy, and the U.S. Nuclear Weapons Complex*. New York: Lexington Books.

Tellis, Ashley J. 2006. "Atoms for War? U.S.–Indian Civilian Nuclear Cooperation and India's Nuclear Arsenal." *Carnegie Endowment for International Peace*, June 27.

Temple, David. 2009. "Politics and Lobbyists: The Internal Political Dynamics Influencing US Congressional Approval of the Nuclear Deal." In *Indo–US Nuclear Deal: Seeking Synergy in Bilateralism*, edited by P. R. Chari, 46–59. New York: Routledge.

Thakur, Ramesh. 2000. "Envisioning Nuclear Futures." *Security Dialogue* 31, no. 1: 25–40.

Thomas, Raju G. C. 1998. "Should India Sign the NPT/CTBT?" In *The Nuclear Non-Proliferation Regime: Prospects for the 21st Century*, edited by Raju G. C. Thomas, 284–309. New York: St. Martin's Press.

Thompson, Edward. 1982. "Notes on Exterminism, the Last Stage." In *Exterminism and the Cold War*, 1–33. London: Verso.

Tickner, J. Ann. 1993. *Gender in International Relations: Feminist Perspectives on Achieving Global Security*. New York: Columbia University Press.

Titus, A. Costandina. 2001. *Bombs in the Backyard*. Reno: University of Nevada Press.

Todorov, Tzvetan. 1999. *The Conquest of America: The Question of the Other*. Norman: University of Oklahoma Press.

Tuchman, Jessica Matthews. 1989. "Redefining Security." *Foreign Affairs* 68, no. 2: 162–77.

Ungar, Sheldon. 1992. *The Rise and Fall of Nuclearism: Fear and Faith as Determinants of the Arms Race*. University Park: Pennsylvania State University Press.

Vanaik, Achin. 2004. "Unravelling the Self-Image of the Indian Bomb Lobby." *Economic and Political Weekly,* November 20, 5006–12.

———. 2009. "Regional and Global Nuclear Disarmament." *Economic and Political Weekly* 44, no. 16: 18–24.

Van Evera, Stephen. 2006. "Assessing U.S. Strategy in the War on Terror." *Annals of the American Academy of Political and Social Science* 607: 10–26.

Varadarajan, Latha. 2004. "Constructivism, Identity, and Neoliberal (In)security." *Review of International Studies* 30: 319–41.

Walker, R. B. J. 1993. *Inside/Outside: International Relations as Political Theory.* New York: Cambridge University Press.

Walker, Ronald. 2000. "What Is to Be Done about Nuclear Weapons? A Rejoinder." *Security Dialogue* 31, no. 2: 179–84.

Walker, William. 2000. "Nuclear Order and Disorder." *International Affairs* 76, no. 4: 703–24.

———. 2004. *Weapons of Mass Destruction and International Order.* Adelphi Paper 370. New York: Oxford University Press for the International Institute for Strategic Studies.

———. 2007. "Nuclear Enlightenment and Counter-Enlightenment." *International Affairs* 83, no. 3: 431–53.

———. 2012. *A Perpetual Menace: Nuclear Weapons and International Order.* London: Routledge.

Wallerstein, Immanuel. 1979. *The Capitalist World Economy.* Cambridge: Cambridge University Press.

———. 1984. *The Politics of the World Economy: The States, the Movements, and the Civilizations.* Cambridge: Cambridge University Press.

Walt, Stephen. 1985. "Alliance Formation and the Balance of World Power." *International Security* 9, no. 4: 3–43.

Waltz, Kenneth. 1981. *The Spread of Nuclear Weapons: More May Be Better.* Adelphi Paper 171. London: International Institute for Strategic Studies.

———. 2012. "Why Iran Should Get the Bomb?" *Foreign Affairs,* July/August, 2–5.

Weldes, Jutta, Mark Laffey, Hugh Gusterson, and Raymond Duvall, eds. 1999. *Cultures of Insecurity: States, Communities, and the Production of Danger.* Minneapolis: University of Minnesota Press.

Wesley, Michael. 2005. "It's Time to Scrap the NPT." *Australian Journal of International Affairs* 59, no. 3: 283–99.

Wheeler, Nicholas J. 2009. "Beyond Waltz's Nuclear World: More Trust May Be Better." *International Relations* 23, no. 3: 429–45.

———. 2000. *Saving Strangers: Humanitarian Intervention in International Society.* Oxford: Oxford University Press.

Williams, Raymond. 1982. "The Politics of Nuclear Disarmament." In *Exterminism and the Cold War,* 65–85. London: Verso.

Wills, Garry. 2010. *Bomb Power: The Modern Presidency and the National Security State*. New York: Penguin Press.

Wilson, Ward. 2013. *Five Myths About Nuclear Weapons*. New York: Houghton Mifflin Harcourt.

Wirtz, James J., and Peter R. Lavoy, eds. 2012. *Over the Horizon Proliferation Threats*. Stanford, Calif.: Stanford University Press.

Wolaver, Adrianna. 2010. "The Real Price of Nuclear Weapons." *Waging Peace Today Blog*, August 6. http://wagingpeacetoday.blogspot.com/2010/08/real-price-of-nuclear-weapons.html.

Yih, Katherine, Albert Donnay, Annalee Yassi, James A. Ruttenber, and Scott Saleska. 1995. "Uranium Mining and Milling for Military Purposes." In *Nuclear Wastelands: A Global Guide to Nuclear Weapons Production and Its Health and Environmental Effects*, edited by Arjun Makhijani, Howard Hu, and Katherine Yih, 105–68. Cambridge, Mass.: MIT Press.

Yost, David. 2007. "Analysing International Nuclear Order." *International Affairs* 83, no. 3: 549–74.

Young, Iris Marion. 2003. "The Logic of Masculinist Protection: Reflections on the Current Security State." *Signs: Journal of Women in Culture and Society* 29, no. 1: 1–25.

Young, Oran R. 1982. "Regime Dynamics: The Rise and Fall of International Regimes." *International Organization* 36, no. 2: 277–97.

———. 1986. "International Regimes: Toward a New Theory of Institutions." *World Politics* 39: 104–22.

Young, Robert. 2001. *Postcolonialism: An Historical Introduction*. Oxford: Blackwell.

Zeller, Tom. 2011. "Nuclear Agency Is Criticized as Too Close to Industry." *New York Times*, May 7.

Žižek, Slavoj. 2008. *The Sublime Object of Ideology*. London: Verso.

Index

ABM (Anti-Ballistic Missile) Treaty, 12, 34, 38–39, 60, 66, 69–70, 81, 177, 218n17, 239n6
Aboriginal lands, 165, 237n61
Abraham, Itty, 131, 190, 222n37, 225n12, 225n17, 228n38
absolute enemies, 83, 92–95
"accidents" (nuclear), 1, 135–39, 151–70, 183–84, 226n19, 229n3, 233n26, 234n45. *See also specific disasters*
ACDA (Arms Control and Disarmament Agency), 51, 70
ACDIS (Program in Arms Control, Disarmament, and International Security), 55
Acheson-Lilienthal Report, 85, 210n7
Acronym Institute for Disarmament Diplomacy, 56
Additional Protocols, 71–72, 80, 237n60
Adelphi Papers (monograph series), 54, 80, 82–84
Adler, Emanuel, 31–32, 34–35, 66, 70, 214n42
AEC (U.S. Atomic Energy Commission), 152–53
Afghanistan war, 91
Africa, 42–45, 51, 97, 124, 164–67. *See also specific countries*
Agency for the Prohibition of Nuclear Weapons in Latin America, 42

Ahmedinejad, Mohammad, 3, 179
Albright, David, 62
Alliance for Nuclear Accountability, 57
Allison, Graham, 163, 210n6
al-Qaeda, 28, 83. *See also* September 11 attacks; terrorism
Alsos Digital Library for Nuclear Issues, 59
alterity, 19–21, 104. *See also* post-colonial theory; subaltern, the
American Israel Public Affairs Committee, 61, 157
anarchy, 18, 28–30, 74, 119, 174, 187
Anderson, Benedict, 95
Anghie, Antony, 98
Antarctic Treaty, 41
Anti-Politics Machine, The (Ferguson), 19
Appadurai, Arjun, 23, 117, 127–29, 228n34
Areva, 158, 164–66
Argentina, 45, 111–13
arms control, 10–11, 27–41, 48–59, 64–76, 87–94, 99–110, 174–77. *See also* disarmament; NNP; NPT; nuclear capabilities
Arms Control and Disarmament Act, 51
Arms Control Association, 54, 67
Atomic Obsession (Mueller), 8
Australia, 113, 164–65

SHAMPA BISWAS is Paul Garrett Professor of Political Science at Whitman College.